MIDWAY IS.

HAWAIIAN IS.   Oahu
Honolulu
Pearl Harbor

NORTH PACIFIC OCEAN

Makin

GILBERT IS.

ELLICE IS.

RUZ IS.

WESTERN SAMOA

HEBRIDES IS.   AMERICAN SAMOA

SOCIETY IS.   Tahiti

P O L Y N E S I A

SOUTH PACIFIC OCEAN

CORSAIR

CORSAIR

The F4U in World War II and Korea

BY BARRETT TILLMAN

NAVAL INSTITUTE PRESS
Annapolis, Maryland

To Yellow Leader
From Yellow Two

Other Books by Barrett Tillman
The Dauntless Dive Bomber of World War II
Hellcat: The F6F in World War II
TBF-TBM Avenger at War

Contents

Chapter opening photographs:

Frontispiece: Early Corsairs, probably of VF-17, over the East Coast in 1943. Note the canopy bulge to accommodate a rear-view mirror. (Ling-Temco-Vought)

Pages 2–3: Vought test pilot Lyman Bullard in the prototype Corsair, the XF4U-1 in the summer of 1940. (Ling-Temco-Vought)

Pages 24–25: Marine Corsair pilots race to their planes in response to a scramble alert at Guadalcanal. (Ling-Temco-Vought)

Pages 42–43: Maintenance on a Corsair of VMF-222 on Bougainville in March 1944. (R.M. Hill)

Pages 72–73: A napalm-loaded FG-1 taxies out for a strike mission from Peleliu in support of Marine infantry. (R.M. Hill)

Pages 92–93: Twenty-six Corsairs of the Royal Navy's Eastern Fleet, probably in the Indian Ocean. (Imperial War Museum)

Pages 106–7: An F4U-1D of VMF-124 or 213 lands aboard the *Essex*, as a TBM-3 of VP-4 passes by the port quarter during operations in early 1945. (U.S. Navy)

Pages 126–27: An F4U-1D of VMF-216 or 217 launches from the USS *Wasp* for the first Tokyo strike on 16 February 1945. (R.M. Hill)

Pages 158–59: Complete with heraldry, cannon-armed F4U-4Bs of VMF-214 are parked at Pohang, Korea, in October 1951. (U.S. Marine Corps)

Pages 176–77: AU-1s of the French Navy's squadron Flotille 14F under preparation for service in Indochina, 1954. (Icare)

Foreword

"Capable of or adapted for turning with ease from one to another of various tasks." That was the Vought F4U Corsair. A day fighter and a night fighter. A dive bomber and a reconnaissance plane. Land-based and carrier-based.

But before the Corsair demonstrated its full potential and versatility, it was deployed where it was needed most—Guadalcanal. And carrier suitability had nothing to do with that. At the time, the F4U was the only fighter available to the Navy and Marine Corps for replacement of the obsolescent F4F Wildcat. Therefore, Marine Fighter Squadron 124, equipped with twenty-four F4U-1s and a cadre of twenty-nine pilots, was sent to Guadalcanal. There the Corsair made its combat debut on 12 February 1943.

But long before Guadalcanal became a household word, the F4U was being developed for its ultimate role in World War II. It is here that the author begins the chronology with due recognition of the test pilots. They were the first to fly what was once a schematic, they proved its design, and continued with test flights until the aircraft was ready for military service. It was up to the Navy to prove carrier suitability, and this the Navy did. Fighter Squadron 17 contributed materially to this project, and more will be said of this famous squadron. For the Marines, it would be another year before fleet carrier operations; there was enough to do in the Solomons.

As the author continues this chronicle—through several decades—the full potential and versatility of the Corsair will be realized. But its niche in naval aviation history will more reflect its role with the early squadrons in the changing tide of war in the Pacific. There it challenged the enemy in air combat: intercept, bomber escort, and fighter sweeps. The F4U was a formidable weapon, and its six .50-caliber guns with the Mark 8 gunsight did the job! The trigger was literally at the pilot's fingertip, and another switch on the console recharged the guns hydraulically. A mere two-second burst would fire approximately 150 rounds. One can imagine the deadly results when locked on to a Zero for two to three seconds of gunfire, or when in range behind a formation of Vals.

In reading this book one can understand why Barrett Tillman is so well established in the ranks of contemporary aviation and military writers. Moreover, one can appreciate the research and the endless hours necessary to produce a manuscript. His analyses are splendid, and he

opens some doors to a scenario of the world in the turmoil of conflict—
and in this conflict, the story of that remarkable and rugged aircraft,
the F4U Corsair.

Kenneth A. Walsh
Lieutenant Colonel,
U.S. Marine Corps (Retired)

Preface

Thirty-nine years after the first Corsair took off, and twenty-five years after the last was built, it seems remarkable that anything substantial remains to be said about the F4U. At least seven previous publications—softcover, hardcover, monographs, and profiles—have dealt with the long-lived U-Bird to some degree. The Corsair has even starred in an otherwise undistinguished television series.

Despite this abundance of publicity, I felt the Corsair story had still not been fully told. And while this volume may not tell the entire story, I have attempted to touch upon each phase of the bent-wing bird's lengthy career.

This includes perhaps the most neglected aspect of Corsair history—not its combat record, but the story behind the delay and near-cancellation of this outstanding aircraft's appearance aboard U.S. aircraft carriers. Though the F4U was conceived and built as a carrier fighter, it spent the first three years of its wartime life ashore. I suspected there might be a lesson to be learned here and make no apologies for dealing with the subject in some detail.

With the Grumman Hellcat, the Corsair was the first true fighter-bomber flown by the U.S. Navy. The phrase in vogue today, as with the Northrop A/F-18 Hornet, is strike fighter, but it amounts to the same thing. Military services have never been able to resist hanging bombs on fighter planes, and they probably never will. For in today's world, with prohibitive prices for military hardware, there is little alternative but to employ aircraft in dual roles. Thus, the Corsair's story provides some lessons from the past. Superb as an air superiority fighter, the F4U was also outstanding in the air-to-surface role. It is safe to say that only the now-legendary McDonnell-Douglas F-4 Phantom series has rivaled the Corsair as a proven multi-purpose combat aircraft.

So this volume attempts to cover the varied facets of the Corsair story, giving full attention to the "glamorous" air combat role while examining the lesser-known but important aspects of administrative decisions, operational problems, and strike capability. Inevitably, some conclusions and observations have been made, and not all may meet with wide agreement. In self-defense I will make one observation: the purpose of studying history is to learn from the past in order to avoid repetition of similar errors in the future.

Admittedly, my long and close association with that breed of aviators sometimes called "arrogant fighter pilots" has been a factor. An author's final arrogance, and perhaps his responsibility, is to impose his own values and judgments upon his subject. Where I have done so, I have been either arrogant and dutiful or arrogant and reckless. But I hope that mainly I have let the Corsair tell its own story. And what a story it is.

Barrett Tillman

Athena, Oregon
June, 1979

CORSAIR

chapter 1

Bent-wing legend

Corsair: a privateer; hence, a pirate.

Webster's

Test pilot Boone Guyton had his hands full. Flying low over the Connecticut countryside, he alternately peered through his rain-streaked canopy and glanced at his fuel gauge. After nearly an hour of high-speed cruising tests, he was farther than expected from the Chance Vought Company's field at Stratford. The radical new fighter was fast—faster than he'd anticipated—and in the course of taking notes, Guyton hadn't noticed how far he'd flown. But now the July rainsqualls blocked his way home. And to complicate matters, he had no radio contact with any other airport.

Unable to locate an alternate landing strip, Guyton selected the longest fairway of the Norwich golf course. There was no other choice; he was running out of fuel. A former Navy pilot, Guyton knew about landing airplanes in short spaces. He set up a carrier landing pattern with full flaps and a nose-high, power-on approach. He was still unfamiliar with the experimental fighter, but it felt responsive and stable. Guyton could almost imagine the *Lexington* stretched out before him as he turned from base leg to final.

At 80 knots indicated, Guyton closed the throttle and three-pointed the long-nosed airplane onto the manicured green turf. For a moment he was filled with relief. It was a good landing. He carefully applied the brakes.

Abruptly his mood changed. He was not slowing perceptibly, and the trees at the end of the fairway seemed to be growing taller every second. Guyton decided to ground-loop the airplane as a desperate means of stopping it. He jabbed one foot down on the rudder pedal. No response. The sleek, silver Vought continued straight ahead toward the looming trees. The fighter's own inertia had formed a silent conspiracy with its smooth tires and the slick grass to prevent effective braking. Guyton saw the inevitable and his reactions took over. He cut the switches left and right, turned off the fuel, and barely had time to brace himself.

With speed hardly diminished, the Vought went through the rough and headlong into the trees. There was a series of loud cracks as the heavy aircraft splintered tree trunks. Branches snapped off, mingling momentarily in midair with pieces of aluminum. The abrupt deceleration lurched the airplane on its nose, and the momentum brought the tail forward and down. Guyton's ship slid inverted, tail first, partway down a shallow ravine until the remains crunched into a large stump.

Guyton's Navy training had paid off. As a routine precaution before landing, he'd shucked off his parachute harness and locked the canopy back. There was just enough room for him to crawl out of the cockpit. Except for cuts and bruises he was unharmed. But as he stood up to survey the scene, he felt sick. An airman's concern for his plane often exceeds his joy at being alive. Boone Guyton felt that ambivalence now.

What seconds earlier had been a sleekly beautiful flying machine was a pitiful, tangled mess. The starboard wing had been wrenched off, the empennage mangled, the cockpit crumpled. The XF4U-1 seemed destroyed.

Forty-four days previously, on 29 May 1940, the experimental fighter had flown for the first time. Vought's chief test pilot, Lyman Bullard, was at the controls. Known as a careful, calculating flier, Bullard had spent days learning the intricacies of the big, gull-winged prototype. Engine and taxi tests were conducted before Bullard finally decided to fly the beast. He was by then well acquainted with the Pratt and Whitney R-2800-4 engine, and when he advanced the throttle he stampeded off the runway behind 1,805 horses. The takeoff and climb were astonishing.

Bullard had climbed to 9,000 feet and executed some standard tests. He made shallow-banked turns, cycled the landing gear, tested the flaps, and made notations on instrument readings. In a brief test of the new fighter's speed range he slowed to a near-stall, then resumed normal fast cruise. Some of these maneuvers were visible from the field, and the assembled engineers, mechanics, and officials saw nothing unusual when the bent-wing Vought entered the traffic pattern and landed.

When Bullard had shut down the engine and climbed out, he seemed nervous and on edge. He asked for a cigarette. The onlookers soon learned why. One was Boone Guyton, who recalled, "Upon inspection, we noted that the spring tabs on the elevators were not there. They had been carried away because of a brief flutter mode. Bullard commented that the airplane had shaken slightly and vibrated, but that control forces were not so high that he could not handle the landing. The tabs had fluttered off at a normal cruising speed of about 180 knots."[1]

With this discouraging beginning did the Corsair launch its career. But the F4U's origin dated to early 1938 when the Navy Bureau of Aeronautics sponsored a design competition for a new carrier fighter. Vought submitted its entry in April—designer Rex Biesel's design V-166B, better known as the Corsair.

Pratt and Whitney's new Double Wasp radial engine was the soul of the Corsair. The radical configuration was based upon use of the Double Wasp and its three-bladed Hamilton Standard propeller. The inverted gull wing solved four problems at once. It caused the least possible aerodynamic drag with a right-angle juncture at the fuselage. It allowed a shorter landing gear than would have been possible with a straight-wing design, thereby giving sufficient ground clearance for the 13-foot, 4-inch prop. Also, the shorter landing gear could retract straight aft, avoiding space problems near the internal wing tanks. And finally, as a carrier aircraft, the F4U could fold its wings directly over the canopy with room to spare on a hanger deck. In this configuration, however, the lower overhead on British carriers would cause problems for storage.

Vought won the contract in June 1938, and by February 1939 the full-scale mockup was completed. The prototype XF4U-1, Bureau of Aeronautics number 1443, was built with the original armament specifications. They reflect the Navy's uncertainty about aviation ordnance at the time:

one .30-caliber and one .50-caliber machine gun firing through the propeller arc with one .50 in each wing. Wing racks for ten light air-to-air bombs and an aiming window in the bottom of the fuselage were also provided.

After the forced landing on 11 July 1940, Vought's experimental shop spared no effort in rebuilding the first Corsair. Close inspection had revealed that the center section, engine accessory section, and landing gear remained intact. This fortunate development simplified the formidable task of restoration, which proceeded on a round-the-clock basis.

The job was done in something under three months. On 1 October the Corsair set a record. On a flight from Stratford to Hartford, a distance of some 40 statute miles, the XF4U-1 clocked a blazing 405 mph, or 350 knots. The exact figure was withheld for some time, but the press learned that the U.S. Navy probably had the fastest fighter plane in the world. Since 1940 the claim has been made that the Corsair was the first American fighter to exceed the magical 400 mph mark in level flight. This was not strictly accurate. The Army Air Corps' Lockheed P-38 Lightning is the legitimate holder of that title. The Corsair was the first U.S. single-engine fighter to break the 400 mph barrier.

Some bugs remained to be excised from the F4U's big, beefy airframe. The speed and ceiling both exceeded specifications, but lateral stability and spin recovery required attention. There was also a persistent prop surge. Navy pilots flew the prototype at NAS Anacostia in October and November, presenting a long list of desired improvements. They stressed changes in armament, internal fuel, armor plate, and aileron design for greater roll rate. Meanwhile, the company conducted dive tests in January 1941, achieving speeds of 515 mph. Eventually the F4U's maximum dive speed was calculated at a Critical Mach number of 0.73. This translated to 536 mph, or 465 knots, at 10,000 feet.

One of Boone Guyton's major chores throughout the war was describing the phenomenon of compressability to new F4U pilots. He explained the technique for recovering from terminal velocity dives in which the controls seemed frozen at high and medium altitudes. The best procedure was to avoid using the elevator trim tab, which could induce a violent pitch-up in the denser air at lower altitudes and overstress the airframe. Instead, power reduction and slow, steady back pressure on the stick were advocated after waiting long enough for the controls to become effective.

The Navy's requests were complied with and met the satisfaction of BuAer during final demonstrations at Anacostia in late February 1941. The Corsair was then on its way to production. In March and April Vought and the Navy concluded contract negotiations, and on 30 June the F4U-1 was ordered into manufacture.

At this point the Corsair became caught in a time warp. The world was changing, and not at all for the better. In 1938, with no immediate threat of war, the F4U seemed destined for limited production, not unlike the P-38. Vought's emphasis was upon speed and performance, leaving production methods a secondary consideration. Therefore, thousands of engineering man-hours were devoted to the construction of the inverted gull wing and reduction of parasitic drag. And similarly, the F4U contained numerous forgings and castings. Its tailwheel forging was the largest employed in any fighter of the era. There seemed little need to solve these problems on a mass-production basis.

Three years later, the world had turned over. Europe was either under Axis occupation or waging full-scale war. Japan was on the march in Asia. America was preparing for what many saw as an inevitable entry into the conflict. Under these circumstances, it was not difficult to imagine that the Corsair would be needed before long, and needed in large numbers. The parent company simply could not provide as many of the new fighters as the Navy and Marines could absorb. Therefore, during November and December two other manufacturers were brought into the Corsair production scheme. These were Brewster Aircraft and Goodyear. Both companies required over a year to reach production, but their subsequent records contrasted markedly.

Brewster was the hard-luck company of the aviation industry. When it did win military contracts, as with its SBA dive bomber, it often could not meet the desired quota and had to sublet some of the work to other factories. The designs which reached the fleet—most notably the much maligned F2A fighter—suffered from obsolescence. Early in the war it was suspected that Brewster's Long Island plant had been infiltrated by German agents who sabotaged the production line. Whether true or not, the fact remained that Brewster didn't build many airplanes. Its Corsairs were designated F3A-1, duplicates of the F4U-1 series. The first one flew in April 1943. Deliveries lasted from June of that year to July of 1944, at which time the contract was canceled. Only 735 Brewster-built Corsairs were delivered, counting Long Island and Pennsylvania production.

Goodyear was another matter entirely. The Akron, Ohio, factory delivered 377 FG-1s in 1943, boosting the next year's figure nearly sixfold to 2,108. Another 1,453 were accepted in the eight months of hostilities during 1945, for a wartime total of 4,006. This amounted to over one-third of all Corsair production during World War II. Many FG-1s were built with nonfolding wings during the period before Corsairs were put aboard carriers, and these aircraft inevitably went to land-based Marine squadrons.

Vought's own production began slowly. Partially this was due to the number of changes implemented before the program began. The cockpit

Completed F4U-1s awaiting acceptance test flights. (Ling-Temco-Vought)

was moved three feet aft to accommodate more fuselage fuel capacity, and the engine in the F4U-1 was the updated R-2800-8(B), providing 2,000 horsepower on takeoff. The first production Corsair, BuAer 02153, was flown on 25 June 1942. With a gross weight of 12,060 pounds, the early dash one demonstrated a sea-level climb rate in excess of 3,000 feet per minute, a service ceiling of 37,000 feet, and a maximum level speed of 360 knots, or 415 mph.

The Navy accepted its first two Corsairs in July 1942, with nine following in August. By the end of the year 178 had been delivered. During 1943 the production rate showed a slow but steady increase, exceeding 200 units by November. F4U deliveries peaked in July 1945 with 303 aircraft, though 300 or more Vought-built Corsairs were accepted during three other months. Total Corsair production was topped in May 1944 when the Navy accepted 254 F4Us, 220 FGs, and 122 F3As—a total of 596.

8

Even after Brewster ceased production, combined Vought and Goodyear acceptances were seldom much below 400 per month.

Vought's flight-test section was kept working full-time during the war, and not surprisingly. Quite aside from experimental flying, production flight testing was a continual project as new Corsairs came off the assembly line. In 1940 the flight-test roster included two names: Lyman Bullard and Boone Guyton. But Guyton took over from Bullard as chief test pilot late that year, and during the war the ranks swelled to about twenty-three at any one time. These included six in experimental flight test and as many as seventeen in production test.

Vought's test pilot recruitment was a story in itself. During wartime, experienced aviators were a rare commodity. As Guyton said, "The draft left us with little to choose from for most of those years." There were general aviation instructors, former crop dusters, private pilots, and a few "young engineer types or close to engineer types."[2] Their flight time varied from as little as forty hours up to several hundred. After check rides in Piper Cubs, the aspiring test pilots were brought up by stages through OS2Us and SB2Us. Considering that there were two fatalities in some 20,000 F4U test flights, spanning fourteen years, the program must be considered exceptionally successful.

Engine failure was the single leading cause of test-flying crashes. Guyton, who logged 1,754 Corsair flights, had two engine failures in three days during 1943. The first ended in a safe dead-stick landing from 20,000 feet. The second time, his Corsair hit short of the runway, broke in two, and spilled him out, still in his seat. He spent two months recovering in a hospital. Bill Boothby was over rough terrain when his F4U-1 suffered engine failure. Boothby bailed out but apparently snagged his ripcord on the emergency canopy release, causing his chute to catch on the tail. He went down with the airplane. Dick Burroughs made a dead-stick landing in an F4U-5 at New Haven Airport but landed short and was killed instantly when the Corsair flipped inverted.

The U-Bird first tried its sea legs on 25 September 1942. The seventh F4U-1 was flown by Lieutenant Commander Sam Porter to Chesapeake Bay where the escort carrier *Sangamon* (CVE-26) waited to receive him. Vought's project engineer Russ Clark and service manager Jack Hospers were both aboard to observe and lend advice. The CVE had 28 knots across her deck, and Porter made four takeoffs and landings. In a conventional deck run the takeoff distance was 280 feet.

This experiment, however brief, showed up some serious problems which would plague the Corsair for two years. Visibility, already hampered by the long nose, was further diminished by hydraulic fluid leaking from the cowl flap actuators and by engine oil from the valve push rods. It not only streaked the windscreen, but spattered on the pilot's goggles

9

The landing signal officer waves a Corsair aboard an escort carrier during carrier trials in the fall of 1942. (U.S. Navy)

when the canopy was open. This problem was easily solved. Beginning in December, F4U-1s were built with a different flap actuator and the top portion of the cowling was permanently faired over.

The other problems remained. The Corsair's rigid landing gear oleo caused a potentially disastrous bounce in any but a smooth touchdown. It was not only noted on carriers, where hard landing are the norm, but also on runways. Though some pilots considered the F4U no more difficult to land than some other planes, many had serious trouble. Additionally, the F4U-1's low tailwheel put the big flaps close to the ground, making directional control erratic. Until these discrepancies could be cured, the Corsair would face serious opposition about going to sea.

Meanwhile, the first squadrons had been formed and deployed, with varying degrees of success. The original F4U outfit was VMF-124, commissioned 7 September 1942 at Camp Kearney, California. Led by Major William E. Gise, 124 was a scratch-built unit formed around a nucleus of personnel from Marine Air Group 12. Late that month the initial batch of F4U-1s arrived, and Gise's pilots began feeling out their new fighters.

Like thousands of pilots after them, the men of VMF-124 stood almost in awe of the Corsair. Its initial impression was one of size and power. Compared to the chunky little Grumman Wildcat, the F4U was huge—three feet taller and a ton and a half heavier. The F4F's cockpit was comfortably compact. Many pilots felt lost in the Vought's spacious cockpit. And the two footrails running forward to the rudder pedals only heightened the sense of size. Looking down between his knees, a pilot saw only a deep darkness. It was almost an eerie sensation—you didn't know exactly what was down there. One way to find out was to roll inverted. Anything was likely to fall to the top of the canopy: dust, screwdrivers, comic books, nuts and bolts, cigarette lighters.

Breaking in a high-performance aircraft always takes time. But that was one thing VMF-124 didn't have. Gise's unit was scheduled to depart the West Coast during the first week of January 1943, bound for the Solomon Islands. New Corsairs arrived a few at a time, and by early December it seemed doubtful that the full twenty-four-plane complement could be readied before sailing date. In order to comply with the dozens of modifications and directives required before each plane was declared combat-ready, a West Coast establishment was set up by Colonel Stanley Ridderhoff and Jack Hospers. Using Chance Vought modification kits, Hospers worked full-time with Marine mechanics while persuading senior air officers that the job could be done. At one point the project was in danger of cancellation.

Early production F4U-1s on the Vought assembly line in December 1942. (Ling-Temco-Vought)

But the task was accomplished, with precious little time to spare. Gise's personnel worked twenty-five days straight preparing their F4U-1s. The last aircraft was declared combat-ready on 28 December. Barely a week later VMF-124 sailed from San Diego, bound for Guadalcanal via Espiritu Santo in the New Hebrides. As a result of the frantic maintenance and modification program, Gise's pilots averaged only twenty hours of flight time in their F4Us while in California. Some had never fired their guns.

Serious problems still remained when VMF-124 arrived in the South Pacific. Pilots complained of limited visibility, due to the F4U-1's original "birdcage" canopy, and the nose-high three-point attitude due to the short tailwheel strut. But there were other, more pressing difficulties. The ignition system was particularly troublesome. The R-2800 engines in the early dash ones had faulty ignition shielding which allowed considerable interference with radio reception. And insufficient pressurization of the distributors led to complete engine failure on some flights above 29,000 feet.

Since altitude is everything in aerial combat, the latter problem was especially urgent. It was traced to faulty pressurization from the Pratt and Whitney supercharger, which sometimes allowed the spark to "jump the gap" and burn out the distributor points. The Marines solved both ignition system problems while at Espiritu Santo, and production-line changes prevented similar difficulty in the future. But not before a Corsair went into the water.

On 1 February 1943 Lieutenant Kenneth A. Walsh, a former enlisted pilot, suffered engine failure on a high-altitude flight. He made the first water landing of an F4U, and though he would shortly put several other "firsts" in the Corsair record book, this one left an indelible impression: "I went down with the plane and had extreme difficulty freeing myself from the cockpit. Finally free, I had barely the strength to inflate one half-section of the Mae West, which brought me to the surface. I would estimate I went down about 150 feet and doubt if I would have survived another five seconds underwater. As it turned out, I was flying again the next day. An attempt to salvage the plane was abandoned since it went down in something like a thousand fathoms!"[3]

The second Corsair squadron was the first Navy unit to receive F4Us. This was VF-12, formed at NAS North Island, San Diego, in October 1942. The CO was Lieutenant Commander Joseph C. Clifton, and his Corsairs arrived more slowly than Gise's. Not until mid-January did Fighting 12 have ten combat-ready aircraft. Commander Fleet Air West Coast directed that four Corsairs be delivered per day until Clifton's unit was brought up to strength, and by 22 January there were twenty-two aircraft declared operational. But the same high-altitude problems which bedeviled VMF-124 also plagued VF-12. More delay ensued.

But training continued. Fighting 12 did its initial night flying in late February, and commenced field carrier landing practice on 3 March. Next day, "Jumpin' Joe" Clifton and Lieutenant (junior grade) John Magda made four landings aboard the escort carrier *Core* (CVE-13) 100 miles offshore. More problems. The conventional pneumatic tailwheel tires were subject to blowouts under the stress of deck landing, and it was some time before hard rubber tires were employed. Other VF-12 pilots qualified during the rest of the month. One Corsair was lost over the side in a bad landing, but the pilot was rescued.

Carrier training continued after Clifton took his squadron to Hawaii. A pilot was killed landing aboard the USS *Enterprise* (CV-6), and when VF-12 reached the South Pacific that summer, it exchanged its Corsairs for Hellcats. The squadron was already assigned to operate from the *Saratoga* (CV-3), thus the conversion. But the change in equipment was not due entirely to the F4U's deck-landing problems. The main reason was apparently that no Corsair parts or equipment were in the supply pipeline for carriers.

Though fourteen pilots had been killed in training, VF-12 remained impressed with the F4U. The exec and later CO, Lieutenant Commander Robert G. Dose, considered the Corsair "a beautiful bird. We estimated it had about 50 knots on the F6F. The F4U-1 with its flashy performance was, however, a tricky plane to fly. It had a vicious stall for one thing. If you stalled thirty feet up you wound up on your back. By comparison the Hellcat was a baby buggy, but we loved the 'hog.' "[4]

The third Corsair squadron also had problems. However, VF-17 under Lieutenant Commander John Thomas Blackburn exerted a major influence on future Corsair design. His engineering and maintenance departments experimented with field modifications at East Coast bases which eventually became production-line standards.

Originally part of Air Group 17, Blackburn's squadron was intended to operate from the new *Essex*-class carrier *Bunker Hill* (CV-17). Despite six fatalities in training on the East Coast, VF-17 believed in the new fighter's potential and worked towards the goal of sea duty. The engineering officer, Lieutenant M. W. "Butch" Davenport, worked with Vought representatives in solving the landing gear oleo problem. Experimentation with the oil level and air pressure in the gear strut eventually found the right combination. It was a relatively easy procedure to correct the rigid oleos as they arrived from the factory. With a softer oleo piston stroke owing to greater air pressure, the jolt and consequent landing bounce was alleviated.

But not without hard-won experience. Unmodified F4U-1s were employed on the *Bunker Hill's* shakedown cruise to Trinidad in the summer of 1943. There were no losses, but one Corsair was written off when

A VF-17 F4U-1 lands aboard the USS *Bunker Hill* during her shakedown cruise to the Caribbean in July 1943. (R.M. Hill).

it bounced high and was smashed back onto the deck by the engagement of the arresting hook. Other planes suffered tire blowouts, but the F4U was demonstrated to be a viable carrier aircraft.

Shortly before deployment to the Pacific a batch of thirty-six new F4U-1As was received, incorporating the new landing gear setup and starboard wing spoiler which, among other mods, effectively "tamed" the Corsair. Then en route from San Diego to Hawaii, VF-17 was ordered detached from the air group. A Hellcat squadron, VF-18, was waiting to replace Blackburn's outfit in Hawaii. Recalled Butch Davenport, "We were extremely disappointed because there was no doubt in our mind that the Corsair was superior to the F6F."[5] Tom Blackburn tried to get the order revoked, but to no avail. The same supply considerations which thwarted VF-12 applied to Fighting 17. When Blackburn took his squadron into combat in November 1943, it was a land-based unit in the Solomons.

In all, seven major changes were made to the F4U over a year and a half, and each involved considerable research, engineering, and testing. The first was introduced in November 1942 when the fifth production aircraft was modified to raise the pilot's seat eight inches and improve forward visibility. Further development brought about the frameless, clear-vision "bubble" canopy, made standard in the F4U-1A. This was the model VF-17 took into combat.

Controllability was a major feature of the Corsair design and test program. Positive aileron control through the range of the F4U's speed was sought and achieved. But not without hard work. Some 110 test flights were devoted to aileron design alone. By January 1943 this project had also been incorporated into the production line. Test pilot Wolfgang Langewiesche recalled that "the roll rate was terrific; the ailerons were the factory's pride and joy."[6] He knew whereof he spoke. Langewiesche's 1944 classic, *Stick and Rudder*, remains the definitive how-to-fly book.

In March 1943 larger tail-wheel bearings were introduced. That fall saw several production-line changes incorporated. These included a new tail hook to prevent skipping over a carrier's arresting wires, and an extended tail wheel strut. Perhaps the most important addition made that fall was formalized in November. It was the installation of a small spoiler on the leading edge of the starboard wing, outboard of the guns, to reduce the violence of accelerated stalls and provide better stall warning. Again, VF-17 had pioneered this work.

Finally, the new landing gear oleo setup was made standard in May 1944. This period of twelve months between the first efforts to solve the bounce problem and its incorporation into production aircraft (as op-

Landing gear retraction tests on the Vought production line. (Ling-Temco-Vought)

A factory-fresh F4U-1A in 1943, resplendent in the new tri-color paint scheme. (Ling-Temco-Vought)

posed to field mods) has come in for considerable comment. No single explanation exists. Part of the blame falls upon the higher echelons of BuAer, despite the efforts of F4U partisans within the bureau. It is an unfortunate fact that administrative inertia dogs all human endeavors, up to and including full-scale war. But there were other factors as well. Field modification kits handled the problem during that period, so most F4Us were "debounced" by the time they reached the squadrons. And there was no particular need for Corsairs aboard carriers until the advent of the kamikazes. Grumman provided enough F6Fs to fill the fleet's fighter requirement during 1943–44.

And there remained some technical matters. Boone Guyton recalls, "The oleo metering problem was somehow tough to overcome. We did not know all we do now about oleo and orifice action, for this alone took many weeks to cure. That flaw, causing a bouncing action—which exhibited to the green pilot a cause for alarm because of the left wing sag tendency on landing—I am certain caused the 'let's keep it off the carrier' attitude."[7]

The production line change was initiated under Program Dog, one of four such suggestions made by Vought engineers in the face of possible condemnation from carriers. In March 1944 the Chief of Naval Air Operational Training at NAS Jacksonville, Florida, was said to be preparing a letter which could have prevented F4Us from operating at sea. The accident rate, particularly among younger pilots, was unacceptably high. Not only were valuable aircraft being destroyed, but lives were being lost.

Three men were credited with forestalling the potentially deadly letter. They were Captain John Pearson of BuAer's fighter design desk in Washington, Captain Hugh Duckworth of the Fleet Air Jacksonville staff, and Vought's service rep, Jack Hospers. Finally faced with a now-or-never situation—or at least what appeared to be—the company drafted the four alternative measures. Dog was selected and implemented ten days later. Flight tests at Jacksonville were conducted by Commander T. K. Wright and Lieutenant Colonel John Dobbin, a Marine veteran of Guadalcanal. The Corsair was then endorsed for carrier duty on a regular basis, whenever the need should arise.

Substantiation of this decision came from other sources at the same time. On the West Coast a training squadron, VF-301, conducted a lengthy series of landing tests with newly modified F4U-1s during April. Operating from the escort carrier *Gambier Bay* (CVE-73), the pilots of VF-301 made 113 landings with no serious problems. Consequently, all West Coast Corsairs were slated for oleo strut mods.

Another Corsair booster was Lieutenant Commander William N. Leonard, an experienced combat pilot with two tours in F4Fs. He recalled, "At Guadalcanal in the spring and summer of 1943 we operated VF-11 alongside U-Birds. The way the Marines bounced on occasion could be quite thrilling. They got into some very bad habits of landing fast and tail high to remedy the bounce, and had to be untaught later.

"My first flight—in November 1943—was in a low-canopy bouncer, but it never bounced for me. I used my F4F antigroundloop technique and it was great for field work. You land full stall, then raise the tail and run-out on the main gear. Later I was given a debounced F4U-1A for a rocket assist takeoff project, and its behavior was definitely different. It felt like falling into a feather bed when you stalled in."[8]

On 22 April the Navy accepted its first F4U-1D, basically a -1A with two underwing pylons for external stores. Tests conducted in Hawaii during May showed the new Corsair to be perhaps the most versatile carrier aircraft of the period. The Naval Air Forces Pacific Command received an F6F-5 and an F4U-1D for the purpose of fleet evaluation. Three combat-experienced pilots were named to an evaluation board. They were Lieutenant Commander Gordon Cady, CO of VF-11; Lieutenant Commander Bernard W. Strean, CO of VF-1 recently returned from Tarawa; and Lieutenant Colonel John L. Smith who had led VMF-223 at Guadalcanal. Cady and Smith had flown the F4F-4 in combat, Strean the F6F-3.

"Smoke" Strean recalls, "The three of us decided that carrier suitability was the most important concern. We were given wide latitude as to

The F4U-1D, first Corsair fighter-bomber variant delivered as such. Here the two underwing pylons carry 1,000-pound bombs. (Ling-Temco-Vought)

how to accomplish the comparison. To give these planes the severest carrier test, we selected a CVE. All three of us made many landings in both airplanes. We determined that the F4U-1D was equally as good a carrier airplane as the F6F-5, if not better. The evaluation lasted perhaps three weeks."[9]

At the end of that time the board was generally agreed on most findings. The F6F-5 was more maneuverable than the F6F-3 because of the spring tabs on the former's ailerons, but it was not more maneuverable than the F4U-1D. Control forces on the Corsair also seemed lighter than on the Hellcat. There was no doubt that the Corsair was faster than the F6F, and it possessed better zoom-climb characteristics than the Grumman.

In the all-important realm of gunnery and ordnance delivery, the F4U-1D was also judged superior. The three pilots—who so far had all their combat experience in Grummans—believed the Corsair was a steadier gun platform and a better dive bomber. There was some uncertainty as to relative visibility, but the Hellcat probably gave a wider field of view, and it was generally conceded easier to land aboard ship, owing to better forward visibility.

These tests reinforced the informal comparison which VF-12 ran against the Hellcats of VF-3 a year earlier. Joe Clifton and another VF-12 pilot had engaged in mock combat with Lieutenant Commander Edward "Butch" O'Hare and a wingman near San Diego. Clifton's F4U-1s had proven faster and more maneuverable than O'Hare's F6F-3s, and the playful hassling must have made an impression upon O'Hare. When he

18

took his squadron to Hawaii that summer, he managed to take an F4U-1 with him. For some time it was the only Corsair in the islands, and O'Hare would only let one other pilot fly it. Such are the privileges of a Medal of Honor winner.

The Army Air Force got its first good look at the Corsair during the Fighter Evaluation Meet at Eglin Field, Florida, during May 1943. Below 10,000 feet the bent-wing Vought was superior to any Army fighter and held its own up to 15,000 or 20,000 feet. At higher altitudes where they were designed to perform, the Republic P-47 and North American P-51 held the advantage. Along the East Coast, Thunderbolt pilots tired of losing races and dogfights to Corsairs and sought other sport. Pulling alongside the F4Us, they would hold up their oxygen masks and point upwards. A smart Corsair pilot would shake his head and break off.

Perhaps one of the greatest tributes to the Corsair came from an Army pilot. Major (later Colonel) Rex T. Barber was an exponent and devotee of the twin-boomed P-38. His combat tour in the Solomons ended with a key role in the interception of Japan's premier naval leader, Admiral Isoruko Yamamoto. Rex Barber flew a wide variety of fighters, but his assessment of the F4U was typically succinct: "If the United States had to pick one fighter-bomber to produce during the war, it should have been the Corsair."[10]

No matter how the F4U stacked up against other American aircraft, it was an unrealistic comparison. The only comparison that really mattered was how the U-Bird stood up against its main opponent, the Mitsubishi Zero series of Japan.

In early January 1943, just before VMF-124 left for the Solomons, Joe Clifton gave a briefing to the Marines. He had flown an A6M2 (Zero) which was found damaged but intact in the Aleutians during June 1942. It was repaired at North Island and used extensively in technical and tactical tests. His findings went a long way towards helping Major Gise's pilots through their first few combats. The Corsair's greatest advantage over the Zeke was speed. Clifton advocated use of that speed to dictate the rules of engagement and disengagement. A hard diving turn to starboard at 240 knots would lose the Zero every time.

In late 1944 a detailed test was run between an F4U-1D and a captured A6M5, or Zeke 52. From sea level up to 30,000 feet the Corsair proved faster by an average of 55 knots, or 64 mph. This was from a minimum advantage of 36 knots at 5,000 feet to a maximum of 69 knots at 25,000. Top speeds were 413 mph (355 knots) for the F4U-1D at 20,400 feet, and 335 mph (290 knots) at 18,000 for the Zeke.

Unlike the F4F, the Corsair was capable of matching or exceeding the Zeke's rate of climb. Vought and Mitsubishi were equal up to 10,000 feet, after which the Corsair pulled ahead. In fact, at 18,000 feet, the -1D climbed 750 feet per minute better than its opponent. The best climbing speeds were 135 knots for the Corsair and 105 for the Zero.

"The maneuverability of the Zeke 52 is remarkable at speeds below about 175 knots, being far superior to that of the F4U-1D," said the report. "Its superiority, however, diminishes with increased speed, due to its high control forces, and the F4U-1D has the advantage at speeds above 200 knots." Tests showed that in slow speed turns at 10,000 feet, the Zeke gained one turn in three and a half. But the Corsair, by maintaining an airspeed of 175 knots (200 mph) could use full flaps to stay with the Zeke for a half-turn. By that time, however, airspeed was down to 150 knots (173 mph) and it was high time to disengage.

The Corsair's magnificent ailerons gave it an important advantage over Zekes. The two fighters' roll rate was equal at speeds under 200 knots, allowing the F4U to change directions on an equal basis. Above 200 knots, the Zeke's ailerons became heavy while the Corsair's were still effective. The time invested in those engineering test flights to perfect the ailerons paid handsome dividends in combat.

In dive comparisons, both fighters were approximately neck-and-neck in the very early stages. After that, the Corsair was vastly superior as it accelerated with astonishing speed. Few Japanese fighters had any hope of escaping an F4U in a dive, and even then it was only over short distances.

Since a fighter plane is a gunnery platform, a word is in order about armament. The Zeke employed a typical mixture of weapons found in Japanese fighters. In the A6M5 this consisted of two 20-mm cannon with 200 rounds and a pair of 7.7-mm machine guns with 1,400 rounds. The F4U series was mainly armed with six Colt-Browning M-2 .50-caliber machine guns. Between the prototype and production the nose guns had been deleted, and a suggestion was considered for use of four wing-mounted .50s. However, the standard American fighter armament of six .50s was the final choice. They carried a total of 2,350 rounds: 400 for the two inboard guns in each wing, with 375 for each outboard weapon owing to wing contour.

This was a formidable battery. The M-2 fired a bullet measuring .511 inches in diameter, weighing up to 709 grains, or about 1.6 ounces. It was nominally propelled by 253 grains of IMR-5010 powder at a muzzle velocity of 2,840 feet per second. Sighted to converge at 300 yards, six .50 calibers could do terrific damage not only to aircraft, but to light naval vessels as well. As production of specialized bullets increased, a greater mixture of ammunition types became available. By 1943, most aviation .50-caliber ammo was belted in the ratio of one armor piercing, one incendiary, one armor piercing, one incendiary, one tracer. By efficient use of ammunition, Corsair pilots could and did destroy four, five, even six Japanese aircraft in one mission.

Early in the program, some thought was given to arming F4U-1s with Danish 23-mm cannon. In the fall of 1943 limited production began on F4U-1Cs, a total of 200 being produced. These were -1As armed with four 20-mm cannon. Using IMR 4831 powder, the 20 millimeters fired a shell over three-fourths inch in diameter which was shorter ranged and of lesser muzzle velocity than the .50 caliber. It also possessed a somewhat slower rate of fire, but was more lethal with fewer hits. Later model Corsairs, most notably the F4U-4B and the French F4U-7, also employed 20 millimeters, but the large majority of all Corsairs retained the sextette of .50 calibers.

Among other specialized Corsairs were late-model photo planes and night fighters, such as the F4U-4P and -5N. At a time when the need for carrier-based night fighters was recognized, only the Corsair possessed the necessary attributes: a high-performance single-engine aircraft capable of carrying a radar set. The F6F was still in the design stage during early 1942, hence the adoption of the F4U as a night fighter.

Thirty-two F4U-1s, including the first production plane, were modified as night fighters at the Naval Aircraft Factory in Philadelphia. This was accomplished under Project Roger, since Chance Vought's work load was far too heavy just dealing with normal Corsair problems in the fall of 1942. The modified aircraft were designated F4U-2s. They were equipped with new instrumentation and cockpit lighting, flame dampeners, a tailwheel extension, and AIA (Airborne Intercept, Type A) radar sets. They featured a scanner in a bulbous pod on the leading edge of the starboard wing. To offset the additional 308 pounds and make room for electronics, the outboard starboard gun was removed. And the ammunition load was reduced to 250 rounds per gun. The result was a net saving of some 230 pounds. Top speed was reduced by about ten knots but handling characteristics were unaffected.

The main drawbacks were monetary and administrative. The conversion process took the NAF about six weeks per plane and nearly doubled the cost of each F4U. It was the Navy's first major experience with the high price of aviation electronics. But the need was great, so the program continued. The mods were completed on the last of the batch in September 1943.

The AIA set possessed a blind-fire mode made possible through the radar-controlled gunsight, but it was not employed in combat. Operational procedure required visual identification of each target as a precaution against destroying a friendly aircraft. But the sets proved generally reliable within their limitations. The early AIA sets were literally handmade, and proved more effective at ranges under two miles than the rated three-mile range.

Experience demonstrated that the five .50 calibers were most effective in nocturnal combat when boresighted to 250 yards instead of the standard 300. They were adjusted to fire slightly upward since most approaches were made from six o'clock low. No tracer ammunition was loaded in most squadrons in order to preserve the pilot's night vision and avoid giving away the fighter's position.

Three squadrons finally flew F4U-2s in combat: VF(N)-75 was commissioned in April 1943 at NAS Quonset Point and VMF(N)-532 formed at MCAS Cherry Point that same month. Both these squadrons flew from island bases. A split-off component of VF(N)-75 went to sea in early 1944 as VF(N)-101. Among them, these pioneer night fighters accounted for only thirteen confirmed victories, but the technical and tactical information they developed would prove invaluable.

Much more of the Corsair's development could be told—another book's worth. The F4U-4 was probably the most popular of the mass-produced U-Birds, with the R-2800-18W and -42W engines, also known as the Twin Wasp C, which drove it at speeds of 450 mph, or 390 knots. The postwar F4U-5 was faster yet, officially clocked at 469 mph. The sensational F2G-1 and -2, with 3,000 horsepower engines, were experimental interceptors with a sea level climb rate of 4,000 feet per minute. Their greatest success came in postwar air racing, where they captured the prestigious Thompson Trophy.

In its long career the F4U underwent 981 major engineering changes and approximately 20,000 minor ones. When development, engineering, and production costs were figured, an F4U-1D cost the taxpayers about $75,000. This was neither the highest nor the lowest figure for single-engine fighters of the era. But it was roughly $12,000 more than the F6F-5, and comparable to the SB2C-5. The only U.S. Army Air Force fighter-bomber which cost more was the Republic P-47.

Vought moved F4U production to Dallas in 1946–47, but the intense effort of the previous five years was no longer required. The bent-wing fighter was a proven winner, though a long evolutionary process had been required to bring the design to its perfected state. Some may argue, with reason, that it took too long. Particularly when the press of wartime need was so urgent. But few would argue about the final result. Of the initial complaints, only the spin characteristics remained potentially troublesome.

There was ample stall warning in the entire Corsair line: tail buffeting and left wing heaviness. Any pilot sensitive to the aircraft's feel could anticipate the approach of a stall. The F4U broke abruptly when it quit flying. The -1A stalled from 66 to 87 knots indicated, depending upon power setting, flaps, and landing gear positions. In landing configuration, with power off, gear down, and thirty-degree flaps, the Able usually stalled at an indicated 77 knots.

Stalls were one thing—spins something else. Boone Guyton, lecturing VMF-124 in December 1942, was asked about spinning the new fighter. He offered sage advice when he bluntly replied, "Don't." The pilot's handbook reinforced this message with a bold notice: "WARNING—no intentional spinning is permitted." A one-turn spin could usually be corrected within a quarter turn. But into a third or fourth gyration, the Corsair wanted to poke its long nose down and wrap up ever tighter. A related problem was the inability of some new pilots to recognize an inverted spin soon enough to correct it. As usual, experience was the best teacher—if one survived to learn the lesson.

Once understood, the stall-spin characteristics were but a part of the U-Bird's personality. As an aircraft and as a weapon it offered an exceptional range of performance and mission options. Fast, robust, long-legged, and hard-working, it was tremendously versatile. Perhaps the ultimate word on the F4U came from Major General Marion Carl, the Marine aviator who has himself been called "the ultimate fighter pilot." Twenty-five years after World War II, Carl concluded, "The Corsair was a great mount, head and shoulders above its contemporaries. An airplane like the Corsair only comes along occasionally. Today the Phantom is in the same category—the best flying machine in its time."[11]

chapter 2

Cactus Corsairs

. . . a blue ball bat with inverted wings.

Captain John A. DeChant
Devilbirds

Guadalcanal was the watershed of the Pacific air war. Virtually every Allied aircraft type during 1942–43 operated from one of the island's airfields. First had come the urgently needed Wildcats and Dauntlesses two weeks after U.S. Marines occupied "The Canal" in August 1942. Shortly Navy and Marine TBFs augmented what became known as the Cactus Air Force, after Guadal's code name. Then came Army Air Force P-39s, with American and New Zealand P-40s. And late that year arrived the twin-boomed Lightnings which would kill Japan's greatest admiral.

But there was more. The ubiquitous, beloved PBY and the big, glamorous B-17. The long-range, versatile Liberator series, flown by all three services, was also present. There were C-47 and R4D transports which flew in fuel, food, and ammunition and departed with wounded, sick, or exhausted men. There were Army B-25 and B-26 medium bombers, Navy Kingfisher floatplanes, and twin-engine Australian Hudsons.

In the fall of 1943 there arrived more of the new generation of warplanes—land-based F6F Hellcats which shared the Solomons war while their carrier-borne counterparts won victories and headlines in the Central Pacific.

But even before the Hellcat, there was the Corsair.

By early 1943 there were three airfields on Guadalcanal: Henderson Field, where the strike aircraft were based, and two fighter strips. These fields became the springboard for aerial operations farther up the Solomons.

Much of the Solomons were within reach of Guadalcanal-based F4Us. The big Japanese airfield at Kahili on Bougainville's south coast was 300 miles northwest of Henderson Field, at the limit of the Corsair's tactical radius. But all the mid-Solomons came within easy grasp of the gull-winged fighter, and it would inevitably shape the course of the long-drawn, hard-fought campaign.

So gradually, Corsair pilots came to know the Solomon Islands well. For in this setting of diverse geography, the F4U would fly well over two-thirds of its combat sorties during the Second World War. Most Corsair squadrons staged up through "Buttons," the Allied base at Espiritu Santo some 500 miles southeast in the New Hebrides. Following B-24 navigation planes, their first sight of the Solomons was San Cristobal at the near end of the island chain, and beyond, Guadalcanal's high central mountains. Once established at Cactus, on the grass-covered plain of Guadal's north coast, they began learning the area.

Immediately north across Ironbottom Sound, where so many warships died, were the Floridas. The main base here was Tulagi, home of the PT boats, and known to airmen as "Ringbolt." Malaita to the northeast was seldom of concern to Cactus pilots, but Santa Isabel to the northwest was another matter. Much longer and narrower than Guadalcanal, Isabel

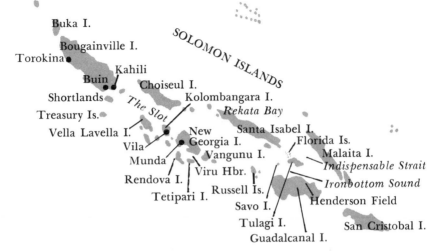

The Solomon Islands.

harbored a pesky, notorious flock of Japanese floatplanes at Rekata Bay on the north coast.

Just south of Isabel, 60 miles northwest of Henderson Field, were the Russells. This two-island group eventually stocked Allied fighters at the advance base called "Knucklehead."

Farther up the chain, still on the south side of the open strip of water known as The Slot, was the New Georgia group. Named for Britain's reigning monarch at the time of its discovery, the southernmost of the Georgias was nearly 150 miles from Henderson. The island of New Georgia itself boasted a Japanese airfield at Munda.

Immediately across Kula Gulf on Kolombangara was another field at Vila. There was Rendova with its distinctive hook at the south end where Tetipari formed Blanche Channel. And there were the oddly alliterative names of islands and places in the Georgias: Vella Lavella island with Baka Baka, Kila Kila, Lambu Lambu and Mundi Mundi; Vange Vange on Kolombangara; Visu Visu Point on New Georgia itself.

Thirty miles across The Slot was Choiseul, with Boe Boe on the south coast. Then even closer, across the strait, was the southern tip of the big island, Bougainville, named for the French explorer who found it in 1767. Clustered at its south end were the Shortlands, in honor of the Royal Navy lieutenant who came along the next year and named Indispensable Strait—between Guadalcanal and Malaita—for his ship. There were also

Fauro Island, which was to the east of Shortland, and the Treasuries, which were slightly to the southwest.

On Bougainville's south coast the Japanese had airfields at Kahili and Buin. Well up the west coast, on the north shore of Empress Augusta Bay, was Torokina where Corsairs would eventually operate. And finally, appended almost as an after-thought, was Buka Island standing straight north across the narrow neck at Buka Passage.

These islands were all south of the equator. The tenth degree of south latitude barely nicks Cape Henslow on Guadalcanal's southeast coast.

In size and topography the Solomons varied greatly. Tiny pinpoints of coral jutted here and there, many too small to support human life. The larger islands could vary from low, flat kunai grass plains to rough, ir-regular mountains reaching 8,000 feet.

The days could be oppressively hot, with temperatures at 95° Fahren-heit and humidity not much less. These were days when condensation trails streamed from wingtips, marking the passage of any aircraft flying in contrail altitudes. But nights often had an edge to them, a startling contrast to the ideal of the tropics. And there was the rain. On some islands the rainfall reached eighty inches a year, but it was mostly sea-sonal. Guadalcanal during late summer received as little as three inches per month. But it could also be deluged, making even pierced steel mat-ting dangerous as a runway.

Dominating the entire chain was The Slot. During latter 1942 this long stretch of open water was one of the busiest arenas in the war. Jap-anese destroyers made almost nightly runs down to Cape Esperance where the "Tokyo Express" unloaded its cargo. PT boats churned up 40-knot wakes trying to keep track of the Express, and not infrequently American men-of-war clashed with the Imperial Navy in brief, brutal, bloody noc-turnal gun and torpedo duels. Thus did Ironbottom Sound acquire its name.

For aviators, The Slot was the main battleground. Japanese air raids were intercepted as far north as possible, thanks to the superbly dedi-cated band of rugged individualists known as coast watchers. Stationed on every main island from Guadalcanal to Bougainville, these Austral-ians eluded the Japanese and radioed Cactus the warning it needed to scramble its fighters.

Hundreds of American and Japanese aircraft fell into The Slot or on islands around it. But this aerial arena had none of the foul odors or wretched sights of the jungle. To James Michener, then an aviation maintenance troubleshooter, this "home of great battles . . . is the most beautiful I know in the world. This may offend those who struggled in its skies. It may cause a shudder to those who fell into its waters and paddled their way on rafts to dismal islands. But during the war I flew

The Slot, and so help me it was beautiful, passionately wonderful with craggy islands, spangled lagoons and towering clouds."[1]

Into this scenic, deadly environment the first Corsair squadron appeared on the morning of 12 February 1943. Major William Gise led the 24 F4U-1s of VMF-124 into Fighter One, and just in time. Informed of the Corsairs' impending arrival, the Cactus air staff already had the squadron scheduled for a mission. Only an hour after the crank-winged fighters set down, a dozen were winging north on a 230-mile Dumbo escort—protecting a PBY which rescued two Wildcat pilots shot down on 31 January. The F4Us orbited overhead while the Catalina picked up the fliers at Sandfly Bay, Vella Lavella.

Next day 124's Corsairs went even farther. This time it was to escort a formation of PB4Ys attacking Japanese shipping in Buin Harbor, a full 300 miles out. It was the farthest Allied fighters had yet gone up the Solomons, a portent of things to come. Leading one four-plane division was First Lieutenant Ken Walsh, a twenty-six-year-old New Yorker with a Brooklyn accent, pale blue eyes, and a fondness for classical music. Walsh

First lieutenant Kenneth A. Walsh of VMF-124 became the first Corsair ace in May 1943. He finished the war with twenty-one victories and the Medal of Honor. (U.S. Marine Corps)

was a mustang. He had enlisted in the Marines ten years before, became an aviation mechanic, and then earned his wings as a private in flight training at Pensacola in 1937. Now he had over 1,600 hours in his logbook. He would shortly put all his skill and experience to use.

Though this first long-range escort brought no combat, it did attract one curious Zeke. The enemy fighter dropped down on one side of the American formation and looked over the Corsairs. Then, curiosity satisfied, it broke away.

Next day the Japanese were more than curious. Returning to Bougainville for a strike on Kahili airdrome, 124's Corsairs were part of a mixed fighter escort to more Liberators. The bombers flew at 20,000 feet with Army P-40s low in front, F4Us above the PB4Ys, and P-38s as top cover.

An estimated 50 Zekes were up and waiting. They shot down all four P-38s, engaged the frontal P-40s and downed two, then broke through to the bombers and hacked down a pair of Liberators. Two F4Us were also lost with their pilots, Lieutenants Lyon and Stewart. Against the loss of these ten American planes, only three Zekes were destroyed, and one of them had collided with Lyon's Corsair. It would be forever remembered as the St. Valentine's Day Massacre.

Stewart's element leader, First Lieutenant Lloyd B. Pearson, reported what happened. It proved that 124 was playing in the big leagues, where the opposition played for keeps: "Stewart's plane was racked with machine-gun fire diagonally across the main fuel cell. When Stewart rejoined me after the melee, I could see the gasoline spraying out of the numerous bullet holes. He appeared to be okay. After approximately ten minutes with us his fuel gave out, he waved goodby and nosed down to the water from about 20,000 feet. The Zeros then followed him down, shooting at him all the while. He made a successful water landing and I thought I could see a yellow spot (his life raft) beside the cockpit. However, the Zeros continued to strafe him. We never heard from Stewart again."[2]

The 15th was scheduled as a repeat of the previous day's mission. It was not greeted with much enthusiasm by any of the aviators. "We were all rather apprehensive," said Ken Walsh. "There was little conversation among the pilots, all of us sensed what it would be like in the target area."[3] The Marines were just starting their engines when ground crewmen gave the cut signal. The mission was canceled. Bomber Command had decided against further strikes on Bougainville until heavier fighter protection was available.

It was probably just as well. The pilots of VMF-124 had averaged only about thirty hours in their planes before arriving at Guadalcanal. A few like Gise and Walsh had fifty hours of F4U time, but most required more experience before they could get the most from their aircraft.

30

As Solomons Fighter Command gained strength, the pressure on Bougainville was increased. By summer a typical strike would include 24 to 28 bombers escorted by 50 or 60 fighters. The same formation was generally employed: bombers at 20,000 feet with P-40s providing low front cover, the Corsairs stacked up to 30,000 feet and P-38s as high as 35,000. The F4Us mostly flew two or three divisions per squadron on these missions, averaging four hours in the air for a round trip to Bougainville. In order to save fuel, rendezvous with the bombers was nearly always accomplished on course up The Slot.

The flying weather was usually good, VFR as much as 85 percent of the time. But spectacular, looming cumulus clouds occasionally forced a detour, and at such moments the fighters could get separated from the bombers. This was an ideal setup for Japanese interceptors, which employed clouds and sun expertly to strike at the bombers when they were most vulnerable.

One of the Corsair's first big dogfights came on 1 April during a Knucklehead patrol over the Russells. Sea Bees were constructing an airfield at Banika, and the Japanese viewed the setup with displeasure; they attempted to bomb the field out of existence. In this combat Ken Walsh scored his first victories, as VMF-124, Wildcats of 221, and some P-38s became heavily engaged with 58 Zekes. The enemy fighters were sent south as part of the huge "I Operation" which Admiral Yamamoto launched in an all-out effort to regain air superiority over the Solomons and New Guinea. Walsh latched on to a tan-colored Zeke and shot it down, then quickly dropped another Zeke and a Val into the blue-green waters of The Slot.

In larger context, "I Operation" was a failure. Though six Marine fighters were lost, 18 Zekes fell to Wildcats and Corsairs, and Banika remained unharmed.

During the next three months, seven more Marine squadrons entered combat with F4Us. The first after VMF-124 was Major Wade Britt's 213 in March, followed by Major Ray Vroome's 121 in mid-April. But Britt was killed in a takeoff accident on 13 April and Major Greg Weissenberger assumed command.

The manner in which 121 re-equipped with Corsairs was typical. The squadron was one of the old-line F4F units on Guadalcanal, dating from October 1942, but by spring few of the veterans remained. The pilots were rushed down to Espiritu Santo where F4U checkouts were conducted at Turtle Bay, since none had ever flown a Corsair. Most of them had time for only ten or fifteen hours in their new fighters before taking them into combat.

Other Corsair squadrons—either by transition or arrival—became operational at the rate of about two per month. Major Paul Fontana's VMF-

A rare combat mission photo showing an F4U-1 of VMF-121 escorting SBDs on a mission up "The Slot" from Guadalcanal in mid-1943. (R.M. Baker)

112 was flying F4Us by 19 May, as was VMF-221. During June, VMF-122 under Major Elmer Brackett had its Corsairs in service. Two-Fourteen, eventually the Black Sheep, also transitioned in June under Major H. A. Ellis. And when Major Richard Baker's VMF-123 flew its first Corsair mission on 2 July, all eight Marine fighter squadrons in the Solomons were equipped with F4Us.

Many of the squadron commanders came and went during this period. A few were killed, but most were rotated or reassigned as experienced leaders were shifted around. VMF-112 had three COs during July alone, and 221 had three in August.

The second Corsair squadron in combat, VMF-213, staged a frantic free-for-all quite unexpectedly on 25 April. A division led by Major Monfurd Peyton was returning from a bomber escort when a large Japanese formation was seen. It consisted of 16 dive bombers and 20-plus Zekes, apparently headed for the Russells or Henderson Field. Despite the lopsided odds, the four Hellhawks attacked. In the short, deadly dogfight which ensued, two Corsairs and five Zekes went down, but the bombers were routed. One Marine was rescued, and Peyton landed with nearly eighty holes in his plane.

In one of the last major Japanese flights against Guadalcanal, at least 25 Zekes escorted recon aircraft down The Slot on 13 May. The enemy formation was intercepted near the Russells by 15 Corsairs of VMF-112 and 124, led by Major Gise. The Marines claimed 15 Zekes for three F4Us, and a "poaching" P-38 dropped one more. But it was a day of mixed fortunes for 124, which lots its skipper, Bill Gise. Ken Walsh killed three Zekes and brought his total to six. He thus became the squadron's first ace, and the first pilot to achieve that status in the Corsair.

After his third kill of the fight, Walsh saw another Zeke flying abreast of him off his port wing. Next thing Walsh knew, tracers were flashing past his wingtips and canopy. The Japanese pilot had barrel-rolled into a firing position 500 feet behind Walsh's tail. The Marine was having none of that. He split-essed, firewalled his throttle, mixture, and prop controls, followed by a hard right turn, and went straight home. Upon landing back at Guadalcanal, Walsh found two 7.7-millimeter "arrows" in his plane's tail. But more importantly, he learned that not all of the enemy's skilled, experienced aviators had died at Midway or Guadalcanal.

Captain Archie Donahue, a twenty-seven-year-old Texan, became 112's first ace in this same combat. He splashed four Zekes to add to his single F4F victory with the Wolfpack back in November. Gise's place at the head of 124 was taken by Captain Cecil Brewer, who would remain in command for the next six weeks.

The 112-124 team was in action again on 5 June. Escorting 15 Navy SBDs and 12 TBFs, 21 Corsairs thoroughly worked over a Japanese destroyer, a corvette, and a troop transport off Buin. The latter two vessels were set afire by bombing and strafing while the DD was badly shot up before the Zekes arrived to contest the issue. Ken Walsh's division escorted the strike director, Commander Weldon Hamilton, leading Air Group 11 in a TBF. Hamilton sat above the strike planes, calmly ordering his planes to their targets. The admiring Walsh thought that Hamilton performed as if he'd been flying combat for five years.

The Marines saw six SBDs sink the moored corvette and then followed Hamilton down as he dropped his bombs on a cargo ship. Walsh strafed a barge in the harbor, watching his .50 calibers churn the water white and chop big chunks from it. Still in the target area, he chased a Zeke off one of his wingmen, who had lost altitude switching fuel tanks, and won a climbing contest with the Mitsubishi. When the Zeke stalled and nosed down, Walsh easily gained a firing position and destroyed him within sight of his own field.

By this time the combat was nearly over and about a dozen Zekes had gone down, along with five Navy and Marine planes. Departing the target area near the Shortlands, a Pete floatplane attacked Hamilton's TBF and damaged it. Walsh chased the Pete as it scurried back north. He caught up and exploded the Mitsubishi, but doubted the victory would be confirmed.

Rejoining Hamilton above the broken clouds, Walsh saw that an SBD had linked up. The Dauntless gunner called out a Zeke approaching from astern and Walsh chandelled into the threat. He pounced on the bandit "like a vulture on a mouse,"[4] and found it was another Pete, not a Zeke. Walsh had the outclassed Japanese completely at his mercy, but when he pressed the trigger his guns wouldn't fire. An electrical circuit had come loose. The floatplane split-essed and escaped.

When he rejoined the CAG section for the trip home, Walsh noticed the SBD gunner gesturing. The Corsair pilot slid in close and discerned the rear-seatman clasping his hands over his head in a gesture of triumph. After debriefing, Walsh learned the gunner had "confirmed" the Pete for him. Total Marine claims amounted to fifteen.

The off-again-on-again sparring continued till mid-June. By that time, two more large Japanese attacks had been foiled. On the 7th, 112 raiders were intercepted and 23 claimed destroyed. Only VMF-112 made any kills among the Corsair squadrons, with seven tallies, while four F4Us and a P-40 were shot down. One Wolfpack pilot, Lieutenant Sam Logan, had a horrifying taste of aerial combat. Attempting to break through a flock of Zeros which had trapped a New Zealander, Logan's plane was set afire and he bailed out at 18,000 feet.

Logan's parachute deployed safely but left him a helpless, dangling target for one bloodthirsty Japanese. The Zeke pilot proved a poor marksman, failing to hit Logan in several passes, then changed tactics. He decided to chop the Marine to pieces with his propeller, and succeeded in amputating part of each foot. Before the Japanese could complete his aerial butchery he was driven off by another Kiwi P-40. Logan splashed safely into the water and was rescued by a J2F amphibian.

During this same engagement Lieutenant Gilbert Percy had an even more harrowing trial—if possible. Surrounded by five Zekes, Percy fought back and sent one spinning out of sight. But the others shot out his controls, engine, and hydraulic systems, forcing him over the side at about 3,000 feet. The stricken Corsair was indicating 350 knots when Percy jumped, and when he pulled his rip cord, the parachute canopy streamed behind him, not opening. Spinning wildly, the Marine cooly stabilized himself by holding his arms and legs stiff.

Seawater is about three-fourths the consistency of cement when struck at terminal velocity. But Percy hit with such force that he went feet first far below the surface. The impact broke both ankles, his pelvis, and inflicted internal injuries. He passed out from the pain but had presence of mind to pull the CO-2 bottles in his life vest and bobbed to the surface. Unable to swim, fighting constant nausea, Percy back-stroked for seven hours toward a nearby reef. He was washed up on the beach early next morning where friendly natives found him and sent for help. The indestructable Mister Percy returned to active duty twelve months later.

The last enemy daylight bombing raid on Guadalcanal came on 16 June. It involved at least 90 planes, mostly Zekes and Vals, which split in a two-pronged attack to get at Allied shipping anchored between Guadalcanal and Tulagi. U.S. and New Zealand fighter direction stations—"Recon" and "Kiwi" respectively—estimated the raid at 120 bandits, and every available fighter was scrambled. But the fortunes of war belonged to the Army and Navy this day, especially the Sundowners of VF-11 with their F4F-4s. The Wildcats clawed down 31 raiders, while Army and New Zealand fighters, with AA gunners, accounted for most of the other claims. Three Corsair outfits—VMF-121, 122, and 124—reported an aggregate eight victories. Two American ships were hit, but at a cost of six aircraft Solomons Fighter command had destroyed nearly all the raiders and convinced the Imperial Navy that further daylight raids on Cactus were useless.

After this mid-June fling, the war progressed at a more-or-less steady pace. Additional bases were seized, built, or occupied. Already operating F4Us and other Allied fighters was Banika in the Russells, known fondly to airmen as "Boomtown." It was all of that. The amenities of civilization included a free hamburger stand and a steam laundry. VMF-121 and 124 operated there for a time before returning to a quieter, safer Guadalcanal. Banika was mainly used as an advance field to top off fuel tanks for escorts to Bougainville.

By now both the Americans and Japanese had ample opportunity to evaluate the Corsair. To Strike Command, the F4U's range—about twice that of the Wildcat—was its greatest virtue. The Japanese probably would have agreed, since the long-legged P-38 was never available in comparable numbers in the Solomons. Noted the Zero's designer, Mitsubishi engineer Jiro Horikoshi, "The first single-engine American fighter to seriously challenge the Zero was the Chance Vought Corsair. In a short period of time the excellent qualities of the Corsair became only too evident. . . . Faster than the Zero in level flight and capable of infinitely greater diving speeds, the Corsairs soon proved to be a great nuisance to our fighters."[5]

The first major move up the Solomons occurred at the end of June when amphibious troops went ashore in the New Georgia group, on Rendova and Vangunu. To handle the anticipated Japanese reaction, a 32-plane CAP was kept on station over the landing beaches. It was barely enough.

Early on the 30th, two determined enemy attacks were repulsed. The third raid came in the afternoon, and though the 28 Japanese torpedo planes were destroyed almost in total by fighters and flak, they sank Rear Admiral Kelly Turner's flagship, the transport *McCawley*.

Major Greg Weissenberger's VMF-213 had the best of the Marines' shooting during the day. He took his division into a flock of Zekes and spent an exceedingly eventful sixty seconds. The CO shot down three bandits, then fell prey to a fourth and bailed out from about 800 feet. Weissenberger dropped into the water close to a destroyer which reeled him in just as a Corsair splashed a Betty intent on crashing into the ship.

Lieutenant Wilbur J. Thomas, originally an SBD pilot, destroyed four Zekes in his first dogfight. But other types of Mitsubishis were engaged, as one 213 division came across a formation of nine Petes and dropped them all. It amounted to 20 kills for the squadron.

The Corsairs tallied fifty-eight victories during the 30th, slightly more than half the entire Allied total. And though the claims were undoubtedly optimistic, they reflected the intensity of the combat. Captain Robert Bruce's VMF-121 had a rugged fight near Rendova when a gaggle of Zekes dropped unseen onto two divisions. Four F4Us were shot down by the estimated 40 hostiles, which hit the Corsairs at 12,000 feet. Lieutenant Bruce Porter, a former USC swimmer, had a typical experience. He shot down one Zeke and hit another which evaded, trailing smoke, then went after a third. But another Zero sneaked up unseen and put several rounds through his starboard wing and one through the canopy. Porter's wingman, Lieutenant Jim Leeds, smoked the Zeke and drove it off. In all, VMF-121 claimed eighteen victories during two combats. Captains Bob Baker, Ken Ford, and Perry Shuman contributed half of this figure with three apiece. VMF-221, now under Major Monfurd Peyton, was next most successful of the engaged F4U squadrons, with sixteen victories.

Though the Japanese failed to repulse the New Georgia landings on the first day, they kept trying. The battles over the beaches continued for the next two weeks, but the Allied air defense held tight. During the entire month of July, only four ships of the invasion force were hit by enemy bombs or torpedoes—testimony to the skill of both fighter pilots and radar controllers.

Two days in particular are worthy examples. On the 7th, Corsairs were vectored to a forward interception on 70-plus hostiles. They completely broke up the attack. Three F4U squadrons, paced by VMF-122, knocked down 16 Zekes or Bettys. Then on the 15th, 122 was again at work when planes of the newly formed ComAir New Georgia claimed forty-four kills. Two divisions of 122 made first contact and splashed 14 raiders in about fifteen minutes. Then 8 Corsairs of 213 arrived and reported the destruction of 16 more.

The F4Us had other missions besides air defense, however. On one occasion a flight of VMF-124 was sent out to hunt down and sink a troublesome Japanese yacht which had been nosing around a coast watcher's position. But more typically the Corsairs escorted bombers in strikes against Japanese bases. Kahili was brought nearer at the end of July when the fighter strip at Segi Point became operational on southern New Georgia. But Kahili was already within range of Guadalcanal-based F4Us, and Cactus aircraft returned there regularly after the New Georgia landings got underway. On 17 July four Corsair squadrons escorted three dozen Dauntlesses, an equal number of Avengers, and seven Liberators in an attack on enemy shipping off Kahili. While the bombers sank one destroyer and damaged three others, the Allied fighters locked horns with the numerous Japanese interceptors. Again the Marines did most of the shooting, with forty-one of the fifty-two aerial victories claimed. The potent team of VMF-122 and 213 tied for top score with fourteen each while Captain Albert Hacking made four of 221's six kills.

In mid-August VMF-124 moved temporarily to the still-uncompleted strip at Munda. Now under Major William A. Millington, the squadron had just returned from R and R in Sydney, where high-strung young aviators indulged in not much rest, but considerable recreation. It was a popular spot. The joke went that many fliers were glad to get back into combat, where they could regain their strength.

Millington's outfit, along with VMF-123, moved into Munda on 14 August, just in time for the invasion of Vella Lavella. Only 90 miles from Kahili, the landing beaches were subjected to incessant attack, and a quick-response fighter force was needed. To save weight and improve rate of climb, many of the Munda F4Us had their arresting hooks removed, along with other equipment including CO_2 bottles used for purging fuel tanks. Reduced ammo loads and empty wing tanks were also a method of lightening the interceptors' weight.

The practice of fighter scrambles, however, was shortly discontinued. Experience showed that the haste and harried atmosphere of such circumstances produced an environment for disaster. Some pilots tended to skip through the check list, or ignore it altogether. And taxi or takeoff collisions resulted from the rush to get airborne. In short, a scramble temporarily made the fighters more dangerous to one another than to the enemy.

But for the moment the old ways prevailed. On the 15th, VMF-124 launched two divisions on CAP over the beach at Vella Lavella, 40 miles to the northwest. Three planes dropped out with engine trouble, and when Ken Walsh arrived on station he reported to the fighter direction ship that he had five "chicks" at angels ten. Shortly thereafter the FDO, call sign Cracker Base, notified the Marines of 30-plus bandits inbound, headed for the shipping offshore.

As usual, Walsh scored multiple kills. Bounced by five Zekes, his flight became dispersed and he chased down one bandit five miles north of Cracker Base. Now alone, Walsh responded to the FDO's new vector which put him on to a flight of nine Val dive bombers. Approaching from six o'clock low, the Marine closed in and fired several long bursts which flamed two of the Aichis.

Then a vengeful Zeke dropped onto Walsh's tail. Before he could evade, the Japanese hit the Corsair hard. One 20-mm shell exploded in the starboard wing tank, exiting in fifty-seven pieces, but the depressurized fuel system prevented a larger explosion. Another 20-mm entered the right wingroot, severing the aileron control rod on that side. Machine gun shells perforated the horizontal stabilizer, cut hydraulic lines, and punctured the right tire. But Walsh shook the Zeke and managed a safe landing back at Munda. Pilots and mechanics actually cheered the display of flying skill, then pushed the shot-up Corsair aside. It was too badly damaged to fly again.

None of the Japanese aircraft had broken through to attack the invasion force.

Two weeks later, on 30 August while escorting B-24s to Kahili, Walsh's supercharger quit over southern New Georgia. Recalling the still-untidy Munda strip, he landed there.

Almost as soon as Walsh climbed from his plane he was met by an old friend, Major Jim Neefus, who had charge of the field. Anxious to complete the mission, which was sure to bring combat, Walsh quickly explained his situation and asked if there were a spare F4U available. Neefus told him to climb in a jeep and they sped off to the alert flight's area, where four Corsairs were parked. "Take your pick," grinned Neefus, and Walsh did.[6] Barely ten minutes after landing at Munda he was climbing at full power to rejoin the bombers.

Walsh knew the Liberators would fly past Kahili, then turn southeast on their bomb run. By cutting the corner he arrived at 30,000 feet over Bougainville just as the twin-tailed Consolidateds began their attack. He was in perfect position to hit the rear portion of about 50 Zekes, and he dropped 2 within a few miles of each other.

The aerial clash followed the bombers' progress, and Walsh drifted with the tide of battle. About 70 miles southeast of Kahili he became engaged with another group of Zekes and shot down two more. But the Japanese had a numerical advantage which could not be negated. Walsh saw a Lib go down, from which no parachutes emerged, and a P-39 pilot bailed out when Zekes set his Airacobra afire.

Set upon by numerous hostiles, Walsh's borrowed Corsair was thoroughly shot up. He was forced to set it down in the water off Vella Lavella, the second time he had ditched an F4U. Sea Bees on shore had seen the crippled fighter splash, and sped to the scene in a Higgins boat. Walsh was hauled aboard and next day returned to Guadalcanal on an LST. A companion was one Lieutenant Fowler, the same P-39 pilot he had seen bail out, suffering a broken leg in the process. Three days later Walsh was flying again.

This raid on Kahili cost seven fighters and two bombers, but the bombing results were good. In addition to enemy planes shot down, the field was hard hit. Japanese air power in the northern Solomons was being beaten down.

When VMF-124 completed its tour in early September, the pattern for Corsair operations was well established. The CO, Major Bill Millington, took his squadron back to the States with an enviable record. In seven months 124 had been credited with 68 victories in aerial combat. Seven pilots had been killed—three lost to enemy action and four operation-

"Knucklehead" Corsairs. F4U-1s, probably of VMF-214, at Russell Island in September 1943. (R.M. Hill)

ally. Nine more sustained serious injuries or wounds. The squadron had lost or written off 32 F4U-1s or -1As, but only 11 were attributed to enemy action.

By this time Ken Walsh was the clear leader among Marine fighter pilots in the post-Guadalcanal campaign. He had run his personal total to twenty kills—16 Zekes, 3 Vals, and a Pete. But there was another record yet to come. Upon return home, Walsh was assigned to training command at NAS Jacksonville, Florida. In early February he was summoned to the White House, where he received the Congressional Medal of Honor from President Roosevelt. The citation specified Walsh's single-handed combats of 15 and 30 August, making him the first of four Corsair pilots to win the nation's highest award for valor.

Behind every fighter ace there is a wingman, who usually receives precious little credit for his crucial services. Speaking of Lieutenant Bill Johnston, his usual number two, Walsh said, "If it wasn't for him, I'd still be somewhere in the Solomon Islands! He was always there when I needed him."[7]

Other F4U pilots were also piling up good scores in the Solomons. The Hellhawks of VMF-213 counted seven aces among their number, led by Lieutenants Gus Thomas with sixteen victories and Edward O. Shaw with thirteen, and Captain James N. Cupp with an even dozen. Finishing its tour in December, the squadron claimed over 100 aerial victories.

Jim Cupp undoubtedly expressed many a Marine fighter pilot's feelings for the Corsair. During a hard-fought combat over Vella Lavella on 17 September, his division battled eight Zekes, jumped "a massive formation" of Vals, and engaged more Zeros. Cupp saw four of the Vals he

A Marine F4U-1A in a bulldozed revetment on Vella Lavella in January 1944. (R.M. Hill)

selected hit the water, but ended the fight with four Zekes on his tail. Caught at an altitude disadvantage with a badly mauled Corsair, the Iowa pilot decided his only chance was to run for it. The Pratt and Whitney responded, despite battle damage, and Cupp left his assailants behind. He landed "that beautiful, faithful greyhound of a plane"[8] at Munda without flaps or brakes.

As Allied air power gained ascendancy, fighter pilots were forced to seek the enemy more often on his own airfields. By far the single most spectacular such episode was the result of a quirk of nature.

Lieutenant Alvin Jensen, a former enlisted pilot, was separated from VMF-214 on 28 August while flying through a storm. Purely by chance, Jensen's Corsair was spit out of the storm, inverted, right over Kahili. Jensen was a second-tour pilot with five aerial victories to his credit, but he had never seen anything like this. Through the top of his cockpit canopy he could see that Kahili was loaded with Japanese aircraft.

Rolling his Corsair right side up, the Marine pressed down to the treetops beneath the darkened sky. His abrupt, unconventional appearance caught the enemy unprepared. Keeping low and kicking the rudder to spread as much destruction as possible, he clamped down on the trigger as he raced the length of the 5,000-foot strip from north to south. Tracers lanced through aircraft, gun pits, and facilities. Once beyond the field, Jensen stayed low over the water near Ballale and kept going. He didn't realize it at the time, but photo reconnaissance next day confirmed that Alvin Jensen had single-handedly burned two dozen enemy aircraft. Four Vals, 8 Zekes, and 12 Bettys were destroyed as a result of his unintentional exit from the dark, broiling storm cloud. The Tennesseean received a Navy Cross for his expert strafing.

Strategically, the central Solomons were secured in October with the Japanese evacuation of Kolombangara. Bougainville was still to be occupied, but by the early fall of 1943 it was apparent where the bulk of Allied air power would shortly be directed. For beyond Bougainville lay the Bismarck Archipelago.

And Rabaul.

chapter 3

The upper Solomons

If I were a king, the worst punishment I could inflict on
my enemies would be to banish them to the Solomons.

Jack London

Island hopping was the name of the game in the Pacific. There were few rules and any number could play. But by the early fall of 1943, the contest showed signs of stalemate.

The major objective in the South Pacific was still the naval-air complex at Rabaul on New Britain, main island of the Bismarck Archipelago. As long as Rabaul remained an effective Japanese base, the upper Solomons would be the scene of a prolonged attrition campaign. It was a type of conflict the Allies would eventually win, but only at considerable expense of time and blood.

One of the few rules in the Solomons island-hopping game was that each hop was limited within the range of land-based air power. Aircraft carriers were too precious a commodity in 1943 to divert from the Central Pacific offensive which had just begun. True, carriers would make a contribution to securing the upper Solomons with strikes against Rabaul, but these were special operations, limited in time and number. If Rabaul were to be neutralized, it would have to be done by the Solomons Air Command from the south and the Fifth Air Force from the west, on New Guinea.

Therefore, part of Bougainville would have to be taken. Largest and northernmost of the Solomons, Bougainville was desirable for basically one reason. It was an excellent position from which to strangle Rabaul. Airfields near Cape Torokina on the island's west coast were within 250 miles of Rabaul. From this complex, Allied air power could pummel the harbor and airdromes, rendering them untenable to the Japanese. Occupation of Rabaul would be unnecessary, as would occupation of all Bougainville. The airfields were what mattered.

The prerequisite for seizing the Cape Torokina area on Empress Augusta Bay was to trample Japanese air power elsewhere on Bougainville. This meant depleting the stock of enemy aircraft at Kahili airfield near Buin, on the south coast, and Ballale, a small island near the Shortlands. Numerous heavy raids had struck these facilities, causing damage and destroying aircraft. But the damage seemed to be repaired with frustrating ease—the runways were kept open. And replacement aircraft were funneled down from Rabaul and Truk. In early November over 170 enemy carrier aircraft were flown from the Carolines to Rabaul, meeting the new threat.

Flying mainly from Vella Lavella, but also from Munda and the Russells, Marine F4U squadrons went to work on Bougainville's Zekes. One of the new COs was instrumental in perfecting the technique which accomplished this goal. He was Major Greg Boyington of VMF-214.

Boyington was, if nothing else, a fighter. Relentlessly aggressive, he never refused a challenge—real or imagined. He had studied aeronautical engineering at the University of Washington, then became a Marine fighter pilot. He had flown with the American Volunteer Group in China during late 1941 into early 1942, where he led a checkered career. Boyington returned to the States claiming he'd shot down six Japanese aircraft while flying the shark-nosed P-40s. Back in the Marines, he still hadn't found his niche. He flew a full tour in the Solomons without seeing an enemy airplane and then suffered a broken ankle in a barroom fight.

At this juncture, fate took a turn. Boyington was knocking around Espiritu Santo in the New Hebrides at the same time VMF-214 came up for reorganization. The CO, Major William Pace, had been killed in action during August, near the end of the squadron's second tour. Under these circumstances, the pilots were reassigned and 214 became a squadron in name—or number—only.

Bored beyond endurance with administrative work, Boyington went looking for a new command. He sought out the group commander, Lieutenant Colonel Lawson Sanderson, and asked permission to form a new 214 from pool and replacement pilots yet unassigned. Sanderson took a liking to the rough, rebellious Boyington, and consented.

On 7 September VMF-214 was reorganized with forty-eight other pilots. Contrary to popular notion, they were representative of many Marine aviators at this stage of the war—a combination of newcomers and old hands. They ranged in age from twenty-one to thirty-one, and nearly half had previous combat experience. Fifteen had already flown in the Solomons and another five were veterans of the Royal Canadian Air Force. At age thirty, Boyington was not quite the oldest man in the squadron, but before long his troops began calling him "Pappy." Before the war he'd been known as "Rats" in the Marines, but from now on the new moniker was permanent.

Boyington's pilots were dubbed the Black Sheep, but not for the popularized reasons. For instance, none faced charges or court-martial. There were other problems, however. The Corsair was "a sweet-flying baby if ever I flew one," Boyington said,[1] but some of his pilots were new to the F4U. One former SBD pilot torque-rolled a Corsair on landing, with predictable results, and was considered fortunate to escape with his life. Others like Lieutenant Bob McClurg, also a dive-bomber veteran, took right to the bent-winged bird and became one of the Black Sheep aces.

Boyington and company arrived at Munda in mid-September and immediately set to work. Their first mission was a bomber escort to Ballale on the 16th. Boyington was so intent on watching the bombers and the flak patterns that he belatedly realized "we were right in the middle of about forty Jap fighters."[2] A Hamp flew past the lead Corsair, wagging

45

its wings in the join-up signal, and Boyington was happy to oblige. The Japanese pilot's poor recognition cost him his life as Boyington added power, caught up, and sent the Mitsubishi flaming towards the water.

The combat descended toward sea level where Zekes were attacking SBDs and TBFs as they re-formed after the attack. In the next several minutes Boyington shot down another four bandits, becoming the first Corsair "ace in a day." The other Black Sheep knocked down six more Zekes with a further eight claimed as probables. One 214 pilot failed to return. He was later found dead in his raft.

In their first four weeks the Black Sheep claimed forty-seven confirmed kills in strikes against Kahili and vicinity. On 4 October a near-solid undercast prevented TBFs from bombing accurately, and the Avengers turned for home without molestation. Ever aggressive, Boyington led five pilots back north and orbited Kahili, seeking combat. The Corsairs found nothing but billowy clouds.

Then, in perfect, unaccented English, came an inquiry over the radio: "Major Boyington, what is your position?"[3] Recognizing a trap, Boyington turned it to advantage. He informed the Japanese controller he was at 20,000 feet over Treasury Island, due south of Buin. When 30 Zekes appeared, the 214 pilots had a 6,000-foot altitude advantage. The Corsairs hit the Zekes from above and behind, Boyington exploding the leader and pursuing the others in a descending port spiral. In a half-minute 360° turn, Black Sheep One splashed two more Zekes, and his pilots claimed others probably destroyed.

Black Sheep F4U-1As on Bougainville in February 1944, at the end of VMF-214's Solomons tour. (R.M. Hill)

46

Kahili was also a favorite hunting spot of VMF-213. On 23 September the Hellhawks had tangled with Zekes over the airdrome and fought them southwards towards the Treasuries. Lieutenant Gus Thomas, one of the deadliest fighter pilots the Corps ever produced, split one Zeke with his wingman and bagged three more which were threatening two F4Us. But somewhere in the frantic hassle Thomas's Corsair took hits in an oil line. His engine began to seize, and he glided towards the water, unscrewing his instrument panel clock as a souvenir.

The R-2800 quit cold at 3,000 feet. Thomas expended his remaining airspeed in a loop and fell free at the top. When he opened his parachute he decided to keep the ripcord as another momento and stuffed it in a pocket. Corsairs circled overhead as the twenty-three-year-old ace inflated his rubber raft and climbed in, pulling his chute canopy after him. When the F4Us departed to summon help, Thomas bailed out his raft and field-stripped his .45 automatic, oiling it to prevent corrosion. Then he settled down to five hours of paddling, trying to keep away from hostile waters. By 1500 he was exhausted and pulled the canopy over him, trying to rest.

"As I was dozing off, I heard something overhead," he said. "I looked up just in time to see a large bird, I think it was an albatross, light on my toe." Thomas tried to make friends with the bird, but it bit his finger. It refused to leave, however, even when Thomas fired tracer bullets trying to attract a passing PBY. But the albatross overstayed its welcome when it "exhibited a lack of housebreaking, and I shooed it away." Trying his fishing line, the downed flier decided the fish weren't as friendly as the bird—he got no bites at all.[4]

Finally, after about ten hours in the water, Thomas spotted another PBY. He spread dye marker and flashed his signal mirror, and was relieved to see the Catalina splash down and taxi towards him. Two weeks later, on 11 October, he killed three Zekes over Bougainville. It was his fifth and last combat in the Solomons, running his score to sixteen and one-half confirmed. When 213 finished its tour soon after, Thomas was the ranking Marine fighter pilot still in combat, but he confessed that his greater desire was to return to Kansas in time for duck season.

During the second half of October, AirSols mounted sixty missions against southern Bougainville. Eight of these, mainly fighter sweeps, netted claims of 47 Japanese planes shot down in exchange for 9 Allied aircraft lost to enemy action.

Largely by being in the right place at the right time, VMF-214 had been responsible for most of the successes during this period. When Boyington herded his Black Sheep south to Espiritu for R and R late that month, the situation was well in hand over Kahili. Meanwhile, another

Corsair squadron was just going operational in the area, and it too would make a name for itself.

This was VF-17 under Lieutenant Commander John T. Blackburn. In late October the unit had staged north through Espiritu and Henderson Field to Ondonga, New Georgia. The Corsairs with small Jolly Rogers painted on their cowls landed on the 4,000-foot white coral runway where they were met by VMF-215 mechanics. Blackburn's own maintenance personnel had not yet arrived.

Fighting 17 was one of the first two Navy squadrons to fly the F4U in combat. But the circumstances surrounding its arrival tended to mar the honor. The Corsairs had been detached from the *Bunker Hill* in Hawaii, despite a proven record of safe carrier operation. However, BuAer had made its mind up, and Air Group 17 went to combat with Hellcats instead of F4Us.

Ironically, in spite of being orphaned from ship and air group, VF-17 beat both into the war zone. Tommy Blackburn had worked his pilots and mechanics hard during training on the East Coast, and they were ready when they began operations on 29 October 1943. The skipper's previous combat experience was brief and disappointing. As CO of VF-29 aboard an escort carrier during the North African invasion in November 1942, he'd run out of fuel and ditched his F4F. It had been his only mission in the war so far, and he was anxious to take a more active role. Almost one year later to the day, he got his wish.

On 1 November 1943 the Allied forces claimed one more rung up the Solomons ladder, putting troops ashore at Cape Torokina on Bougainville's west coast. Fighter Command provided 32 aircraft in considerable variety over the landing beach, and fought a day-long battle with Rabaul-based Japanese planes.

Bougainville was now within range of several Allied airfields, allowing U.S. and New Zealand P-40s to stand medium-level CAP with P-38s and P-39s at high and low level respectively. Still, the Corsairs got in some shooting.

Young Captain James E. Swett of VMF-221 was by now a veteran in the Solomons. In his first combat back in April he had bagged seven Vals before his Wildcat was shot down near Guadalcanal. On the early CAP over Empress Augusta Bay he was again attracted to the fixed-gear dive bombers. Separated from his wingmen during the first of four Japanese air attacks during the day, Swett joined forces with some Lightnings. He shot down two Vals, then dived to the aid of a lone P-40 being pursued by Japanese Army fighters. Swett lined up a Kawasaki Tony, hit it, and saw it smoke. But when tracer "arrows" flashed past his canopy he disengaged and set course for Vella Lavella.

Less than a half-hour later, Tommy Blackburn led his bearded, piratical-looking pilots into combat. He had eight Corsairs as top cover at 25,000 feet when many bandits were sighted at 0745. There were an estimated 40 Zekes and Vals stacked from 16,000 to 18,000 feet. Blackburn took in the spectacle, playing it safe for the moment. He intended to send one division down on the dive bombers while the other tackled the Zekes, but it didn't work out that way. All eight Skull and Crossbones Corsairs went for the nearest targets—the Zekes.

At least VF-17 achieved surprise. Ensign Ray Beacham made the first kill, a spectacular flamer. Blackburn overhauled another Zeke and opened fire at 200 yards, continuing his run down to 100 yards. The enemy pilot gave no appearance of realizing his danger right up to the moment the pretty little Zero flamed and dropped away. Blackburn then spotted a Zeke on a Corsair's tail and made two runs without result. When the bandit disengaged, Blackburn chased it down and again burned his victim from 100 yards astern. Two other pilots also made kills, putting VF-17's initial tally at five to nothing. During debriefing back at Ondonga, Blackburn was vocal in his displeasure. He took part of the blame himself for taking a cautious approach. But with better air discipline, he said, the Corsairs would have made a bigger killing.

During a later CAP the exec, Roger Hedrick, added to the toll. Cool and calm, Hedrick was perhaps the best fighter pilot in VF-17. His flying and shooting were exemplary, as he demonstrated over the invasion force when he led a bounce upon nine Zekes escorting bombers. Conserving ammunition, Hedrick used only four of his six .50 calibers to torch a Zeke in the one pass which time allowed. Two other pilots observed hits upon another bandit but no claim was made, and the others rapidly dispersed.

During the noon hour a division from Lieutenant Colonel Herbert Williamson's VMF-215 fought 8 of an estimated 25 fighters and torpedo planes. First Lieutenant Robert M. Hanson, the India-born son of Massachusetts missionaries, took on six Kates low over the water. During the short, close-range combat, Hanson splashed two Kates before one of the rear gunners put his F4U out of action. Hanson made a safe water landing and spent the next several hours in his rubber raft. He sighted a U.S. destroyer that afternoon and began paddling toward it. When the ship hove to, the sailors were treated to the spectacle of a big Marine aviator lustily singing "You'd Be So Nice to Come Home To."[5] Bob Hanson rejoined his squadron a few days later. He'd had a good day, but had not yet hit his stride.

The Torokina landings were completely successful. Japanese aerial opposition was defeated by Fighter Command pilots, who turned in an unusually accurate assessment: twenty-two kills, which was the exact number the Japanese admitted losing. Shipboard gunners claimed another four planes shot down. Four Allied fighters were lost during the Torokina landings, including a plane and pilot from VMF-215. And VF-17 also suffered its first casualty. That evening while strafing barges near Shortland Island, one of Blackburn's pilots was hit by flak, landed in the water, and never got out.

Japanese air attacks continued against the Torokina beachhead for the next two weeks. There were losses on both sides, but the Japanese suffered the greater casualties, and they could ill afford them. The aircraft carrier squadrons sent from Truk to Rabaul were being slowly annihilated in missions over Bougainville.

On 11 November the second of two carrier strikes on Rabaul was launched by the *Essex, Bunker Hill,* and *Independence.* The first had occurred six days before, with the intention of destroying enemy warships in the harbor. The Armistice Day strike, it was hoped, would finish the job.

For Tom Blackburn and his displaced VF-17, the second Rabaul strike involved a bittersweet reunion with Air Group 17. The Skull and Crossbones squadron was to provide CAP for the carriers, land aboard to refuel, and then resume patrol over the task group. Almost before dawn, 23 F4Us departed Ondonga and overflew the south coast of Bougainville. By 0600 Fighting 17 was on station, in company with a dozen F6Fs of VF-33 from Segi Point. Beneath this umbrella of 35 fighters, the three carriers launched their strikes 160 miles southeast of the target. Two and a half hours after taking station, the Corsairs began dropping into the carriers' landing patterns. Blackburn led three divisions onto the *Bunker Hill*'s 800-foot flight deck, eager to see some old friends and to prove the F4U capable of operating from carriers in combat. The other 11 Corsairs were taken aboard the *Essex* while the Hellcats put down on the *Independence.*

While VF-17 and 33 were refueling, Marine F4Us arrived to take up the CAP. In the brief time available, VF-17 availed itself of the hospitality, showers, and cuisine aboard the two CVs. Compared to the tents, dust, and spam which characterized life back at Ondonga, the Corsair pilots realized just how much they missed the *Bunker Hill.* Then all too quickly the F4Us were launched to protect the task force as its strike planes returned and VMF-212 and 221 returned to Barakoma and Munda. But three of Blackburn's pilots almost immediately set course for New Georgia, aborting with mechanical problems. The other twenty remained overhead, waiting for the second strike to be launched.

At first there was nothing to report. The only excitement occurred at 1130 when Lieutenant (jg) Jim Streig, element leader in Lieutenant Paul

Cordray's division, sighted a lone aircraft ten miles north of the task group. Streig closed on the bogey, identified it as a Tony, and chased it in a 23,000-foot dive. It took that long for the Corsair to catch the sleek Kawasaki, but when Streig came within range he disintegrated it with one short burst.

For almost two hours nothing more happened. Then at 1313 it seemed everything happened at once.

A fighter director reported many bogeys 120 miles out and closing fast. The carriers swung into the wind to clear their decks, and Blackburn found another lone Tony. He engaged it, set the port wing afire, and saw it spin towards the sea. Then a few miles away, Cordray's division contacted roughly 100 enemy aircraft. There were at least 40 Vals at 18,000 feet with as many or more Zekes above. Torpedo planes were following at lower altitude.

Fighting 17 was acutely conscious of its fuel situation. The Corsairs had been airborne for three hours and were very nearly at the end of their leash. They could not land aboard any of the carriers because the flattops were busily launching aircraft. There would be only time for one or two quick gunnery passes, then a direct course to Ondonga. Even then, it was going to be tight.

Big Jim Streig shot down a Zeke from 24,000 feet and immediately attracted the unwelcome attention of several more. The F4U's superior high-altitude performance saved him. He honked back on the stick and climbed at full military power, finally losing his pursuers at 28,000. Now with an altitude advantage, Streig pounced on a Zeke and a Hamp. He shot pieces off both but could not press the issue. He set course for home.

Few others had time for more than one chance at a bandit. Roger Hedrick flamed a Zeke and disengaged. Some like Lieutenant C. D. Gile got in among the speedy Kate torpedo planes. Gile made two passes at one Nakajima, chasing it into the *Bunker Hill's* AA fire. In three bursts he set the Kate afire, and it exploded.

Within minutes most of Blackburn's pilots were headed home. As they departed, a wild sea-air battle raged. The air was full of Zekes, Vals, and Kates pursued by Hellcats and a few Corsairs as flak bursts dotted the sky. Bomb splashes and crashed airplanes littered the sea.

Lieutenant (jg) Ira Kepford was already headed for Ondonga when the Japanese attacked. Noting the flak bursts over the ships, Kepford reversed course. Highly competitive—he'd been a star quarterback at Northwestern—Ike Kepford was drawn to combat. He found a line of Vals retiring from their dive-bombing attack, and the situation suited him. He was on his own, free to fight individually. In his first aerial combat, Kepford dropped three Vals and damaged a fourth. When the attack ended he turned for Ondonga.

51

Minutes later the second strike arrived. Again Kepford turned back, and again he found a target. A Kate was boldly flying up the *Bunker Hill's* wake, intending to torpedo her from astern. Flying low through the "friendly" AA fire into the Kate's slipstream, the Corsair was hard to handle. Kepford bored in to rock-throwing range to be sure. He fired from fifty feet and saw the Nakajima fall off to one side. It splashed in the big carrier's wake.

The Corsair was now desperately short on fuel and Kepford informed the *Bunker Hill* that he needed to come aboard. Besides, he was out of ammunition. But a third enemy attack developed and the twenty-four-year-old Illinois pilot was forced to circle and wait. When the raid was finally over, Kepford gratefully landed and had his plane refueled. By 1630 he was airborne again, landing at Ondonga at 1800. Kepford had flown nearly eleven of the previous fourteen hours, made two carrier landings, and destroyed four enemy aircraft. He earned a Navy Cross for his long day.

In all, VF-17 recorded eighteen and one-half victories on 11 November. Three F4Us were damaged in combat but all were repairable. The only losses were two planes which ditched en route back to New Georgia, but both pilots were recovered.

Two days later the Japanese Third Air Fleet had had enough. Only 52 aircraft remained operational of the 173 which had flown south from Truk two weeks before. The survivors were recalled to the Carolines. But the remaining Rabaul planes were still active. On 17 November VF-17 claimed ten kills in two combats, losing two planes and a pilot. Then early in the morning of the 19th and 20th small Japanese formations attacked the Torokina beachhead, prompting Tom Blackburn's crew to do some thinking.

The engineering officer, Lieutenant Butch Davenport, had a plan. A popular officer respected for his technical knowledge and tactical savvy, Davenport reasoned that he might catch the Japanese early birds by surprise if his division arrived ahead of the Zekes.

The four Corsairs took off before dawn on the 21st and orbited at 3,000 feet in the shadow of the mountains overlooking Empress Augusta Bay. After a prolonged wait, they gave it up as a good try and headed for base. They were over the beach when six Zekes "in beautiful tight formation"[6] passed close by at eleven o'clock level. Davenport turned in behind the leader and exploded him from close astern, astonished to see the pilot parachute to safety. He didn't know how anyone could survive such a violent explosion.

Simultaneously, another Zeke pulled around and fired at Davenport from the port beam. The deflection was too wide for accurate shooting, but Lieutenant (jg) "Chico" Freeman had a good shot and blew the bandit apart. In the rat race which followed, Davenport destroyed another Zeke while his second section bagged two more. The lone survivor fled northwest, and Davenport let Freeman take him. One burst and the Zeke crashed, mysteriously ejecting a parachute with no pilot.

Later Davenport learned that his first victim had been picked up by a PT boat. The enemy pilot was an air intelligence officer sent to learn why so many Japanese fighters were being lost to Corsairs!

When VF-17 was rotated to Espiritu Santo at the end of the month, it tallied forty-five confirmed victories. Three pilots had been killed and five F4Us lost to enemy action, including two in aerial combat.

The Navy's first night-fighter squadron was also the Navy's first F4U squadron in combat. This was VF(N)-75 under Lieutenant Commander W. J. Widhelm. Like many VFN pilots, Gus Widhelm had flown SBDs in the carrier battles of 1942. Cheerful and popular, he was one of naval aviation's more colorful characters.

Night Fighting 75 was commissioned in April 1943. It grew out of Project Affirm, the Navy's aerial radar program at Quonset Point, Rhode Island. Widhelm's pilots were experienced fliers by wartime standards. All those who went to the Solomons with him had logged at least 1,000 hours. The squadron average was 2,000 hours. By August VF(N)-75 had six F4U-2s fresh from the modification program at the Naval Aircraft Factory. Widhelm soon split the squadron in two, turning over half to his exec, Lieutenant Commander R. E. Harmer, who became CO of VF(N)-101.

The first contingent took all six Corsairs to the West Coast for embarkation to the South Pacific. On 11 September VF(N)-75 arrived at Espiritu Santo with six planes and pilots, two radar officers, twelve enlisted men, and an engineer from the Sperry Gyroscope Company. Two weeks later the squadron was established at Munda. Though no ground-control radar was yet operational, patrols began the night of 2 October. This was nearly thirty days before VF-17 started flying combat.

Japanese activity remained nil during the first three weeks at Munda. Though Widhelm and his pilots flew some dusk-to-dawn patrols, they mainly sat "scramble alerts"—meaning they sat around waiting for something to happen. But at least a Marine GCI station, call sign Moon, was operating on Vella Lavella by late October.

About this same time the Japanese became more active at night. Between 20 and 31 October, fifteen single-plane raids pestered Munda. Though only two hostile aircraft actually dropped bombs, there were plenty of chances, but VF(N)-75 failed to make an interception. Delayed takeoff orders, inexperienced fighter direction, and enemy countermeasures foiled each opportunity.

Of seven attempted intercepts on the nights of 31 October and 1 November, five were spoiled when the experimental AIA radar sets failed during final approach. The other two efforts were made visually, and one target escaped. The other didn't.

Lieutenant H. D. O'Neill took off from Munda at 2310 on the 31st. An hour and a half later GCI Moon vectored him onto a bogey southeast of Shortland Island. But the night was so clear that O'Neill saw the exhausts of a Betty bomber at 10,000 feet. Hunter and hunted passed one another on opposite headings with the Corsair 2,000 feet above the Betty.

O'Neill made a diving turn which brought him behind his target. The Betty made a couple of slow turns which did nothing to throw off O'Neill's aim. He fired a burst from about 200 yards astern and the bomber's engine gushed flame which quickly abated. O'Neill came around for his second pass at 7,500 feet. He fired from 150 yards dead astern and the Betty dropped burning into the water. Searchlights from Shortland Island followed the bomber all the way down.

When O'Neill landed at 2340 the armorers reported he had fired only 128 rounds. It had taken time and experience, but Fighting 75 was now in business.

And business slowly picked up. From 10 December Widhelm kept two planes on detached duty at the newly won Torokina fighter strip on Bougainville. At least one Corsair was scrambled each night through the end of January 1944, and five more Japanese planes were destroyed. In one of the most bizarre night fighter incidents of the war, O'Neill shot down a second Betty on 11 December. At 2300 he was under the control of Tiki GCI when he saw flares descending at 3,000 feet about ten miles south of the field. The bogey was not visible but O'Neill tested his guns in anticipation of contact. Tiki then said the target had dropped right off the scope, and moments later an LST reported a Betty falling into the water. Lieutenant O'Neill stated that he shot down this unseen bomber "with the aid of Superman."[7]

Torokina-based F4U-2s accounted for two Rufe floatplanes destroyed and one probable during the balance of December, and a pair of Vals in January. Most contacts occurred between 2300 and 0500 hours at altitudes from 3,000 to 8,000 feet. Four of Widhelm's pilots scored victories, with O'Neill and Lieutenant R. L. Johns each credited with two kills.

But as much was learned from the problems as from the successes. Operating at night from the narrow runway at Torokina was not easy, but it was done safely. Oil leakage onto the windscreen reduced the already marginal visibility from the F4U-2's birdcage canopy, and it was not solved in the Solomons. Widhelm suggested the development of a speed brake to prevent night fighters from overshooting their targets during a fast approach—something which was never done. But otherwise the

F4U-2 seemed well suited to the night role. It had the speed and climb necessary to close most bogies, and could hang in a turn at 95 knots with many slow-flying Rufes or Vals. And the Corsair carried the extra electronics comfortably. Many other F4U night fighters would follow, but the -2 remained *the* nocturnal Corsair of World War II.

It took sixty-one days to defeat Japanese air power at Rabaul.

The vast complex on New Britain boasted five airfields ringing Simpson Harbor and Karavia Bay. The westernmost was inoperable due to drainage problems, but the others were big, well-built facilities with concrete runways. Among them, Lakunai, Vunakanau, Tobera, and Rapopo had revetments for some 430 aircraft—265 fighters and 166 bombers. Approximately 300 were on hand in mid-December. And some of the Zero pilots were tough opponents. Lieutenant (jg) Tetsuzo Iwamoto of the Imperial Navy's 204th Fighter Group, for instance, already had fourteen victories from his combat in China. During two months at Rabaul he claimed 40 victories over Allied aircraft, including 11 Corsairs. Iwamoto survived the war with something over 80 planes to his credit.

Advance elements of two F4U squadrons arrived at Torokina while the Sea Bees were still finishing the airfield on 9 December. Ground crews from VMF-212 and 215 had things well enough organized to support the first Bougainville-based aircraft, which landed the next day. Major Rivers Morrell, formerly exec of VMF-223 in the early days at Guadalcanal, brought in 17 Corsairs of 216 almost before the bulldozers and rock crushers were clear of the runway.

Morrell's squadron was intended mainly for local air defense. Other fighter units would fly from their bases farther south or stage through Torokina in preparation for each big raid. The first of these was scheduled for 17 December, the fortieth anniversary of the Wright Brothers' first flight.

At this time AirSols had nearly 270 fighters on hand. But 69 were Bell P-39 Airacobras, ill-suited to aerial combat with their short range and mediocre performance at altitude. Of the remaining 200, the majority were F4Us and F6Fs. The 71 Corsairs represented one-quarter of all AirSols fighters, followed by 58 Hellcats. There were also 39 American and New Zealand P-40s, and 31 U.S. Army P-38s.

The F4U still suffered from an overall low in-commission rate, despite excellent records in some squadrons. Forty-seven Corsairs were operational on 17 December compared to 53 Hellcats and 36 Warhawks. In other words, the Corsair squadrons maintained an average two-thirds in-commission rate compared to over 90 percent for F6Fs and P-40s. The complex, sophisticated Lockheed Lightnings were lowest with 38 percent operational.

Half of the 150 operational fighters (excluding P-39s) were allotted to the 17 December mission against Rabaul. The Torokina strip, running east-west for 5,000 feet along the water's edge, was crowded with 76 Marine, Navy, and New Zealand fighters. For AirSols had determined that the fighter sweep, which had conquered Kahili, was the tactic to use against Rabaul. And the same man was chosen to lend his expertise: Greg Boyington.

The Black Sheep were back in the area for their third and final tour, still based at Vella Lavella. The first sweep against Rabaul got underway as Boyington received a green light from the tower and pulled onto the steel mat between two lines of tightly packed fighters. He gunned his Corsair down the runway and was followed by 30 more F4Us, 22 Hellcats, and 23 P-40s. While the Marine and Navy squadrons formed up, the New Zealanders pressed on.

It was a disappointing start. The two Kiwi P-40 squadrons tangled with 30-plus bandits a few minutes ahead of the American formations. Numbers 14 and 16 Squadrons, RNZAF, sent five Zekes down over New Ireland but lost three of their own number.

Boyington, spoiling for a fight, resorted to his radio again. Turning the knob of his "coffee grinder" to 6050 kilocycles, he orbited Lakunai Field south of Rabaul Town and implored 40 Zekes to come up and play. All he accomplished was a retort to "Come on down, sucker."[8] The only successful F4U pilot was Lieutenant D. J. Moore of 214 who dispatched a pair of Zekes.

By this time, Boyington and other senior airmen saw the disadvantage of such large fighter sweeps. They intimidated the opposition into remaining grounded, which was the opposite reaction desired. A set of guidelines was drawn up for future operations. It specified that the maximum number of fighters should be limited to no more than 48. As few aircraft types and squadrons should be employed as possible, for better coordination and mutual support. And the sweep leader should fly at the approximate altitude where initial contact was expected. If surprise were achieved, and the sweep arrived with an altitude advantage, it was considered safe for the leader to fly in the lowest layer of fighters. This enabled him to observe the developing situation and more effectively control it. Scouting, flanking, and ambush should also be used.

During the two days before Christmas the new tactics were put to work. Ninety-two Allied fighters went to Rabaul on the 23rd, half of them escorting a heavy bomber formation intended to draw up the Zekes. About 40 bandits were still airborne when the 48-plane sweep arrived, and 30 Japanese were claimed shot down. Again VMF-214 led the way, reporting 12 kills. Greg Boyington himself shot down 4, running his wartime claim to 24.

Among the Corsair squadrons active that day was VMF-223, back in the Solomons for a second tour. Now under Major Marion E. Carl, 223 was based at Vella Lavella with several other units. Carl led his squadron over Rabaul on the 23rd and shot down a Tony. To many observers, Marion Carl looked like a good bet to win the ace race in the South Pacific. With sixteen and one-half kills in 1942, he was well placed among all Marine fighter pilots—only Boyington was now ahead of him of those still active. The tall, twenty-eight-year-old Carl had all the skill and ambition needed for an ace of aces. And despite the fact he was married to a stunning Powers model, he remained aggressive as ever. Some pilots grew cautious when the love bug bit. Marion Carl was still a hunter.

Staging through Torokina, four Corsair squadrons kept up the pressure on Rabaul's defenders. Escorting bombers and flying sweeps, VMF-214, 216, 223, and 331 had the best of the shooting on 27 and 28 December. On these two days AirSols fighters reported 52 Japanese planes shot down—33 by Marines. On the 27th Boyington and Carl each splashed a Zeke.

In the two weeks from 17 to 31 December, Allied squadrons thought they had shot down 147 defenders over New Britain. The actual toll was certainly somewhat less, for the Japanese retained 200 aircraft around Rabaul on New Year's Day 1944.

Too much emphasis should not be devoted to the scoring race, but it was a fact that for the first time Greg Boyington was feeling some pressure. His claim of six victories in China had been universally accepted (though AVG records differ), and his total score amounted to twenty-five—only one short of Joe Foss's year-old record for the Marines. But time was running out. The Black Sheep were scheduled to finish their third tour in mid-January, and if Boyington were to break the record, he would have to do it soon. A period of bad weather had curtailed several missions.

By 2 January Boyington was more irritable than usual. For a week, war correspondents had been asking him when he was going to bag number twenty-six. Finally most men kept out of his way. Few realized how tired he was. He'd been putting bits of tobacco in the corner of each eye to keep from falling asleep on recent missions.

At Vella Lavella Marion Carl was scheduled to lead several divisions up to Torokina for a sweep to Rabaul on the third. But realizing what the record meant to Boyington, he offered the mission to the 214 skipper. Boyington gratefully accepted Carl's sporting gesture. The two were temperamentally about as different as a pair of humans can be—neither friends nor enemies, but professionals who respected one another's ability.

In truth, Carl thought he was giving away little. "I had lots of time left in combat," he recalled, "and figured I'd still get my chance at the record."[9] As it was, fate played tricks on both men—dealing more cruelly with Boyington.

Boyington led the sweep to Rabaul next day, 3 January. An estimated 60 bandits were encountered climbing at 12,000 to 15,000 feet. With an altitude advantage, the Corsairs attacked and 214 saw the CO flame a Zeke from an overhead run. After that, the other Black Sheep lost sight of the lead section. Boyington's element leader, Lieutenant Bruce Matheson, shot down another Zeke and the fight dispersed. Upon landing at Torokina, the pilots compared notes. In all, six Japanese planes were known shot down, but Boyington and his wingman, Captain George Ashmun, were missing. Though Boyington had tied the record, nobody even knew if he was still alive. It would remain a mystery until the end of the war.

Two principals in the Corsair legend: designer Rex Beisel and Major Greg Boyington. (Ling-Temco-Vought)

After the first flamer, Boyington and Ashmun dove on a lower formation of Zekes, only to be pounced upon by several more. The two surrounded Corsairs weaved in a defensive scissors at 12,000 feet as the combat worked its way toward the water. Each Marine shot a Zeke off the other's tail, then Ashmun's F4U nosed down streaming smoke. Boyington followed, trying to scare off several Zekes pursuing Ashmun "in a sort of Aerial Banzai charge."[10] Kicking rudder and shooting indiscriminately, Boyington shot another Zeke out of formation just as the stricken Vought hit the water.

Racing from the scene at low level, Boyington's plane was hit again, and the fuel tank caught fire. He rolled inverted and dropped from the blazing fighter at about 300 feet. His chute opened just in time—"I felt one tug and then slammed into the water without even time to swing once."[11]

The Japanese spent the next quarter-hour and the rest of their ammunition shooting at Boyington in the water. When they tired of this sport and flew off, Boyington remained wary. He waited two hours before inflating his rubber raft. Though suffering from numerous wounds, he was hopeful of drifting into St. George Channel where the coast watcher was likely to find him.

Shortly before dark a submarine surfaced next to the raft. For a second Boyington was elated. Then he saw the rising sun insignia. He only had time to throw his .38 revolver into the water before he was hauled aboard the sub. The soft lead bullets in his gun were a direct violation of the Geneva Convention.

The Japanese never reported Boyington a POW, and he was awarded a "posthumous" Medal of Honor three months after his disappearance. But he astonished the Corps by emerging from a prison camp at the end of the war and returning home to collect his rewards. At a reunion in a San Diego bar, the Black Sheep traded knowing smiles. Old Pappy had put over another one on the system.

At the time, Boyington's claims for the last two Zekes were allowed even though no witnesses could confirm them. Boyington was therefore recognized as the top Marine fighter ace with a wartime total of twenty-eight credited victories.

Two-Fourteen completed its tour five days after Boyington went down. Under his leadership, the squadron was credited with 97 planes confirmed, 32 probables, and 21 aircraft destroyed on the ground. Twelve Black Sheep had been lost and six wounded. Combined with the thirty victories credited during its first two tours, VMF-214 finished as the seventh-ranked Marine Corps fighter squadron.

Marion Carl, who had unknowingly allowed Boyington to fly into captivity, remained in command of 223 for only thirty more days. Then he was unexpectedly transferred to the staff of MAG-12. "It was the end of my shooting," he lamented.[12]

But other pilots got in plenty of shooting. Foremost among the early 1944 Corsair squadrons was VMF-215, now led by Major Robert G. Owens. The "Fighting Corsairs" first operated from Guadalcanal and Munda, then from Vella Lavella. In late January the squadron moved up to Torokina, where it completed its third tour.

All of January was eventful for 215, but particularly for its two top guns, Lieutenant Bob Hanson and Captain Don Aldrich. Beginning in mid month, the squadron really made its presence felt. Aldrich, who hailed from Chicago, had scored five kills on the first tour but was blanked on the second. On 11 January he proceeded to make up for lost time; he nailed two Zekes and got another confirmed and two probables on the 13th. Next day Owens's pilots had their best mission, and Lieutenant Hanson earned his nickname, Butcher Bob.

Two-Fifteen took off from Vella Lavella at 0605 and landed at Torokina little more than an hour later. The pilots were briefed for a bomber escort to Rabaul and departed at 1010. One Corsair crashed on takeoff but the other 21 met the TBFs at 1115. Over New Ireland's coast some 60 Zekes were sighted in several batches. A running fight developed during the approach to the target.

Hanson and his wingman, Lieutenant R. V. Bowman, stayed with the Avengers through the attack, pulling out at 200 feet over Simpson Harbor. "There were lots of Zekes cruising around low, and their speed did not seem to exceed 180 knots," Hanson reported.[13] The two F4Us came up astern of a pair of Zekes at 1,500 feet, and opened fire. Hanson's target immediately caught fire. Bowman's dived into a cloud and dropped out all aflame. Then the Corsairs became separated.

Hanson saw two more Zekes, pursued one into thin cloud, and exploded it. Returning to the cloud layer, he chased two bandits off the tails of two F4Us. Then, with about 30 Zekes in the area, Hanson began to climb, ducking from cloud to cloud. At 3,000 feet he saw two more Zekes crossing his course 500 feet below. He dived and the Japanese turned towards a cloud bank, allowing a 45-degree deflection shot on one. It flamed instantly. Hanson pulled out of his dive and once more regained altitude. "At 2,500 feet I looked out of the clouds again and saw I was right on the tail of a Zero and just a little below him," he related. "I ran right up on him and fired. My tracers went into his belly and he burst immediately into flame. I think this is the best way to shoot them: from astern and below."[14]

After a few more inconclusive passes at scattered Zekes, Hanson turned for the rendezvous. But he spotted one more Zero, dived on it from 3,000 feet, and set it afire from behind. Exiting the area, he noticed two Zekes behind him, so, "I ducked into the clouds and beat it for home."[15] Hanson landed at Torokina twenty minutes after the others, with twenty gallons and 400 rounds of ammo remaining. He had doubled his previous score by burning five Zekes while Captain A. T. Warner splashed four. In all, 215 was credited with 19 confirmed and 6 probables while losing 3 planes and two pilots in combat.

The rest of January was much the same. In his next five missions to Rabaul, Bob Hanson shot down 15 more bandits: 12 Zekes, 2 Tojos, and a Tony. Don Aldrich downed nine fighters during the same period. Between them, these two pilots notched one kill over New Ireland for each day of the month.

Late January was also a busy time for VF-17. Back for a second tour, Blackburn's Irregulars were based at the new Piva complex north of Torokina. Piva Uncle was a bomber strip, while a half-mile away was the parallel Piva Yoke fighter field which also housed VMF-211, 321, and a New Zealand P-40 squadron. The Navy F4Us flew their first mission from their new base on 26 January when they escorted SBDs to Rabaul. A stiff dogfight erupted over Lakunai Field in which eight Zekes were destroyed. Tom Blackburn got one and his wingman, Lieutenant (jg) D. H. Gutenkunst, splashed a pair. It was not one-sided, however, as two Skull and Crossbones aircraft were shot down and four others damaged. Ensign R. H. Hill, flying Butch Davenport's plane, had taken numerous 20-mm hits which badly damaged the tail and caused the loss of hydraulic fluid. In a fast no-flaps landing, Hill got "Lonesome Polecat" on the ground, but couldn't slow down. He nosed over and the Corsair demolished itself skidding inverted along the pierced steel mat. Hill survived with head injuries.

The next four days were even more eventful. In a series of bomber escorts to Lakunai and Tobera airfields, Blackburn's squadron turned in a record performance. From the 27th to the 30th, Fighting 17 claimed fifty-four and one-half victories, sharing the fraction with VMF-215. Individual honors went to Ike Kepford and Howard M. Burriss who flew two-plane top cover at 30,000 feet during an SBD strike at Tobera on the twenty-ninth. Kepford's section remained unseen as a dozen Zekes passed 6,000 feet below. By taking turns, chandelling upward after each pass, the two Navy pilots each picked off four bandits in ten minutes. Two more Zekes fell to VF-17, for a score of ten to nothing.

It couldn't always end that way, and it didn't. By month's end VF-17 had lost six pilots and ten aircraft, including one of its aces. Howard Burriss was shot down in a combat near Tobera on the 31st, last seen gliding out to sea. In exchange, Fighting 17 recorded over sixty confirmed

61

victories during the first six days of its second tour. The frantic pace of operations continued into February. Blackburn himself bagged three Zekes and a Hamp on the sixth.

On 3 February VMF-215 flew out of Piva Toke with eight F4Us to escort 30 TBFs and SBDs to Tobera field. Eight Hellcats of VF-38 also flew the mission. Fifteen hostiles were seen near the target but none got through to the bombers, and three were shot down by two of Bob Owens's aces. Captain Harold Spears got two Zekes and Lieutenant Creighton Chandler splashed one. Retirement was via Kabanga Bay and Cape St. George as some of the F4Us strafed targets of opportunity.

One pilot so engaged was Bob Hanson. His score of twenty-five kills—including twenty in six missions over Rabaul—put him in prime position to take the top spot among Marine fighter pilots. But he never got the chance. The reports varied: some said he flew into the sea; others thought

First lieutenant Robert M. Hanson shot down 25 Japanese aircraft while flying with VMF-214 and 215, becoming the top scoring F4U pilot of the war. But his success was not easily obtained, as this photo proves. Hanson was killed in action in February 1944. (U.S. Marine Corps)

his Corsair caught a wingtip on pullup from his strafing run. Whatever the cause, Hanson's F4U went into the water off Cape St. George. His squadron mates circled low over a patch of oil, but Hanson never emerged. He became the third and last Corsair pilot to receive the Medal of Honor in World War II. And the youngest. He died one day short of age twenty-four.

When 215 finished its last tour a week later, it held the Solomons record for fighter squadrons. In eighteen weeks of combat the Fighting Corsairs were credited with 137 aerial victories, including 106 during the final six weeks. The squadron's ten aces—including Major Owen with seven victories—were responsible for 105 kills, over three-quarters of the total. Hanson scored all but two of his with 215 while Don Aldrich and Harold Spears recorded 20 and 15 respectively.

Owens's maintenance crews remained on Bougainville after the flight echelon departed. And when 215 returned to the States, only fourteen of the original twenty-four pilots were on hand. But the attrition did not stop there. As so often happened, experienced combat pilots fell victim to routine flying accidents. Harold Spears died in a 1944 crash and Don Aldrich was killed in 1947. So was Gus Thomas of VMF-213.

In the first part of February the battle of attrition was reaching its peak. AirSols flung 3,000 sorties at Rabaul in less than three weeks. Some maintenance personnel worked forty-eight-hour shifts to keep enough planes operational. Something had to give.

The Japanese gave.

It happened abruptly, without indication. On 18 February there was little combat. Fighting 17's exec, Roger Hedrick, had his division on high cover over Vunakanau when eight Zekes pounced. Outnumbered two to one, the Corsairs out-climbed their opponents and dived to the attack. Hedrick cooly torched two and exploded a third. His three pilots destroyed four more, leaving one to tell the tale. Blackburn's Irregulars had now passed VMF-215's recent record as top-scoring Solomons fighter squadron.

Next day VF-17 was again engaged over Rabaul. Nobody could know at the time that it would be the last major air battle of the campaign.

Like most important days, 19 February began like any other. AirSols put up 145 planes from Bougainville: 72 Dauntlesses and Avengers from Piva Uncle escorted by 20 P-40s from Torokina and 54 Corsairs and Hellcats from Piva Yoke. Twenty-six of 44 F4Us on the mission sported the skull and crossbones insignia as VF-17 provided six divisions for high and medium cover. The other pair repeated Blackburn's previous tactic of advance roving high cover. Lieutenant Oscar Chenoweth and Lieutenant (jg) Danny Cunningham were twenty minutes in front of the main formation, flying at 30,000 feet in position to break up an early interception.

Arriving over the target, Chenoweth led the section spiraling down to 24,000 feet, hunting for the enemy fighters he knew must be climbing. He spotted them far below and led Cunningham down to attack. The combat followed its inevitable descending pattern, working from 18,000 feet down to the deck. Both Corsairs burned two Zekes each before the strike arrived. Then they became separated. Cunningham shot down two more in flames. "Oc" Chenoweth won a turning contest with a Tojo, flying so low that the Japanese army fighter went into the water without an opportunity to fire.

Coming off the target, VF-17's high cover was attacked by 20-plus bandits, a mixed bag of Zekes and Tojos. Three of the former and one of the latter went down, at no cost to the F4Us. Then, with friendly and hostile formations dispersed or departed, many pilots turned for Bougainville.

Five F4U-1As of VF-17 over the northern Solomans near the end of their tour in March 1944. This unit, under Lieutenant Commander John T. Blackburn, was instrumental in proving the Corsair to the Navy, both operationally and in combat. (Ling-Temco-Vought)

Ike Kepford was left alone when his wingman aborted with engine trouble over Buka Passage. The ex-quarterback was en route to base when he sighted a single Rufe floatplane at 1,000 feet off Cape Siar. Kepford dived onto the Mitsubishi's tail, close enough to see it was painted blue, and sent it flaming into the water.

There was no time to enjoy his fourteenth victory. Checking his tail, Kepford noticed about 20 bandits high over New Ireland, and they had seen him. Four peeled off and attacked in line astern. Caught at low level with barely 200 knots on the dial, Kepford pulled one of the oldest tricks in the fighter pilot's handbook. He extended his flaps, further reducing his speed, and allowed the lead Zeke to overshoot him. When the Japanese foolishly pulled up in front of him, Kepford had the Zeke boresighted. It took the full impact of the F4U's firepower and gushed flames.

The first rule in fighting Zekes was never turn with them at low airspeed. The second rule said that violation of the first was punishable by death. Fully aware of this, Kepford maintained his northerly heading, dropped right down on the water, and shoved his throttle, mixture, and prop controls through the gate. This activated the water injection system, allowing the R-2800 to operate at higher power and temperature than normal. The prop wound up to 2,700 rpm, the manifold pressure needle went into the yellow, and the Corsair howled over New Ireland, accelerating rapidly. Kepford checked his rearview mirror and saw he was pulling away from the three Zekes. But they hung on, knowing he was going in exactly the opposite direction from home. Each minute heading north took Kepford six miles farther from Piva.

The ten-gallon water supply was exhausted as the Corsair crossed the western shore, again over the sea. Kepford knew he had to reduce power or risk detonating his engine, and reluctantly eased back on the throttle. The Zekes were still too close, and he maintained his course straight ahead. Sitting there, with plenty of time to imagine what could happen, was an unpleasantly new experience. Usually in combat a pilot was far too busy to allow his mind to wander. But now, with too much time to think, fear could turn to panic which could cause a fatal error.

After twenty interminable, heart-pounding minutes the Corsair's airspeed had dropped from 355 knots to under 300. At this rate, if Kepford didn't run out of fuel the tenacious Zekes would probably catch him anyway. When his gauge registered 100 gallons remaining, Kepford made up his mind.

At 275 knots indicated, Kepford abruptly racked his number 29 into a hard port turn. Pulling big G's at low level, graying out, he ran a serious risk of losing control. The nearest Zeke ran the same risk. It turned to cut the corner and close to gun range. But the enemy pilot lacked Ike Kepford's skill, stamina, or luck. The port wingtip dug into the water and cartwheeled the Zeke into a fountain of foam and spray. As Kepford rolled out on a heading for home, he saw the last two Zekes abandon the pursuit.

When Kepford landed back at Piva Yoke, he'd spent four hours in the air. The fact that his sixteen kills made him the Navy's number one fighter pilot meant little. Both plane and pilot had been to the absolute limits of their endurance. The former athlete slumped in total exhaustion. Number 29 flew again the next day.

But neither VF-17 nor the other squadrons found any opposition on the 20th. Nor on the 21st. The battle of the 19th, in which the Skull and Crossbones F4Us accounted for 16 of the 23 claims, was the end of effective Japanese fighter defense at Rabaul. From now on, enemy aircraft would be seen infrequently, and never in formations larger than six. The aircraft and shipping losses sustained since December were too great. Rabaul's remaining aircraft were flown north on the 20th, and Simpson Harbor was nearly deserted.

Enemy losses were not as great as AirSols thought. During the eight-week blitz, the Japanese lost some 400 planes while AirSols believed its aviators had shot down 730. Marine squadrons were credited with 393 and VF-17 with 107 during this period, for an even 500 claims by F4Us.

Partners in the Solomons air campaign—an F4U-1A and R4D transport at Green Island in March 1944. (R.M. Hill)

But if the numbers were exaggerated, that didn't change the one fact which mattered: Allied airmen now owned the sky over all the Solomons and Bismarcks.

With aerial opposition suddenly nonexistent, the fighter squadrons looked for other employment. They still flew sweeps and escorts, but these became perfunctory duties. Tom Blackburn's plane captain, Aviation Machinist Mate R. K. Condit, helped improvise a bomb rack which he claimed would allow the F4U-1A to haul a thousand-pounder. Before VF-17 finished its tour on 4 March, "Doc" Condit's invention was put to limited use. Some pilots were skeptical of hanging bombs on fighter planes, but the concept prevailed. Marine squadrons in the Central Pacific began using Corsairs as dive bombers several weeks later.

At the end of its tour, VF-17 was the clear leader among Solomons Fighter Command squadrons. From November through February, Blackburn's Irregulars were credited with 152 confirmed victories, the highest toll recorded by an F4U squadron. Nearly 100 kills were recorded by the dozen aces, paced by Ike Kepford with 16 and Blackburn himself with 11. Twenty F4Us and twelve pilots were lost to enemy action, while four planes and one pilot fell victim to operational accidents. It was startling vindication of Blackburn's faith in the Corsair. Surely no other squadron did as much to turn the F4U from a "widow-maker" into a versatile weapon.

By late April Rabaul was finally surrounded. The Green Islands, some 100 miles east of Rabaul, were taken by New Zealand troops on 15 February under an umbrella of Marine Corsairs. Fifteen Vals dived on the invasion shipping while VMF-212 was on CAP. Major Hugh Elwood's pilots disregarded heavy AA fire and splashed six dive bombers in a low-level tail chase. Captain P. C. DeLong shot down 3 on his way to a wartime total of 11.

Lagoon Field on Green was completed the first week in March, and two F4U squadrons arrived on the 13th. Major Alfred Gordon's VMF-222 shared the 5,000-foot strip with 223, now under Major Robert P. Keller.

The Japanese base at Kavieng, on the northern tip of New Ireland, was considered for seizure at one time. But like Rabaul, it was left to wither on the vine. Emirau Island, 90 miles northwest of Kavieng, was captured in late March. Advance elements of MAG-12 set up shop on 5 April, and air ops began late that month. Rabaul and Kavieng would be kept isolated and impotent by the F4Us, SBDs, and TBFs of MAG-12 and Green-based MAG-14.

But Bougainville planes, under the direction of MAG-24, were also involved. The group included six Corsair squadrons at one point, plus two Dauntless and two Avenger units. The operations did not proceed without interruption, however. A large-scale Japanese attempt to recapture the Piva-Torokina area began early the morning of 8 March. Three F4Us were destroyed by enemy shelling on Piva Yoke, others were damaged. In addition to artillery, there were also snipers and stray bullets from both sides. For two weeks Bougainville was Guadalcanal all over again. Pilots flying close support and strike sorties took off under enemy guns. Mechanics worked in the open, exposed to every danger while "keeping 'em flying." One SBD squadron suffered 10 percent casualties among its ground crews. Disease, nerves, and fatigue added to the toll. But despite the hazards and hardships, some maintenance crews excelled themselves. The veteran mechanics of VMF-215 kept their F4Us at 95 percent operational.

By 16 March the Allied air-ground team had broken the enemy ring around the perimeter. "Pistol Pete," the notorious Japanese fieldpiece which lobbed shells into Piva for days on end, was at last silenced. So were the other artillery and mortars. Bougainville eventually settled into the busy, boring business of aerial siege which characterized the aftermath of the Solomons campaign.

And not only Bougainville. Green and Emirau sent strikes against Kavieng and Rabaul for many months after the Japanese were beaten down at both bases. In late May an observer arrived at MAG-14 on Green Island who was to have considerable effect upon the F4U's strike potential. He was a former Army and airmail pilot working as a consultant to several aviation companies: Charles A. Lindbergh.

Denied military service in the Air Corps because of his prewar opposition to the Roosevelt administration, the forty-two-year-old Lindbergh succeeded in flying combat anyway. During May and June he flew at least a dozen missions from Green and Emirau with VMF-115, 212, 218, and 222. Officially his position was that of a civilian technician, as he assisted the services in solving problems with F4Us, P-38s, P-47s, and B-24s.

Lindbergh's status with relation to the Geneva Convention came in for some close scrutiny after his first mission, a strafing flight to Rabaul on 22 May. Upon landing at Green, Lindbergh was met by the MAG-14 CO, Lieutenant Colonel Roger Carleson. The question was not so much Lindbergh "observing" combat operations while flying a Corsair—other civilians had ridden on strikes in bombers—but the legality of his firing his guns. Carleson expressed the opinion that the Japanese would kill a downed civilian who had been shooting at them. This made no impression upon the phlegmatic Lindbergh; he accepted it as part of the risk.

Another pilot interrupted at this point. "It would be alright for him to engage in target practice on the way home," the Marine said. Carleson wavered, then consented, provided that after a day or two nobody "kicks up a fuss."

That night Lindbergh noted in his diary, "The more I see of the Marines the more I like them."[16]

Less to his liking was the impersonal nature of strafing. His journal entries repeatedly express the revulsion Lindbergh felt for shooting up unseen targets. On 24 May he wrote, "You press the trigger and death leaps forth—4,200 projectiles a minute. Tracers bury themselves in walls and roof. Dust springs up from yard and garden. Inside may be emptiness or writhing agony. You never know. Holes in a dirt floor; a machine gun out of action; a family wiped out; you go on as you were before. Below, all is silence again. Death has passed. It is in your cockpit. You carried it in your hands."[17]

Despite his reservations, Lindbergh continued to fly with the Marines, learning more about the F4U and its combat performance. Marion Carl, who once flew with Lindbergh, recalls the man's complex nature: "He was a very good pilot, and he knew an awful lot about the Corsair. But the thing that bothered us when we flew with him was that he was so darned slow. He'd spend thirty minutes inspecting his plane and warming up the engine. All this time the rest of us would be sitting in our cockpits, ready to go. We spoke to him about it, but we never did any good. You just couldn't get Lindbergh to take off before he was good and ready. It probably didn't occur to us young bucks at the time that this was the reason he was still around."[18]

Lindbergh's last F4U mission in the Solomons was a four-hour escort to Rabaul on 9 June. Flying with a division of Major Boyd McElhany's VMF-212, the veteran flier let his airman's eye record the view. "At 6,000 feet we can see over the mountains of New Ireland to the volcanic harbor of Rabaul far in the distance. Clouds float all around—above, below, beside us. To the north there is a squall. All shades of gray and blue and green and white—pale blue sky over Rabaul; patches of deep blue above us; gray, misty clouds on the horizon; dazzling white clouds on our left where the rays of the sun pierce through; the blue water of the South Pacific; the green jungle-covered mountains of New Ireland; the purple volcanoes of faraway Rabaul. And through the limitless space of that sky, above the ocean and the mountains, surrounded by unbroken loneliness, piercing the beauty of land, sea, and air, our four Corsairs float like hawks, the only sign of man or life. . . . We see only the loneliness of the sky, the joy and beauty of the earth. We feel only the companionship of each other, four Corsairs hanging gracefully in the air, moving ever so gently in relation to each other, too high above it to be much concerned about the earth below. . . ."[19]

That same day, Lindbergh was asked to investigate an F4U wing-folding mechanism failure at MAG-11 on Espiritu Santo. He departed on the 10th, having accomplished all he desired except a night flight over Rabaul in a Corsair. No senior air officer would approve the idea, regarding it as too risky.

From the Solomons Lindbergh went to New Guinea to fly combat in Lockheed P-38s. But his association with the F4U was not over. He would return to the Corsair and the Marines during the long, drawn-out campaign of attrition in the Central Pacific.

chapter 4

The backwater war

Round many western islands have I been.

Keats

In the Central Pacific, the Fourth Marine Air Wing was fully occupied during 1944 with an aerial siege of bypassed Japanese islands. But the year began badly for the wing's Corsairs. The loss of an entire squadron in one of the greatest foul-ups in naval aviation history would cost the Japanese not one round of ammunition.

On 17 January VMF-422 embarked in the escort carrier *Kalinin Bay* (CVE 68) at Pearl Harbor. Twenty-four F4U-1As led by Major John S. MacLaughlin were launched for Hawkins Field on Tarawa Atoll seven days later, where all landed safely. The squadron was then ordered south to Funafuti in the Ellice Islands. Takeoff for the 700-mile trip was scheduled for next morning, with an interim stop at Nanomea, northernmost of the Ellice group.

No flying tragedy is caused entirely by the local, immediate circumstances. There is inevitably a lengthy, sometimes devious, trail leading back to the origins. A variety of factors can contribute: inadequate training, poor planning, shabby maintenance. In 422's case, the trouble began the same morning the F4Us landed at Tarawa.

Major MacLaughlin conferred with the Fourth Wing operations staff about the long trip, but unaccountably requested no navigation aircraft, as he could have done. Instead, he contented himself with charts and only the most basic communications data. Meteorologists predicted good flying weather for most of the flight south to Nanomea, with rainshowers and squall lines the rest of the way to Funafuti.

Next morning, the 25th, an updated weather report was posted about an hour before 422 took off. This report indicated poorer flying conditions than had existed on the 24th, but apparently MacLaughlin did not see the update. At any rate, when 23 Corsairs took off at 0930, the odds were already stacked heavily against them. They had no navigation escort plane, their ZB homers remained uncalibrated, the call signs of bases along the route were unknown, and neither the bearings nor quadrants of the Nanomea low-frequency radio range were given. Nanomea wasn't even informed of the flight. The only thing 422 had going for it was a fuel reserve of nearly four hours beyond the estimated two and a half planned. The one pilot who could not get his engine started was unknowingly a very fortunate young man as he watched his squadron mates head south.

At first all went well as MacLaughlin led his pilots down the Gilberts. Then shortly past noon, while only fifteen minutes out of Nanomea, the F4Us encountered heavy clouds. The formation descended to 200 feet, trying to get under the weather, when MacLaughlin unaccountably turned east. None of the Marines knew it at the time, but when the CO made that fatal turn he was only ten miles from his destination. Nanomea radar plotted 422's position from 1225 on, but due to poor communications planning, no radio contact was established until it was too late.

After MacLaughlin made several more turns, the formation became lost and began to disintegrate. Three pilots were separated at this point, and two eventually turned up safe. Lieutenant Walter Wilson pancaked his F4U on a small island, where he found friendly natives and was picked up by a Navy ship. Lieutenant John Hansen finally got a bearing on the Funafuti range and landed with eighty gallons remaining. The planned reserve was 210 gallons.

The other twenty pilots groped through the weather for an hour and emerged over Nui Island, well south of Nanomea. Then Lieutenant Christian Lauesen called that his engine was running poorly and glided towards the water. When Lauesen splashed down, Lieutenant Robert Lehnert courageously bailed out of his own plane to lend assistance. Lehnert spent two days in the ocean but never found his friend.

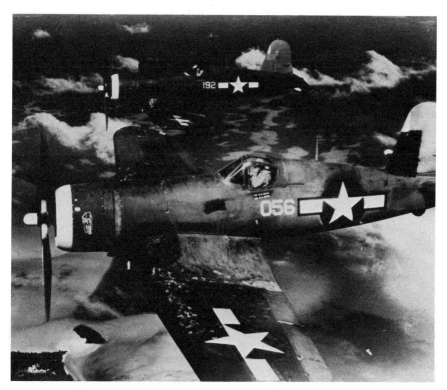

The bleached-out, repainted exteriors of these VMF-114 Corsairs testify to the continuous use they received in a variety of central Pacific sorties. (R.M. Hill)

After circling some more, MacLaughlin led the other seventeen pilots off to the southeast, encountering another storm. At this point Mac-Laughlin turned over command to Captain Cloyd Jeans and shortly disappeared. So did two other pilots.

Two of the surviving 15 Corsairs were now running low on fuel. Jeans, a Guadalcanal veteran, made the only rational decision. He ordered all planes to land in the water as close together as possible. But two ditched seven miles away and one of the pilots was lost. The others bobbed in their one-man rafts for forty-eight hours before they were found by a Catalina flying boat almost 100 miles southwest of Funafuti. The PBY was damaged in landing and at length a destroyer was dispatched to complete the rescue.

The cost of VMF-422's poorly planned flight was agonizingly high. Six irreplaceable pilots and 22 valuable F4Us were lost without inflicting one lick of damage upon the enemy. But Captain Jeans's decision to effect a mass water landing undoubtedly prevented additional loss of life. Reunited at Engebi in Eniwetok Atoll and filled out with replacements, 422 participated in the Marshalls and Okinawa campaigns.

Kwajalein Atoll was the Marshalls base for the Corsair-equipped Marine Air Group 31. Group headquarters was established on Roi Island on 7 February, only five days after the Fourth Marine Division had captured Roi and its twin, Namur. But early in the morning of the 12th, a dozen or so Japanese seaplanes based at Ponape in the Carolines conducted a successful bombing raid against Roi. The Marines and Sea Bees suffered uncommonly heavy personnel and materiel losses.

In order to prevent a recurrence, 17 Corsairs were flown to Roi on 15 February. They were ten planes from VMF-224 and seven F4U-2 night fighters of VMF(N)-532. The balance of 532 came in a second echelon a week later. Then on the 27th half of the night fighters were detached to Engebi, 337 miles northwest. While at Engebi they would see limited but useful service.

So began the aerial siege of the Marshalls. By the first week of March, when operations began in earnest, the Fourth Wing's three groups totaled ten fighter and four bomber squadrons. MAG-13 on Majuro Atoll, some 250 miles southeast of Kwajalein, operated F4Us and SBDs against the same targets as MAG-31, but was closer to most of them. MAG-22, also a mixed fighter and bomber group, was based at Eniwetok some 330 miles northwest of Kwajalein. Thus, the three groups covered a wide expanse of mid-Pacific, from Ponape in the eastern Carolines to Mille in the southern Marshalls—a straight-line distance across the wing's southern target area of over 800 miles.

Most of the Marshalls were unoccupied by Americans or Japanese. The four enemy atolls—Jaluit, Maloelap, Mille, and Wotje—were therefore cut off and surrounded. There was considerable variety in the distances the different groups had to fly to their targets. MAG-31 on Roi, for instance, had 322 miles to Mille. MAG-13 on Majuro was a handy 65 miles from the same atoll. The MAG-31 squadrons averaged 240 miles to their four Marshalls targets while the MAG-13 units, being better situated, had slightly less than half as far to fly.

The first strikes were flown on 4 March, encountering a torrent of AA fire over Jaluit Atoll. Returning pilots described the flak as intense and accurate. For those Marines who had expected otherwise, it came as a shock. Though the Army's Seventh Air Force had been bombing the same four atolls since November, Japanese defenses remained stiff. Taroa Island in Maloelap Atoll, for instance, boasted seventy-three AA guns alone, from 6.5 to 25 millimeter.

Aerial opposition became rare in the Marshalls—at least after VMF-113 was through. The only dogfight worthy of the name came on 28 March when the CO, Major Loren D. Everton, led six Corsairs as escort to four Army B-25s on the first strike against Ponape. It was a long trip for the Eniwetok F4Us—367 miles—but worth the effort. Twelve Zekes attempted to intercept the small formation, and all six Marines scored. Everton was already one of the most experienced combat pilots in the Corps. He'd flown dive bombers at Midway and became a double ace during the Guadalcanal campaign. The two Zekes he splashed raised his wartime total to twelve. Six other enemy aircraft also went down, and one more was destroyed on the ground.

The only other aerial victories recorded by Marines in the Central Pacific during 1944 came barely two weeks later. But the circumstances were considerably different. As different as day and night.

The first and only Marine squadron to fly F4U-2s in combat was VMF (N)-532. This pioneering unit was commissioned at Cherry Point in April 1943 and had been led by Major Everette H. Vaughan since May of that year. A prewar reservist, Vaughan had been a TWA pilot at the time of Pearl Harbor. His instrument flying experience well suited him to command a night-fighter squadron.

Five-Thirty-Two began operations from Tarawa in January 1944 and staged to Engebi via Makin and Roi in February. Its F4U-2s fired their guns in earnest on just one night, the evening of 13–14 April 1944.

One of Vaughan's Corsairs was aloft when an estimated dozen Betty bombers were tracked inbound to Engebi from the west. The night-fighter pilot, Lieutenant Joel E. Bonner, had taken off at 2400 when he was directed to a contact at 20,000 feet. He closed the bogey to near-minimum range and described its dark silhouette to the GCI station on Kwajalein. The controller replied, "Go to it," and Bonner did.[1] He opened fire, found that only his two starboard guns were operating, quickly charged his three port guns, and resumed fire. The Betty showed signs of being hit and dived to starboard, but not before the tail gunner scored. Bonner's windscreen was covered with a film of engine oil and the Marine informed his controller that he would have to bail out. He went over the side at 6,000 feet, 12 miles from base. His parachute opened and Bonner dropped into the water. He spent the night in his rubber raft and was rescued by a destroyer escort next morning.

In the forty-five minutes after midnight, four more F4U-2s were scrambled. First of these was flown by Lieutenant Donald Spatz. A confused radar vector put him out of control range, and despite radio attempts to coach him back to base, he was lost. A five-day search proved fruitless.

Next off was Lieutenant Frank C. Lang, who was foiled by effective Japanese countermeasures. He made successive intercepts on bundles of metal chaff dropped by the marauding Bettys, but found no legitimate targets.

The last two pilots both scored. Lieutenant Edward A. Sovik took off at 0030 and was vectored west, climbing to 20,000 feet in ten minutes. He

By May 1944 the once hotly contested Cape Torokina area of Bougainville was becoming more habitable. Marine ground crews look after an F4U-1A parked near a steel plank taxiway. (Ling-Temco-Vought)

orbited briefly until put onto a bogey 80 miles west of base at 23,000. Sovik bored in to close range and commenced fire at 300 yards, continuing down to 125 yards. In his haste to arm his guns, he missed two switches and fired only three .50 calibers for fewer than 100 rounds. But it was enough; the Betty exploded. Pulling away from his kill, Sovik looked to the south and saw a streak of flame. Captain Howard Bollman was also successful.

Bollman was headed for his bunk when the fifth fighter was requested. He took off fifteen minutes behind Sovik and gained a quick contact. Bollman pressed his attack to absolute minimum range at 22,000 feet and had time for only two short bursts before rolling violently away to avoid a collision. When he came around for another pass Bollman fired once more, and that completed the job. His target broke in two and fell towards the sea.

In barely one hour, 532 had engaged three enemy bombers and shot down two with one claimed a probable for the loss of two Corsairs and a pilot. The other Bettys abandoned their mission and jettisoned their bombs into the sea.

Five-Thirty-Two departed Engebi for Roi in mid-June and subsequently operated from Saipan before returning to the United States. By then, however, the hunting had run out, and Japanese aircraft in the Marshalls were as rare as pinups in a monastery.

During March and April, MAG-22 flew strikes against Ponape, then turned its attention to the Marshalls. During this period VMF-113 established a Corsair record. While covering landings at Ulejang Atoll some 150 miles south-southwest of Engebi, Major Everton's F4Us stayed airborne for nine hours and forty minutes—a long, long time to sit on a hard parachute.

The original Marshalls bombing missions were conducted by SBD squadrons. But the Fourth Wing's primary air power was the Corsair, and in a very short time the F4Us were also engaged in delivering ordnance. With enemy aircraft virtually nonexistent, there was really no other useful purpose for the fighters.

Thus was born the most useful tactical innovation derived from the Central Pacific: the Corsair fighter-bomber. Credit for the "field mod" which made this possible is generally given to VMF-111, at the time under Major Frank Cole. One-Eleven's ordnance crews had manufactured heavy-duty bomb racks for the Makin-based Corsairs, which put them to use for the first time on 18 March. Eight of Cole's planes delivered 1,000-pound bombs against Mille's AA guns on that date. Thus began the F4U's unplanned career as a dive bomber.

Stability and responsiveness are the prime requisites for an accurate dive bomber: a steady aiming platform and the ability to make corrections in the dive in order to line up the sights. The Marines found that by lowering their wheels they could control their rate of descent, and the Corsair's inherent stability and sensitive control response were admirably suited to dive-bombing.

And the F4Us needed all the accuracy they could get. Three-quarters of the Marshalls targets were gun positions of fifty feet diameter or less. Japanese block houses and command posts were likely to be fifty feet square, often reinforced with coconut palm logs. Under such conditions, the Fourth Wing pilots were presented with a formidable challenge.

In bombing with conventional weapons—what are now futuristically called gravity bombs—the standard of comparison is the Circle of Error Probability. The CEP is the radius of a circle about the aiming point within which 50 percent of the bombs are expected to fall. Therefore, scoring a CEP is something akin to golf; the smaller the score the better.

One of the more thorough studies conducted on this subject was made in the Marshalls during July and August, 1944. Three SBD and four F4U squadrons provided the material which formed the basis of comparison between the Dauntless and the Corsair as dive bombers. The results were rather surprising.

The SBD units were VMSB-231, 245, and 331. The F4U squadrons were VMF-111, 311, 422, and 441. After analyzing the combat results achieved by these aircraft, it was conservatively estimated that the CEP for the Dauntless was 175 feet. The Corsair's CEP was estimated at 195 feet. In other words, the SBD—designed and built as a dive bomber—was barely 10 percent more efficient in that esoteric role than the F4U.

With the absence of Japanese air power, the Marines' primary concern was enemy AA fire. But fortunately, both the SBD and F4U had demonstrated an ability to bomb accurately from various altitudes. The survey showed no appreciable decrease in accuracy as release altitude increased, from 1,700 up to 3,000 feet. Tactically, this meant a great deal to the air crews, for the higher their release, the less vulnerable they were to Japanese gunfire.

Further examination of the Marshalls experience only reinforced the conclusions originally derived. In terms of absolute number of hits on targets varying from 25 to 250 feet radius, the F4U and SBD were again almost even. Bombing a 25-foot circle, SBDs could expect to obtain 1.4 percent direct hits while Corsairs scored 1.1 percent. On 50-foot circles the respective figures were 5.4 and 4.5 percent, increasing to 19.9 and 16.7 percent against 100-foot circles. Both types passed the 50 percent margin on 200-foot targets. This was a dramatic increase, for where target size doubled, hits tripled. And attacking 250-foot circles, Dauntlesses recorded 75.1 percent hits while Corsairs scored 68.2 percent.

There was no standard doctrine among Corsair squadrons in achieving these impressive results. Unlike the SBD, which best performed in a 70-degree dive, experimentation showed that the F4U could bomb at angles up to 85 degrees. From the pilot's viewpoint, the difference between 85 degrees and a straight-down 90 degrees was nonexistent. Hanging forward against his shoulder harness, the pilot had a vertical view of his target. The only worry was that at such a steep angle the bomb might strike the propeller upon release.

Different squadrons evolved different techniques. The situation was well stated by Major William E. Classen, who succeeded Frank Cole as CO of VMF-111 in April 1944. Classen avowed that his brand of dive-bombing was more art than science. "It's like playing a violin," he said. "You can't tell a man how to do it. He's got to experiment until he works out his own individual technique."[2]

Depending upon the type of target, some units preferred glide-bombing to dive bombing. One variation was a three-plane division—one bomb-carrying F4U escorted on either side by a strafing wingman. The wingmen suppressed AA fire while the bomber made a fast, shallow run as low as 100 feet. In most dive-bombing runs the Corsair pilots fired their six .50s near the bottom of the dive in order to counter potentially heavy AA fire.

The Fourth Marine Air Wing was active in the Marshall Islands during most of 1944. These F4U-1As have been modified with centerline bomb racks. (R.M. Hill)

The light-caliber AA weapons were most dangerous at low level, but the Marshalls experience showed that gun crews would frequently abandon their weapons in the face of stiff return fire.

But it wasn't always easy. From March to September the Fourth Wing lost 36 Corsairs or SBDs to enemy flak. Half of the downed aviators were rescued by PBYs or destroyers. Wotje and Maloelap were the toughest atolls during this period, but the increasing bomb tonnage was being felt. When the F4U-1D became the standard type, Corsairs began toting 2,000-pound loads. They not only doubled the offensive capacity of the SBD, but matched the normal load of the RAF's twin-engine DeHavilland Mosquito Mark IV.

The man generally credited with increasing the F4U's bombload was Charles Lindbergh. In early September, Lindbergh arrived at Roi to conduct experiments with Colonel Calvin B. Freeman's MAG-31. On the 3rd, Lindbergh took off for an early-morning strike at Wotje, flying ahead of the attack squadrons. His Corsair carried three 1,000-pounders, the first time this had been done in the Marshalls. Lindbergh joined formation near the target and made three dives on Japanese gun positions. Each dive began at 8,000 feet with release at 3,000. The results were satisfying, and Lindbergh spent the next five days working with MAG-31 ordnance officers on a rack to handle a one-ton bomb.

After initial tests, Lindbergh was ready to try the new rack in combat on 8 September. Flying with a regularly scheduled strike, Lindbergh took off from Roi at 1300 into a slight crosswind. It was probably the first time a fighter had carried such a weapon, but the takeoff was normal with no control problems. In a shallow downwind dive from 8,000 feet, Lindbergh put his 2,000-pounder 100 yards from his target building on Wotje. The blast and concussion flattened several smaller structures.

As in the Solomons three months before, Charles Lindbergh remained enthusiastic about flying and ambivalent about waging modern war. "It is impossible to realize as one flies over that Japanese troops crouch hidden in dugouts and concrete houses waiting for the raid of death that we are about to drop from the sky," he wrote. "It is difficult to realize that the sting of death lies coiled in belts of machine gun bullets in those little, harmless-looking circles on the ground. One cannot realize that when he presses the little red button on the stick he releases a bomb that may carry death and agony to a hundred men. . . . In modern war one kills at a distance, and in doing so does not realize that he is killing."[3]

By the 12th, Lindbergh was ready to attempt a takeoff with 4,000 pounds of bombs. But a strong crosswind with 14-knot gusts prompted him to order one of the 1,000-pounders removed. His takeoff with a one-ton and half-ton bomb was still the cause of some concern, as a number of Marines looked on to see how the Lone Eagle fared. But he had little

Marine pilots and ordnancemen experimented with ever-increasing bomb loads in the Central Pacific. This F4U-1A packs a one-ton bomb on a "field mod" wing rack. (Ling-Temco-Vought)

difficulty, making a curving takeoff toward the windward side of the runway. Over Wotje, he grayed out during his dive recovery, but his wingman reported almost a direct hit with both bombs on a radio station.

Next day, 13 September, Lindbergh flew his last Corsair mission. A calm wind allowed him to take off with a 4,000-pound bomb load—a one-tonner in the special belly rack and a 1,000-pounder under each wing. His specific target was a small concrete blockhouse, again on Wotje. As usual, he approached the target at 8,000 feet, but this time rolled into a 65-degree dive, the steepest yet with a heavy load. Committed to an upwind dive, Lindbergh lined up the target, grasping the -1D's manual wing pylon release with his throttle hand, and operating the center-line rack's custom electrical release with his stick hand. But he neglected to compensate for the tail-heavy trim, and the Corsair's nose began rising.

Unable to keep the target in his sight, and knowing he had overshot, Lindbergh released his load just inland from the beach. The F4U abruptly zoomed upward, pulling five or more G's and graying him out. But looking back, Lindbergh saw a black column of smoke and debris over the beach. His bombs had completely destroyed a naval shore battery. "I could not have selected a better target if it had been intentional," he said.[4] His work completed, Charles Lindbergh headed for Hawaii that same day. Though excessive overloads such as he tested in MAG-31 were seldom used, he had probably done more than anyone else to make the Corsair into a true fighter-bomber.

During late 1944 the Fourth Wing underwent some equipment changes. Corsairs replaced Dauntlesses in two squadrons, changing the units designations from VMSB to VMF or, more accurately, VMBF. These squadrons were 231 under Major William E. Abblitt and 331 under Major James C. Otis. But the transition was short-lived, for at year's end both units reverted to Dauntlesses and kept their beloved SBDs.

Regardless of their aircraft, the Fourth Wing aviators continued with their dreary backwater war. They felt "like prisoners on a pinhead,"[5] living and flying in the stultifying equatorial climate, blinking at the glaring sun and coral. The boredom was relieved mainly—and unexpectedly—by flying into sudden tropical storms or encountering heavy Japanese flak. Though enemy food allotments were reduced by 60 percent from spring to fall of 1944 and half the garrison troops died, the Japanese AA gunners remained active and highly practiced to the end. Despite eighteen months of bombing and strafing, nearly 200 AA guns of all calibers remained intact by V-J Day. Most of the heavy-caliber weapons, however, had been destroyed and there was often no ammunition for the others.

There was more to the mid-Pacific campaign than the Marshalls. The next stepping stones to the Philippines were the Marianas and Palaus, and Marine Corsairs saw both island groups up close.

MAG-21 arrived on Guam as an effective force on 4 August, only four days after the first tactical aircraft landed at the newly won airstrip. F4Us of VMF-216, 217, and 225 arrived that day with Hellcat night fighters, all launched from the escort carrier *Santee* (CVE-29). But there was relatively little for the fighters to do in the Marianas. Six weeks after the "Marianas Turkey Shoot," Japanese aircraft were not to be found.

A typical scene from the Central Pacific: Corsair fighter-bombers along a palm-lined runway in the fall of 1944. (Ling-Temco-Vought)

So the Marines contented themselves with occasional strikes on Pagan, 220 miles north in the extreme reaches of the Marianas. And there were 50-mile hops to Rota, "the poor man's Maloelap," where things were a bit livelier. The enemy's twin 25-mm antiaircraft guns hidden in a cave became a local legend, as occasional F4Us and TBMs were shot down over the island. But before long, even the once-formidable Marianas became a rear area as the war moved inexorably westward.

The Palaus lie barely 500 miles east of the Philippines. Therefore, the importance of the island group was well understood by both sides, and the Japanese defenders resisted invasion with all the ferocity and tenacity which characterized their race.

The best-defended island was Peleliu, assaulted on 15 September by the Third Amphibious Corps. Fierce combat ensued, and though the airfield was the first major objective secured—on D-Plus Two—not till the 26th did Second Wing F4Us arrive. They were Major Robert F. Stout's "Death Dealers" of VMF-114, sporting white bands on their cowls. VMF-121 and 122 both arrived in October, supporting operations against nearby islands, so 114 delivered most of the close air support during the Peleliu battle.

And close air support was never closer. Peleliu's main feature was "Bloody Nose Ridge," a craggy, jungle-covered crest running along the island's north-south axis. Corsairs taking off barely had time to retract their wheels before they were over their targets—often a mere fifteen seconds after liftoff. Dive-bombing F4Us frequently never bothered to raise their wheels during these short flights; the extended landing gear made a good dive brake.

Bloody Nose Ridge was full of deep limestone caverns, and formed the enemy's main line of resistance. Not only were the Japanese well defended in their caves; they were often invisible as well, due to the foliage which covered the ridge. The answer to this problem was napalm. Ordnance crews of 114, 121, and 122 occasionally mixed their "hell jelly" with captured Japanese gasoline. The volatile concoction served two purposes. It burned off covering vegetation, and frequently suffocated enemy troops in their caves. Therefore, napalm not only expedited the capture of Peleliu, it substantially reduced American casualties which would have been incurred while digging out the Japanese. And where napalm didn't work, saturation bombing often did. On 30 September VMF-114 smothered enemy resistance with twenty 1,000-pounders in an area only 100 yards square.

Marine aviators lived on Peleliu much as they had on Guadalcanal, but without the satisfaction of air combat. Some Solomons veterans like Major Hunter Reinburg, CO of 122, had anticipated another 'Canal at Peleliu, for the distance from the Palaus to the Philippines was about the same as from Rabaul to Guadalcanal. But aggressive fighter pilots like Reinburg and Stout were disappointed. The only aerial victory of the campaign was recorded by an F6F night fighter at the end of October. Otherwise, old Solomons hands must have felt in familiar surroundings. They swatted mosquitos, fought tropic fever, and ducked snipers—sometimes all at once.

One-Twenty-Two found a unique method of dispelling some of the boredom and discomfort. The skipper, Hunter Reinburg, was an ice cream fiend. His maintenance people devised a technique for manufacturing ice cream, and not surprisingly it soon became the worst of the best-kept secrets on the island.

Originally 122 modified a belly tank, cut open at both ends, to cool the mixture of canned milk and cocoa powder. Flown to 30,000 feet with a stash of beer, the crude machine did an admirable job of providing cold drinks, but the milk and cocoa would not solidify. At first it was theorized that a lengthy descent was responsible, but Reinburg himself showed that by maintaining a steady 200 knots and descending at 8,000 feet per minute, only five minutes were expended from altitude to landing.

The Marines deduced that the underwing tank was too close to the engine exhaust for complete freezing. So the mechanics built a more conventional ice cream machine. They modified a five-gallon can with a shaft which was turned by a wind-driven propeller. Mounted on a removable under-wing inspection panel, the device manufactured soft chocolate ice cream. With one gadget under each wingtip, VMF-122 could provide small amounts of ice cream to about 100 men each day.

Thus began Operation Freeze. Every day at 1400 a different pilot made the flight, accomplishing three objectives at once. First, and most important, it produced ten gallons of chocolate ice cream. Secondly, it gave the pilots continuing experience with high-altitude engine operation and oxygen tests. And finally, by passing over nearby islands, the lone F4U usually prompted the Japanese to waste several large-caliber AA shells. The heavy AA was ineffective above 28,000 feet, while Operation Freeze flew at 30,000 to 33,000.

Only once did anything go wrong. A pilot exceeded 200 knots during his descent and lost both underwing ice cream machines. Reinburg thought some of his men were going to lynch the offender. Then he learned that other interested parties were also aware of the situation. One-Twenty-Two received a call from Colonel Caleb Bailey, the group commander. "You guys aren't fooling me," Bailey intoned. "I've got spies. You tell Hunter I'm coming over there tomorrow and get my ration."[6]

MAG-11 remained in the Palaus till the end of the war, flying CAP and strikes against nearby islands. However, the squadrons within the group came and went. But unlike their Marshalls counterparts, the Sec-

Ordnancemen load a napalm bomb on a VMF-114 Corsair at Peleliu in the Palau group, September 1944. (Ling-Temco-Vought)

ond Wing pilots had a variety of targets almost to the end. For instance, in the last weeks of 1944, F4U squadrons operating from Peleliu claimed the destruction of 112 barges, 30-odd small craft, 58 trucks, and even a locomotive.

Though this activity also developed into a milk-run way of life, it was by no means always easy. Nearly 30 Marine aircraft were shot down over the Palaus and Carolines up to June 1945. Among them was Major Bob Stout, the six-plane ace and CO of VMF-114, killed by AA fire over Koror on 4 March.

General Douglas MacArthur kept his three-year-old promise to return to the Philippines on 20 October 1944 when he waded ashore at Red Beach, Leyte. The first important airfield available was nearby Tacloban —a habitually crowded, narrow landing strip near the ocean. MAG-12 units landed there on 3 and 4 December after a nearly 2,000-mile trip from Emirau, staging through Hollandia and Palau. The four Corsair squadrons, mainly equipped with "stiff-wing" FG-1Ds, were VMF-115, 211, 218, and 313. With the 12 F6F-5Ns of VMF(N)-541, MAG-12 counted

87 aircraft at Tacloban in early December. First Wing SBDs were the most numerous Leatherneck aircraft in the Philippines throughout the campaign, but F4Us ran second, in front of F6Fs, PBJ medium bombers, and an assortment of observation and liaison aircraft.

It was hardly a pleasant environment, but considering some of the places the group's pilots and mechanics had been, MAG-12 considered Tacloban tolerable. The main features were drenching rains which produced thick, oozy mud, and a 70-foot-wide runway. Japanese bombers made frequent appearances until VMF(N)-541 rendered the nocturnal visitations unprofitable.

The Corsair's first action in the campaign came on 5 December when a division of VMF-115 was on CAP over an American convoy off Leyte's east coast. A pair of Zekes dived on the ships and the Marines gave chase. They splashed one, the first Corsair victory in the Philippines. There would be more, but the most successful Marine squadron in the area was VMF(N)-541, which recorded twenty shoot-downs during December.

But however much the Corsair pilots may have complained, at least they were no longer doing the rear area, keep-them-busy type of work which F4Us had performed for the previous year. This time they were right up front.

And a good thing, too. For it was in the Philippines that the precision dive-bombing and close support techniques evolved in the Marshalls and elsewhere became widely appreciated. The Corsair's proficiency as a fighter-bomber would prove a valuable asset, particularly since the kamikaze menace had appeared in late October. One aircraft which could perform both air defense and attack missions was worth two specialized planes.

A large portion of MAG-12's strike sorties were flown against Japanese shipping—sometimes by themselves, sometimes in concert with Army aircraft. On 6 December Major Stan Witonski led a dozen VMF-211 Corsairs against a Japanese convoy of seven ships headed for Ormoc Bay, on the west coast of Leyte. Army fighters were detailed to provide top cover, but they failed to show so the Marines proceeded alone.

The convoy was discovered at anchor in San Isidro Harbor, 30 miles south of Ormoc, and the escorting destroyers were standing out to westward. Despite a flock of Zekes circling above, the Corsairs attacked with bombs, severely damaging one destroyer which was later beached.

But the Zeros and enemy AA gunners took a toll. Three Corsairs were lost, and only one pilot survived. He was the CO, Major Witonski, who bailed out and was picked up. Considering it a lesson learned, from then on the Marines took care to arrange for their own top cover.

Next afternoon, the 7th, aerial pursuit of the convoy continued. Twenty-one bent-wing fighters from VMF-211, 218, and 313 armed with

1,000-pound bombs piled in with the aid of bomb-toting P-40s. The Marines claimed credit for sinking five ships, while postwar analysis attributed four sinkings to the combined efforts of the Corsairs and Army aircraft. Whatever the actual division of the spoils, some excellent bombing was done. The four pilots of VMF-218 put all their bombs on one transport which seemed to break in half and sink by the stern.

The pace quickened during mid-December, despite poor flying weather which curtailed some missions. But fighter-bomber sorties occupied MAG-12 pilots during most of this period, and probably the most eventful day was the 11th.

The catalyst was one of numerous Japanese attempts to reinforce Léyte. A ten-ship convoy—freighters and transports escorted by destroyers—was subjected to seventy-three fighter-bomber sorties in the course of two strikes. The first involved 27 Corsairs which pounced on the convoy 40 miles east of Panay Island. Two ships were hit, and the enemy fighters which attempted to intercept were roughly handled. The Marines claimed nine kills over and around Panay.

That afternoon 56 planes struck, including 16 P-40s. Though the Army fliers were inexperienced in shipping strikes and released their bombs too high, they did help confuse the AA gunners. This allowed most of the Corsairs to penetrate the destroyer screen and deliver their bombs in fast, low, shallow-angle attacks. Four Marine squadrons—VMF-115, 211, 218, and 313—all claimed damage to a variety of enemy vessels. The reports were too confused to sort out who did what.

Not that it mattered. Two cargo ships were sunk, only five miles offshore, and the next day the Marine-Army team returned to dispatch a damaged destroyer and a transport.

Meanwhile, a VMF-313 division covering an Army reinforcement convoy to Ormoc found air combat. At mid-afternoon some 16 Zekes, all laden with bombs, attack the U.S. ships with suicidal intent. For some reason they concentrated on the destroyer *Reid*, and achieved near-surprise due to low clouds. The hostiles came under fire barely a mile from the convoy, and the sailors put up fierce and accurate flak. Four Zekes were shot down or crashed very close aboard. The fifth scored a direct hit, exploding the DD's depth charges, and the ship sank immediately. The 313 division splashed five—too late to save the *Reid*, but preventing further damage to other ships.

In all, Corsairs claimed nineteen aerial victories during the day, a record for their service in the Philippines. There was, however, always a price to be paid. Throughout the 11th, MAG-12 lost six aircraft and three pilots. Two Corsairs collided with Japanese fighters during combats over the enemy convoy. Several other U-Birds returned to base with extensive battle damage and were written off.

The invasion of Mindoro was another prominent Corsair operation. As the amphibious force approached the landing beaches on 13 December, a CAP of three dozen F4Us and FGs orbited overhead. And while they encountered no opposition, there were still losses. The press of operations was such that some shot-up aircraft had received the barest of repairs in the previous few days. One such was flown by Major Theodore Olsen of VMF-313. His Corsair had been seriously damaged by flak on the 11th; mechanics counted 300 holes. When the plane gave out, Olsen jumped over the water but was struck by the tail before he could open his chute.

Air defense of U.S. convoys continued for some time. VMF-211 dropped five Zekes over the Mindoro beachhead on the 14th, but by the year's end things had changed. A variety of installations were targeted on Luzon, and Japanese transport featured prominently. Road, canal, and rail traffic was shot up with near impunity. It was a job many fighter pilots relished. Flying low and fast, firing their guns at close range, was a sensation which neither bombing nor even air combat could provide. The aviators especially relished "train busting," till then a rare sport in the Pacific. Puncturing locomotives' boilers, watching the steam gush high in the air, provided a unique thrill. Trigger-happy pilots of all services were so enthusiastic about it that by mid-January fully half the nearly 160 prewar locomotives in the islands had been destroyed.

There were other diversions at Tanauan, where the Marines moved just before New Year's Day. Chief among these were a swamp with its attendant fever and a pesky dawn sniper who was persistent but fortunately not very proficient.

Another air group, MAG-14, arrived in the Philippines shortly after MAG-12 moved out of Tacloban. On 2 January 1945, 22 Corsairs of VMO-251 under Major William C. Humberd put down on Samar. They were followed by VMF-212, 222, and 223 before the end of the month.

Also before month's end, there occurred one of Marine aviation's most tragic accidents. Taking off from Guiuan on the morning of the 24th, Lieutenant Karl Oerth of 222 blew a tire, lost control of his speeding Corsair, and slammed into a revetment. The F4U caught fire, and the .50-caliber ammunition exploded. Thirteen men were killed and over fifty injured—many while vainly attempting to rescue the trapped pilot. Nor was this the only operational casualty. In its first thirty days on Samar, MAG-14 suffered nearly twenty similar losses.

But there were successes as well. Two footnotes to Corsair history were written by VMF-115 under Major John S. King, Jr. On 23 February Major Eldon Railsback led three other F4Us against an unusual target at Cebu City. Each plane had a 1,000-pounder, and Railsback's division attacked a midget submarine from less than thirty feet altitude. The half-ton bombs skipped off the water directly into the small sub, which was seen to explode. Lack of surviving Japanese documents makes this claim difficult, if not impossible, to verify. But as the action report noted, it was undoubtedly the first submarine sunk by F4Us. And almost certainly the only one.

One-Fifteen's other claim to fame during this period was connected with the occupation of Mindanao. American troops went ashore on 10 March, but MAG-14 pilots had often landed at Dipolog on the north coast, where a small grass airstrip was in control of Filipino guerrillas. It may have been the only instance of more or less regular air operations from an enemy-held island. But the guerrilla movement was large and well organized, and the Japanese never did achieve anything resembling complete occupation of Mindanao.

In the course of these impromptu air operations, an unusual incident occurred on 27 March. U.S. infantry had moved beyond Dipolog, but heavy Japanese pressure was threatening the small airfield. Colonel Clayton Jerome, commanding MAG-12, had little available at the moment, but was anxious not to let the guerrillas down. So he dispatched a division from VMF-115, which landed at Dipolog shortly before sunset. One of the aviators, Lieutenant Winfield S. Sharpe, looked up an Army guerrilla officer, Major Donald H. Wills, to discuss the situation. In the fading light the Japanese were well hidden, but Wills said he knew just where to find them.

So the Army officer climbed into the Corsair and Sharpe sat on his lap. They took off and flew over the enemy-held area where Wills pointed out the Japanese. Sharpe nosed over and made six strafing passes which drove the Japanese away. An Army pilot had shot down a Japanese plane while flying a Corsair in the Solomons, and Sharpe and Wills's sortie was not the only two-man mission flown by a Corsair. But certainly it was the only inter-service flight in an F4U!

Of the seven Corsair squadrons in MAG-12 and MAG-14, four remained in the Philippines for the duration. The other three—VMF-122, 222, and 223—eventually moved north to fight at Okinawa. But between now and then, other F4U squadrons would see combat with the fast carriers. The Corsair had finally gone to sea.

chapter 5

Commonwealth Corsairs

They change their skies above them . . .

Kipling

Among the many statistics on World War II aircraft production is the fact that one Corsair in six was delivered to the British Royal Navy. All told, 2,012 F4Us, FGs, and F3As went to the Fleet Air Arm from 1943 to 1945. In fact, the 430 F3A-1s, called Corsair IIIs by the British, represented 58 percent of the Brewster contribution.

Corsairs were used in larger numbers by the British than any other U.S. naval aircraft. And the need was great. The Royal Navy began the war with wholly outdated fighters. The obsolete biplane Sea Gladiator was, like most subsequent FAA fighters, a "hooked" version of a Royal Air Force type. The Supermarine Seafire and Hawker Sea Hurricane did reasonably well as interim measures, but were clearly not the answer. Nor was the Fairey Fulmar, which though designed as a carrier fighter, was a two-seater employing a radioman-navigator. The Fulmar acquitted itself well in the Mediterranean, but its prewar design philosophy was disproven by comparison with land-based fighters. It simply could not compete.

Grumman Wildcats, called Martlets by the British, were available in small numbers from 1940. They lacked the later Seafire's speed and performance, but were built as carrier aircraft and therefore withstood the considerable strain of carrier operations. Grumman and General Motors eventually built over a thousand Wildcats for Britain, and nearly 1,200 Hellcats went to the Royal Navy. But the Corsair was the fighter which most attracted Fleet Air Arm. It was a generation ahead of anything else in the inventory.

By 1943 the British had acceptance and modification centers at Roosevelt Field, New York, and Brunswick, Maine. The first two Corsair squadrons to join the fleet, Numbers 1830 and 1833, were formed that summer and began "working-up" to operational status. Ninety-five F4U-1s were delivered as Corsair Is while a subsequent 510 One Ables became Corsair IIs. The Goodyear aircraft became Mark IVs in British service.

Apparently the Fleet Air Arm never entertained serious reservations about the Corsair as a carrier aircraft. Almost from the beginning, modifications were made with the specific aim of qualifying the new fighters for embarked operations. These included the oleo strut and starboard wing spoiler mods which became standard on all American Corsairs. But the FAA made other changes, too. Eight inches were clipped from each wingtip in order to accommodate F4Us to the lower overhead of British carrier hangar decks. The Royal Navy pioneered virtually every important feature in carrier design, and armored flight decks were one of the first. But this resulted in smaller hangars, hence the shorter wingspan on British Corsairs. Otherwise the wings could not have been folded.

But the clipped-wing Corsairs brought unexpected benefits. With slightly less wing area, they were not as prone to float on landing, and some pilots detected an increased rate of roll. At last equipped with a modern, first-class carrier fighter, the British were delighted. They considered the F4U "a honey of a ship."[1]

While the first two FAA Corsair squadrons deployed to the Indian Ocean, two more were en route to combat in a vastly different climate. These were Numbers 1834 and 1836 Squadrons, embarked in the HMS *Victorious* as Number 47 Naval Fighter Wing. The wing's 28 Corsair IIs were operational with the Home Fleet in early 1944, preparing for the first in a series of Scandinavian operations.

The *Victorious* was one of seven carriers participating in Operation Tungsten, a massive strike against the German battleship *Tirpitz*. Protected in a Norwegian fjord, the 42,000-ton dreadnought posed a constant threat to Allied convoys in northern waters. Tungsten was intended to end the threat, as 121 aircraft were launched in two waves some 120 miles offshore on 3 April 1944. The fighter escort for the ungainly Barracuda dive bombers included top-cover Corsairs. Surprise was achieved in the early morning light, and this, combined with determined low-level strafing by Wildcats and Hellcats, kept German AA fire suppressed. Only three aircraft were shot down, and the *Tirpitz* was put out of commission for ninety days. The Luftwaffe was spread thin throughout Scandinavia, and the top-cover F4Us met with no opposition. Thus was set the pattern for future operations; Corsairs would never fight German aircraft.

Two more large carrier operations were mounted against the *Tirpitz* that summer. Operation Mascot in mid-July involved one Corsair squad-

Royal Navy operations in the Arctic included landing at "dusk" in the midnight sun. (Imperial War Museum)

ron—Number 1841 aboard the HMS *Formidable*—but the strike accomplished little. The Germans had advance warning and obscured the target area with smoke. Operation Goodwood was conducted during three days of late August, amounting to over 240 sorties, but only minor damage was inflicted on "the lone queen of the north." By this time the *Formidable* embarked 1841 and 1842 squadrons as Number 6 Naval Fighter Wing, and the Corsairs repeated their role as top cover. But a few strike sorties were flown. Among 1841's new pilots was Lieutenant R. H. Gray, who was mentioned in dispatches for his aggressive leadership. During Goodwood, the young Canadian engaged in flak suppression and led his section in an attack against three anchored destroyers. His attraction to enemy escort vessels would climax twelve months later.

Corsair losses were extremely light during the Norwegian operations —only one was known lost to flak. Otherwise, things had gone smoothly. And therein lay the larger importance. The British safely operated F4Us in squadron strength from the spring of 1944—over eight months before their American counterparts put Corsairs aboard ship in similar numbers.

With the last of the *Tirpitz* strikes the Corsair's European combat was ended. The scene shifted from the craggy fjords of the Arctic to the balmy islands of the tropics.

Number 15 Naval Fighter Wing aboard the HMS *Illustrious* had already seen combat against the Japanese. In April 1944 the *Illustrious* completed a sweep of the Indian Ocean with the USS *Saratoga*, seeking enemy commerce raiders. Ironically, 1830 and 1833 Squadrons were flying Corsair IIs while VF-12 aboard the "Sara" was equipped with Hellcats. Fighting 12, now under Lieutenant Commander Bob Dose, had been the first U.S. Navy squadron to receive F4Us, and his pilots missed them.

The Americans found the British appreciative of the F4U's capabilities. Leading Number 15 Fighter Wing was Commander Richard J. Cork, then the Royal Navy's most successful fighter pilot. Cork had flown in the Battle of Britain and ran his string to thirteen victories while flying Sea Hurricanes off the *Indomitable* in the Mediterranean. He came to a tragic end at Ceylon on 14 April, flying into China Bay with other Corsairs. Cork inexplicably landed downwind despite a wave-off from the tower after a previous wrong-way approach. In the early-morning darkness Cork's F4U smashed head-on into another fighter landing normally.

During this period Bob Dose had a chance to fly a Spitfire, courtesy of an Australian squadron leader. He found the British fighter a fun airplane; it turned inside the F4U at low airspeeds, and while the Spit could make two vertical rolls, Dose found the Corsair managed only one. But for speed, range, endurance, and versatility, there was no beating the Vought.

The Allied partnership continued during April, as the Corsairs and

Hellcats struck Japanese facilities at Sabang Island on the 19th. Fighting 12 knocked down three Betty bombers but the *Illustrious* pilots had to be content with burning about a dozen parked aircraft.

In July the well-traveled *Victorious* joined the Royal Navy force at Trincomalee, bringing Number 47 Naval Fighter Wing, reinforced by 1838 Squadron. The *Illustrious* also received a third Corsair unit, 1837 Squadron. The fighter strength of these carriers was thereby increased to 39 and 42 respectively. No FAA Corsairs had yet engaged in combat, but the upcoming operation looked promising. Hence the extra units.

The two Corsair wings provided air cover to a bombardment force which shelled Sabang, off the north tip of Sumatra, on 25 July. Specially trained fighter pilots served as gunfire spotters for the twelve warships, which inflicted heavy damage on Japanese naval facilities. Camera-equipped F4Us also obtained reconnaissance information and took damage assessment photos. Upon retirement, enemy aircraft belatedly appeared, and three of the six fighter squadrons found combat. The *Illustrious* pilots had the best of the shooting, as 1830 Squadron destroyed three Zekes while 1833 claimed two Zekes and a Sally. Number 1838, the *Victorious* reinforcement squadron, got a Zeke.

Though a minor operation in the context of the Pacific War, the Sabang bombardment was important to the Corsair. Seldom was the F4U's versatility so well demonstrated in a single action. The bent-wing Voughts not only defended the task force from air attack, but also conducted effective gunfire spotting and photoreconnaissance. However, the two extra fighter squadrons were removed, and the Barracudas went back aboard.

In October the *Victorious* wing had things more to itself. In company with the HMS *Indomitable*, embarking two Hellcat squadrons, Number 47 Wing Corsairs struck the Nicobar Islands. On the first day, the 17th, 1834 and 1836 Squadrons strafed airfields and AA positions. But the Japanese flak was effective, and two F4Us plus a Barracuda were shot down. Two days later, after waiting out bad weather, the carrier planes returned. And this time there was fighter opposition. Oscars rose to contest the spotter Hellcats, and 1834 Squadron's Corsairs became engaged. The British pilots knocked down seven bandits, losing two F4Us and an F6F. Four Oscars fell to 1834 Squadron, including three to Lieutenant L. D. Durno who made one kill himself and shared two with his wingman.

January 1945 may have been the busiest month of the war in the Indian Ocean. Heavy weather largely negated a December strike against Sumatran oil targets, and upon return to Trincomalee, the British carriers planned a return engagement. The slow, awkward Barracudas had been replaced with TBM Avengers, which gave the three air groups more offensive punch. The *Victorious* retained her veteran 47 Wing Corsairs while the *Indomitable* and *Indefatigable* used Hellcats and Seafires as fighters.

On 4 January Sir Philip Vian launched his strike against the refinery at Pangkalan Brandan. With good visibility and clear skies, the Avengers made a shambles of the petroleum plant. Corsairs and Hellcats flew escort and CAP, encountering more Oscars and a few twin-engine bombers. The *Victorious* F4Us again saw the majority of air combat, with seven of the dozen or so claimed victories. Lieutenant Durno of 1834 Squadron took shares of a Dinah and a Sally. Meanwhile, 1836 knocked down five Oscars, with Sub-Lieutenant D. J. Sheppard claiming two. The only British loss was an Avenger, and the crew was recovered.

On the 24th, four carriers launched 144 strike and CAP sorties on Operation Meridian One, attacking the refinery at Pladjoe in southern Sumatra. It was one of the two largest strikes ever launched by the Fleet Air Arm, involving 32 Corsairs from the *Illustrious* and *Victorious* as bomber escort, and another two dozen "Ramrods" to tie down Japanese planes on their fields. Launch commenced at 0615, 80 miles offshore in clear weather. The Corsairs and Hellcats, escorting 45 Avengers, climbed over the Barisan mountain range along the southwest coast, en route to the target 160 miles inland.

The Ramrods from all four F4U squadrons arrived too late to prevent enemy fighters from taking off. Attacking airdromes around Palembang, five Corsairs were lost, including one in a midair collision. But the others flew through the lethal flak, destroying upwards of 30 planes on the ground. These pilots saw few airborne hostiles, however, as the Japanese interceptors concentrated upon the strike aircraft.

All the top-cover Corsairs became engaged in the target area. Nearly 20 Tojos and Nicks attacked, leaving the close-escort fighters to take the Avengers into Pladjoe. More bandits were drawn to the scene, and a running battle developed which allowed the bombers to proceed.

The 16 top-cover Corsairs fought Tojos and Oscars, downing 8 for the loss of one. The missing F4U was from 1833 Squadron, last seen racing north, pursued by a Tojo. The *Victorious* pilots claimed six of the kills, paced by Major R. C. Hay, a Royal Marine aviator who dropped an Oscar and a Tojo, and Sub-Lieutenant A. French who destroyed two Tojos. Among 1836's two other kills was a Tojo by Sub-Lieutenant D. J. Sheppard, who raised his personal score to three. The close-escort leader, Lieutenant Commander Norman Hanson of 1833 Squadron off the *Illustrious*, shot down an Oscar. Upon return to the task force he crashed while landing and was rescued by a destroyer.*

*As described in Norman Hanson's autobiography of Corsair flying, *Carrier Pilot*, published by Patrick Stephens.

The refinery and storage tanks were hard hit, and though seven F4Us were lost to all causes, overall FAA casualties were fairly light. The eight Corsair victories would remain the one-day record for Royal Navy F4Us. Nevertheless, there was more work over Sumatra, and five days later an almost identical strike was launched against the nearby Soeni Gerong refinery.

Meridian Two on 29 January was even more successful than the first strike, but it was also more costly. The defenses were alert to the probability of a follow-up attack, and interception was made 50 miles out. Despite poor coordination between the Avengers and their escort, owing to lapses in radio and air discipline, the attack went well. Major Hay orbited overhead as strike coordinator, and he put in a full morning's work. He photographed the strike results with a camera pack in his F4U, directed Avengers to the target, and was intercepted by Oscars and Tojos. Hay and Sub-Lieutenant Sheppard accepted combat, and teamed up to shoot down one of each. Hay thus became the Royal Marines' only fighter ace, as his two victories in Blackburn Skuas and Fairey Fulmars early in the war put his total at five. Another Tojo was downed by 1834 Squadron, while 1830 claimed two kills. One was a Sally attempting to crash into the *Illustrious*. Two F4U pilots failed to return from Soeni Gerong, including Lieutenant L. D. Durno of 1834 Squadron, who had done so well over the Nicobars and Pankalan Brandan. He was seen to bail out of his damaged aircraft, but no further information was available.

At a total cost of 41 planes, the two Meridian strikes cut Sumatran aviation gasoline production by one-third. As such, these missions probably represented the Fleet Air Arm's most significant achievement in the war against Japan. But the carriers were needed elsewhere, and they steamed to Sydney, Australia, where they joined the British Pacific Fleet.

Beginning in late March the BPF operated with the U.S. Fifth Fleet under the designation Task Force 57. Actually, with five carriers and a heavy supporting screen, the British contribution was more on the order of an enlarged task group. But it amounted to an interesting assortment of aircraft. The normal strength consisted of some 270 planes, including 83 Avengers, 40 Seafires, some 30 Hellcats, and a dozen Fairey Firefly strike fighters. However, the most numerous type was the Corsair, with nearly 110 embarked in the *Illustrious*, *Victorious*, and *Formidable*.

The British carriers got into the Pacific war on 26 March, launching strikes against the Sakishima Gunto. Corsairs performed their usual flak suppression chores and flew some strike sorties. During the first half of April, Task Force 57 supported the Okinawa landings, and the kamikaze wind blew at gale force. The *Illustrious* was hit in the big raid of the 6th, but there was no serious damage. CAP sorties provided the Corsair wings

A British Corsair from HMS *Victorious* landed aboard the USS *Essex* on 9 August 1945, less than a week before Japan agreed to surrender. (R.M. Hill)

with plenty of interception practice, and from the 1st to the 16th, the *Illustrious* and *Victorious* F4Us splashed five suiciders each.

The campaign continued into May. On the 4th, the *Victorious* Corsairs downed four hostiles, including a Judy by D. J. Sheppard. It was the Canadian flier's fifth kill, making him the only FAA Corsair ace, and the only Royal Navy pilot with five Japanese planes credited. The next day the *Formidable* recorded its first F4U victory when 1841 Squadron downed a Zeke.

On 9 May the kamikazes tagged two BPF carriers, causing substantial aircraft loss. The *Formidable* lived up to her name, shrugging off a hit which destroyed 18 TBMs and F4Us, but leaving her armored deck intact. The *Victorious* was hit twice, losing four Corsairs. When the British carriers returned to Sydney in early June, they were due for a well-earned, but brief, rest period. About two-thirds of their original aircraft had been destroyed or damaged beyond repair, but the replacement escort carriers had kept them supplied with enough planes to finish the Okinawa campaign.

The home stretch of the Pacific war began on 17 July, with Third Fleet strikes against Honshu which were pressed through impending typhoon weather. The two British Corsair wings performed most of the BPF bombing during the two days of operations, expending over thirteen tons of ordnance.

Ramrods against airfields were the normal strike duty of Royal Navy F4Us by now, as aerial opposition was all but trampled. Enemy flak remained the greatest hazard, and the Corsair squadrons began to feel the effect of Japanese AA fire. But there was a change of pace on 24 July when ten FAA aircraft, including two F4Us, found the escort carrier *Kaiyo* during strikes against the Kure naval base. Four Avengers did most of the damage, but the Corsairs helped cripple the 13,000-ton CVE. She was left for Task Force 38 planes to complete the job.

During antishipping strikes at the end of July, the *Formidable*'s 1841 Squadron shot down a Kate, the penultimate British Corsair victory. The same squadron splashed a Grace on 9 August, bringing Royal Navy F4U credits to nearly fifty. But that was the lesser part of 1841's activity on that date.

It was the same day that Nagasaki was pulverized by a plutonium bomb. The BPF carriers launched Ramrods against the bay of Onagawa Wan, on the northeast coast of Honshu. Numerous smallcraft, escorts, and auxiliaries remained there, bottled up and vulnerable to air attack.

One of the *Formidable*'s flights was led by Lieutenant Robert Hampton Gray. A veteran of twelve months in 1841 Squadron, "Hammy" Gray was a twenty-seven-year-old former art student from Trail, British Columbia. He'd made something of a specialty of attacking Axis shipping, having gone after the *Tirpitz* and German destroyers in Norway. As recently as 28 July he'd helped sink a Japanese destroyer, the 1,200-ton *Nashi*, in the Inland Sea.

Corsair IIs prepare to launch from HMS *Illustrious* in the South Pacific. (Imperial War Museum)

Leading his flight in low over the bay, Hampton selected his target. It was identified as a destroyer, but was actually the two-year-old sloop *Amakusa*, a 255-foot escort of 870 tons.

Shore batteries and AA guns of the *Amakusa* and five other ships took the lead Corsair under fire. Their aim was good. Though Gray's plane was badly hit, he continued his slanting dive toward his target. Nearing the *Amakusa*, with her triple 25-mm mounts firing steadily, the Corsair burst into flames. Gray could have swerved away and perhaps saved himself with a water landing.

But he didn't. Other pilots saw the aggressive Canadian release his bombs from perhaps fifty feet. At least one scored a direct hit. There was a tremendous explosion and the scene dissolved into a swirling mass of smoke, spray, and debris. The *Amakusa* sank quickly but Hammy Gray was never seen again. For "his brilliant fighting spirit and inspired leadership," he was awarded the thirteenth Victoria Cross won by a Canadian in World War II.[2]

Gray was only the second Fleet Air Arm pilot in six years of war to earn a VC, and both were posthumous. He was also the second Common-

Lieutenant Robert Hampton Gray, RCN, who earned a posthumous Victoria Cross leading a flight of Corsairs on an antishipping strike over Japan. (Canadian War Museum)

wealth fighter pilot so honored, as the conservative British never decorated their fighter pilots in the manner of the Americans or Germans.

Eighteen FAA squadrons flew Corsairs in the period 1943–45, of which eight actually entered combat. They had been the first to demonstrate the F4U's full potential, and provided one example of the Corsair's dramatic change of image.

Lieutenant Commander Bill Leonard was a staff officer aboard the Task Force 38 flagship *Shangri-La* when a British Corsair landed low on fuel, shortly before the war ended. The Americans gawked at the pilot when he climbed out. Some wondered how long the "limeys" had been letting children fly airplanes. "But he was a great F4U booster," Leonard said, "for all his eighteen years of age and total of about 300 hours!"[3]

Royal Navy Corsairs remained in limited service until 1946, based aboard light fleet carriers. But most of those on hand by V-J Day were unceremoniously dumped into the ocean. The U.S. Navy suddenly had more aircraft than even it could use, and the lend-lease provisions held that all equipment retained by the British Commonwealth had to be paid for. Thus, the British Corsair story ended three years after it began.

While the Royal Navy received by far the most exported Corsairs during the war, it was not the only recipient. The Royal New Zealand Air Force acquired 364 F4U-1As and -1Ds plus 60 FG-1Ds from May 1944 to September 1945—a total of 424 aircraft.

Six RNZAF fighter squadrons operated in the Solomons during 1943–44, all equipped with Curtiss P-40s. They were therefore loosely referred to as the Kittyhawk Wing, and had been credited with ninety-nine confirmed victories. Known as colorful, spectacular fliers, the New Zealanders hungrily looked for their hundredth victim. It is said they nearly came to blows with the crew of an American PT boat which shot down a Japanese floatplane before the Kittyhawks could get to it.

As some P-40 units were rotated home for a rest, Number 20 Squadron was formed in January 1944 under Squadron Leader S. R. Duncan. The unit left for the Solomons in April, but while at Espiritu Santo it was issued F4U-1As, newly arrived from the U.S. Conversion training took until May, when 20 Squadron began operations from Bougainville. The old-line Kittyhawk units also underwent transition while new squadrons formed with F4Us from the beginning.

By the time the Kiwi Corsairs were established in the northern Solomons, things had calmed down. Japanese aircraft were nonexistent and the primary duties were ground support and perfunctory CAP or escort. In all, thirteen RNZAF squadrons flew Corsairs—Numbers 14 to 26 inclusive. They were well scattered throughout the South Pacific, changing

Kiwi Corsairs—sixteen F4U-1As of 18 Squadron, Royal New Zealand Air Force, near Guadalcanal in 1945. (Imperial War Museum)

bases constantly. For instance, in February 1945 there were three on Bougainville, one on Guadalcanal, two at Espiritu Santo, one on Emirau, two on Green Island, one on Los Negros in the Philippines, and two in New Zealand.

Major Marion Carl, the U.S. Marine Corps ace, was familiar with the RNZAF during early 1944. While with MAG-12 on Emirau he overheard a young Marine pilot returning to base in a shot-up F4U. More scared than hurt, the American radioed a running commentary of his difficulties, irritating everyone within range. Finally a New Zealander intoned, "I say, old boy, why don't you shut up and die like a man?"[4]

The Kiwis got one last chance at their century mark during early 1945. Two 20 Squadron pilots on patrol over New Britain saw a bandit—either a Zeke or a Rufe—taking off. They made gunnery runs at the lone Japanese, who escaped into a convenient cloud bank. It was 20 Squadron's last mission of the tour, and no RNZAF Corsairs ever got another shot.

Number 14 Squadron was typical of the RNZAF fighter units. The squadron traded in its P-40s for F4Us between tours in New Zealand. Two planes and pilots were lost in a midair collision near Guadalcanal in June 1944 prior to beginning operations from Bougainville's Piva complex. Most New Zealand units flew successive three-month tours, with rotation home for rest and reorganization, and Number 14 flew several such tours. Between June 1944 and August 1945 the squadron lost nine Corsairs to AA fire and several more to operational causes. In all, the RNZAF lost 150 Corsairs—35 percent of its total—in 1944–45. But only 17 were known attributable to enemy action.

The worst day by far was 15 January 1945. Numbers 14 and 16 Squadrons sent eight flights on a mission to Rabaul. One Corsair was shot down over Simpson Harbor, a victim of the most practiced AA gunners in the South Pacific. The other pilots circled the downed flier, hoping to protect a PBY dispatched on a rescue mission. But daylight ran out and the remaining Corsairs had to depart. Then the weather turned against them. Trying to avoid heavy rain squalls, five Corsairs were forced into the water and one simply vanished. Another was written off in a crash landing at Green Island. Eight F4Us and seven pilots were lost.

But 14 Squadron's job did not end in 1945. It was the lone RNZAF unit to draw occupation duty in Japan. Re-formed with 24 FG-1Ds, the squadron went to Kure aboard the HMS *Glory* in March 1946. Based at Iwakuni and Bofu, there was little excitement aside from rather frequent forced landings. However, five aircraft were destroyed or damaged beyond repair over the next two and one-half years.

Occupation duty ended in October 1948. But the New Zealand government decided against the expense of bringing 19 remaining FG-1Ds home. They were lined up and burned in one huge bonfire. Financial considerations had again prevailed over sentiment and history, and today only one Corsair remains in New Zealand.

chapter 6

With the fast carriers

Oh, pilot, 'tis a fearful night!
There's danger on the deep.

T. H. Bayly

The greatest irony of the Corsair's long career was enacted at Ford Island, Pearl Harbor, on the ninth day of 1944. That was the date on which the reorganized Air Group Ten returned to the *Enterprise* for a second combat tour. Fighting Ten's F6F-3s flew into Ford Island from Kahului to be hoisted aboard the Big E. With the Hellcats were four F4U-2s, and there lay the irony. The Corsair, designed as a day fighter and declared unsuitable for carrier duty, made its combat debut from a flattop as a night fighter.

Leading the four-plane detachment was Lieutenant Commander Richard E. Harmer, skipper of VF(N)-101. The unit's journey to combat had been a long one. It began 5,000 miles to the east, with Project Affirm at Quonset Point, Rhode Island.

Originally part of Commander Gus Widhelm's VF(N)-75, Harmer's team was left to carry on as best it could when Widhelm split the squadron in August 1943 and took the six available F4U-2s to the Solomons. Chick Harmer, a VF-5 veteran out of the Annapolis Class of '35, was left with a half-strength contingent. He had ten ensigns and a former enlisted pilot, Lieutenant Cecil L. Kullberg, as exec. While awaiting delivery of more Corsairs, Harmer's pilots and maintenance crews practiced on radar-equipped twin-engine Beechcrafts.

At last supplied with its own F4U-2s, the second detachment prepared for deployment to the Pacific in December. The first step was a two-day cross-country flight to San Diego. Actually, the Corsairs could have made it in one day, but there were problems in Arizona. One plane force-landed in the desert and another stopped at Tucson with oil leaks. Upon arrival in San Diego, Harmer caught a Martin Mars flying boat to Hawaii to pave the way for his unit. The rest of the squadron—planes, pilots, mechanics—followed by escort carrier.

Once established at Kahului, events accelerated. The detachment was redesignated VF(N)-101 but would shortly be split again. Lieutenant Kullberg took half the planes and pilots and departed for the new fleet carrier *Intrepid*. Harmer was destined for the *Enterprise* and Air Group Ten. He had four other pilots, four planes, and a support crew. The latter included his maintenance chief, Joe Clayton, and his "personal" fighter director, a Yale reservist named Frank Burgess. The one problem during their brief time in Hawaii was that Harmer's pilots were discouraged from flying their Corsairs; the F4U's reputation was too well known in the Navy. Consequently, they flew F6Fs to gain minimal flight time.

There were more problems once aboard ship. This was the first time that carriers had embarked night fighters on a regular basis. The *Enterprise*'s experiment in the Gilberts during November, operating radar-equipped TBFs with conventional F6Fs, had been more promising than conclusive. Except for Kullberg's *Intrepid* detachment, the other CV-

Lieutenant Commander Richard E. Harmer, who led VF(N)-101, the first carrier-based Corsair night fighter squadron. (U.S. Navy)

based night fighters were F6F-3Es, but the reaction to any nocturnal flying was largely the same. At the ship and air group levels, there existed a pronounced reluctance to employ night fighters.

The reason behind such opposition was practical rather than conceptual. A normal working day for a carrier's air department was fifteen hours. By the time the sun set, nobody felt much like putting in more time and effort just to launch and recover one or two night fighters. It meant respotting the entire flight deck.

But VF(N)-101 got a boost from the task group commander, Rear Admiral "Black Jack" Reeves, who insisted on launching one or two "bats" every time a bogey appeared on the radar screen. No intercepts were soon forthcoming but, recalls Harmer, "We even took the duty when the other carriers refused to launch their night fighters." As a result, 101 was not in the running for title of most popular group aboard the *Enterprise.* "Tom Hamilton, the air officer, almost became physically ill every time he saw me," Harmer said.[1]

Prodded from above and resented from below, VF(N)-101 found itself in a peculiar situation. But there were a few bright spots. The quality of electronics maintenance was very good. Harmer found that Chief Clayton and his crew kept the AIA radar sets at about 50 percent availability, "by inventiveness, thievery, and some pure research."[2] The CO never had to abort a flight due to electronics failure.

At first, most of the F4U flying was done in daylight. This chiefly involved ResCap missions, protecting cruiser floatplanes which rescued downed fliers. At least these flights allowed the younger pilots to keep their hand in. Night landings were another matter. The Corsair's notorious bounce was proving too much for the less experienced fliers to safely handle. As a result, Harmer and Lieutenant (junior grade) Robert F. Holden did more and more of the Big E's night flying. Eventually most of the ensigns were returned to Hawaii.

At length a cure was found for the F4U's long oleo stroke which caused the bounce. Independently of VF-17's similar modification, VF(N)-101 added extra air pressure in the main gear legs above the strut, providing more of a cushion. A zerc fitting and what Harmer described as an overgrown bicycle tire pump did the job. The F4U-2 was made nearly as safe for carrier landings as the F6F.

Another problem was solved aboard the *Enterprise*, but not so successfully. The 57-gallon fuel tanks in the wings developed leaks. Maintenance crews determined that the wing-fold mechanism rubbed against the fuel cell, and there was no economical method of solving the problem beyond the production line. Therefore, the Big E's night fighters discontinued use of the wing tanks. The fuselage main and reserve tanks allowed a four-hour endurance, and though this reduced the F4U-2's patrol time, it was adequate.

The big carrier raid on Truk Atoll during mid-February was an important event in the Corsair's life at sea. And it wasn't entirely beneficial. On the night of the 16th a Japanese torpedo plane was chased by a Hellcat night fighter into the *Intrepid* task group. The antiaircraft director held his fire, fearful of hitting the F6F, and the enemy aircraft put a torpedo into the "Evil I." She wasn't badly hurt, but she headed for Pearl Harbor and repairs. Cecil Kullberg's Corsair detachment was thereby knocked out of the war.

Three nights later Chick Harmer got a chance to avenge the insult. He was vectored onto a bogey which he identified as a Betty and closed rapidly. But his speed was excessive and he overshot the initial approach. He took such radical evasive action that it was ten minutes before the

F4U-2 night fighters of VF(N)-101 aboard the USS *Intrepid* during the first Truk strike in February 1944. (R.M. Hill)

controller could steer him into another contact. With good visual sighting at about 400 feet, Harmer opened fire with all five guns. The Betty spiralled off to starboard with a small fire from one engine which was soon extinguished. Harmer found his target again at 5,000 feet and chased it down to 800, where contact was lost for good. So ended the F4U's first carrier-launched interception.

The squadron's next chance came a little over two months later. This time there was more business than one pilot could easily handle. But again the pilot was Chick Harmer, and he handled it.

The *Enterprise* supported the Allied landings in New Guinea and was operating off Hollandia on 24 April. That evening Harmer was launched on sunset patrol. After several vectors, fighter director Frank Burgess put the CO onto a bogey at 30 miles distance. It was a moonless night with scattered clouds and line squalls, so Harmer concentrated on his scope. He gained AI contact at two miles, 30 degrees to port and below. The Corsair descended from 1,500 to 500 feet. In the murky darkness Harmer finally saw his target at a half-mile range, maintaining a steady 120 to 130 knots in a steep bank. It was a twin-engine bomber, either a Betty or a Sally.

Harmer dropped his flaps, slowing to 140 knots indicated, then retracted the flaps and continued. The bandit was now dimly silhouetted

111

against the horizon at 300 yards range. The Corsair nosed down to 300 feet in order to attack from below, but at this point the Japanese spotted their pursuer. At 250 yards the tail gunner opened fire, and Harmer replied with a long burst. The bomber dived for the surface as the F4U swerved to one side, avoiding enemy tracers.

Harmer lost visual contact, went back to his scope, and regained the bomber once more at 300 yards. The tail and dorsal guns both fired at the Corsair, and Harmer returned fire. A small flame appeared from the port engine followed by a large splash behind the Mitsubishi. Apparently the enemy pilot had jettisoned his ordnance. Again hidden by darkness, the F4U pulled alongside its quarry as the dorsal gunner was still shooting erratically. It had gone on long enough. Harmer resolved to finish the affair.

"I slid back on his tail again and gave him another long burst at less than 150 yards," Harmer reported. "The tail gunner took over and threw inaccurate fire at me. I made one more S-turn and closed in again. The dorsal gunner was directing his fire at an imaginary target above me. I was at less than 100 feet and had to depress my nose to fire at the target. I fired a short burst just as he struck the water. I passed over him and saw that he had made a good water landing, as the plane was intact and afloat. I made a couple of orbits over him. When I left, only the tail section remained above water."[3]

But that was not all. Shortly thereafter, Harmer came across five bombers in formation. Incredibly, three had their lights on, and two were fired upon. But they both got away owing to frustrating jams. The *Enterprise* ordnance department had not yet acted upon a recent dispatch which condemned a specific lot of .50-caliber ammunition with defective cases. Harmer's ammunition that evening was from the condemned lot. Nevertheless, it was an encouraging demonstration. In little more than an hour, from 1900 to 2010, Harmer had made three intercepts.

All of May was relatively uneventful for VF(N)-101, but the second half of June brought considerable activity. And small wonder. Most of that month was spent in the Marianas.

By this time Harmer and Bob Holden were doing nearly all the night flying. On sunset patrol on the 15th they contacted at least eight Sallys. Harmer fired at one and damaged it, but was set upon by what Holden thought was a Tojo fighter. The CO's Corsair was already damaged by 20-mm hits from the bomber, but Holden got a good shot at the Tojo. The bandit reacted as if it were fatally hit and Holden was credited with a probable. Harmer recovered aboard the *Enterprise* with one flat tire and a damaged flap.

Four days later came "The Great Marianas Turkey Shoot" in which Hellcats of Task Force 58 annihilated successive Japanese air strikes against the U.S. carriers. During much of the 19th, the Big E's Corsairs were on ResCap, freeing a few more F6Fs for air defense. Four fighters were launched at 1420, with two F4Us seeking a downed SOC floatplane while Harmer and the VF-10 exec, Lieutenant H. C. Clem, headed for another "Sock" rescuing two downed fliers off Orote Point, Guam.

Nearing Guam, Harmer and Clem heard their floatplane, call sign "Ace," hollering for help. It was being strafed on the water by a lone Zeke. Some other Hellcats pounced, but lost the bandit when it zoom-climbed. Lieutenant Clem raced for the scene in his F6F-3, leaving Harmer to cover the SOC. Clem pulled almost straight up after the Zeke and Harmer, watching from the distance, instantly feared the worst. His apprehension was realized. The Hellcat stalled and the Zeke, seeing its advantage, winged over to make a head-on gunnery pass. Clem's plane never recovered and went right into the water.

"They got one of our guys," called Ace.[4] Harmer bent the throttle and hauled into maximum shooting range. He fired a long burst from astern which drew some smoke from the Zero, but the bandit never slowed in its run for home.

Returning to the scene of the crime, Harmer found only an oil slick where the F6 had splashed. He remained over the damaged SOC for an hour before being relieved by a division of *Princeton* Hellcats. ResCaps were not always dull.

The following night the indefatigable Harmer was once more searching for airplanes in the dark—American airplanes. The 200-plane strike at the Japanese carrier fleet on 20 June returned to the task force in complete darkness, and not all air groups were night qualified. Harmer was launched to lead some of the strays back to base, and he succeeded. Using his radar's search mode, he contacted three groups of errant carrier planes and shepherded them to the task force. After that night, whatever plane handlers and air staff might have felt about night fighters, other pilots loved them.

A week later, on 27 June, Bob Holden was vectored onto a Sally cruising at 160 knots at 10,000 feet. The hostile took no evasive action, and Holden dispatched it with 700 rounds of .50 caliber. The next night, the 101 team hit its stride.

Holden and Harmer sat in their Corsairs waiting for a scramble order. As usual, the AIA sets had been tuned on nearby friendly ships while the F4Us sat on deck. With bogies on the screen, Holden was sent off at 1940 when the first blip was 56 miles out, bearing 160 degrees. The Corsair chased vectors for forty minutes before Holden got radar contact at near-maximum range, three miles. Visual acquisition was made at 800 feet. It was a Betty. Holden closed the range to only 200 feet and fired a very short burst from dead astern. He hit the starboard wing, and the target blew up with a terrific explosion. "I was so close I could feel the heat from the flames," Holden reported.[5] Radar confirmed the splash at 22 miles.

Holden's second Betty of the evening proved more alert than the first. Though there was no return fire, the bomber took violent evasive action, bobbing up and down, turning left and right. To no avail. The Mitsubishi caught fire, crashed and burned on the water. Holden had bagged two bombers with a total of 450 rounds.

The scopes were now clear and Harmer launched at 2130. The two Corsairs joined formation and Harmer made a practice interception on his squadron mate. The AIA was working perfectly. But with no more trade the F4Us headed home.

En route to the *Enterprise*, FDO Frank Burgess noticed a third aircraft cruising near the F4Us for a few minutes. When it broke away, Harmer pursued to investigate. He caught it 27 miles out and identified it as another Betty. "I took careful aim at his port wing and fired a short burst," he said. "Incendiaries flashed on the target's fuselage, port wing stub and engine, and the wing appeared to explode. The plane fell off to port and struck the water with a terrific explosion."[6] The armorers had experimented with a new load on this flight. They used two incendiary and two armor-piercing in four guns, while the fifth had one tracer every fifteen rounds. Judging from 101's success this night, one in fifteen was just about right.

The Corsairs remained aboard the *Enterprise* into July when Air Group Ten was relieved. In seven months, VF(N)-101 had lost no aircraft while flying its Corsairs both day and night. Certainly it showed that the way was clear for future F4U carrier operations. And while the squadron's kill record was not spectacular, it was proof enough of the Corsair's effectiveness. Between them, Chick Harmer and Bob Holden had accounted for five confirmed, a probable, and four damaged.

The F4U-2s were left at Barber's Point for use at the night fighter school. Harmer went to Vero Beach, Florida, where he spent most of the remainder of the war on instructor and staff duty. Another five months would pass before Corsairs reappeared in the fast carrier force, but not as night fighters. The Marines were coming.

Before the war, Marine squadrons frequently operated from carriers on a rotational basis. Though they never remained aboard one ship for any length of time, they were at least qualified for sea duty. In fact, as early as 1939 a secondary role for Marine Corps aviation was specified as replacement duty for Navy carrier squadrons.

The real world of 1942–44 was another matter. Except for ferrying operations and a two-month fling by VMO-155 Wildcats on a CVE in

An F4U-2 of VF(N)-101 on the number-two elevator of the USS *Enterprise* in January 1944. (U.S. Navy)

1943, Marine pilots were strangers to flight decks. At first there were too few carriers to make use of available Marine squadrons. Then the Navy's wartime expansion program got into gear and the Leathernecks found themselves land-based in the Solomons and Central Pacific.

Confusing the situation was the ill-defined mission of Marine Corps aviation and an uncertainty as to whether the Corps really wanted its own carriers. Even had a consensus existed and been enumerated, the administrative organization of Marine air did little to further the cause. There was no easy access to the highest levels of naval planning, and Marine Air Wings Pacific had no representatives at CinCPac in Pearl Harbor.

At length General Alexander Vandegrift, Commandant of the Corps, took steps to make use of surplus Marine squadrons. By the fall of 1944 the Marines had 120 squadrons, and some fitted William Allen White's description of the 1916 Progressive Party. They were all dressed up with nowhere to go. Following the reduction of Rabaul and the conquest of the Gilberts and Marshalls, as many as a dozen squadrons waited weeks at a time for deployment orders. Finally fifteen of these units were de-commissioned and their personnel reassigned.

Thus was established Marine Carrier Groups, Fleet Marine Force. Colonel Albert D. Cooley set up his new command at Santa Barbara, California, in late October 1944. His mission was to train two-squadron air groups for escort carriers. Each air group was to contain an eighteen-plane Corsair squadron and a twelve-plane Avenger outfit. Cooley was well qualified for the job. One of the most experienced aviators in the Corps, he had begun the war as an SBD squadron commander, led MAG-14 on Guadalcanal, and most recently had been assistant director of Marine Corps Aviation.

Cooley's command was originally expected to produce four of these two-squadron air groups. An intensive training syllabus was initiated to ensure that the pilots and air crews would be fully qualified by the time they reached their ships. Beginning with a small cadre of combat-experienced fliers, the new squadrons worked hard preparing for ground support duty. They practiced navigation, gunnery, ordnance delivery (including the new 11.75-inch Tiny Tim rockets), and field carrier landing practice. The Corsair pilots, flying F4U-1Ds off and on *Commencement Bay*-class CVEs, knew they would be ready for combat in the new year.

Another Marine CVE scheme with Corsairs had been shot down before it got off the ground. In June 1944 Project Danny was conceived by the Naval Air Atlantic Staff to counter the German V-1 rocket threat against southern England. It was planned to rush five MAG-51 F4U squadrons to Europe, where they would fly from escort carriers in the North Sea and destroy Buzz Bomb sites with Tiny Tims.

But Danny fell afoul of bitter interservice rivalry. Commander Thomas H. Moorer of the NavAirLant staff gave a high-level briefing on Danny in the new Pentagon building. He was interrupted by General George C. Marshall, Army Chief of Staff, who stood up and walked towards the door. Moorer, a future Chairman of the Joint Chiefs, recalled that Marshall said, "That's the end of this briefing. As long as I'm in charge there'll never be a Marine in Europe."[7] Even had Marshall been overruled, Danny was doomed. The V-1 menace largely ceased in July when Allied armies occupied most of northern France, where the sites were located.

But the question of Marines aboard carriers remained. And it was not resolved by the Army, the Germans, or even by the carrier training program. It was dictated by the Japanese.

Less than one week after Al Cooley established his command at Santa Barbara, a terrifying new aerial weapon was introduced in the Philippines. Enemy aircraft made obviously intentional dives into American ships, especially aircraft carriers.

116

The kamikazes had arrived.

They brought with them a whole new problem in fleet defense. In the two years since the new generation of ships and planes entered combat, only one fast carrier had been sunk—the light carrier *Princeton* by conventional bombing in Leyte Gulf. High-performance aircraft, sophisticated fighter direction, and intense AA fire had rendered American carrier decks virtually immune to air attack. The kamikazes changed all that virtually overnight.

Usually flying in small formations at varied headings and altitudes, suicide planes proved difficult to intercept. By their very nature they required few of the bomber's traditional assets. They needed neither large numbers, a strong escort, nor a coordinated plan of attack. And while regular bombers were usually ineffective flying alone, kamikazes were most dangerous as singles. They were much harder to detect and therefore to intercept.

In October of 1944, when the aerial suicide threat emerged, Hellcats already comprised 60 percent of the fast carriers' aircraft. But even this preponderance was deemed insufficient. The most immediate answer to the crisis was increased fighter strength, and plans were quickly laid to enlarge each carrier's F6F squadron at the expense of the bomber and torpedo units. While the authorized strength of each CV fighter squadron was expanded from 54 to 73 aircraft, an unexpected shortage arose.

The shortage was not of Hellcats, but of fighter pilots. The Navy flight training program had been cut back earlier in the year to compensate for excesses in the aviator "pipeline." As a result, many SB2C and TBM pilots were withdrawn from combat for assignment to training air groups where they transitioned to F6Fs. But this took time, and meanwhile the carriers faced long odds off the Philippines and Formosa.

Rear Admiral J. J. Clark, an experienced task group commander, recognized Marine squadrons as the best interim anti-kamikaze defense. Less than two weeks after the suicide menace appeared, Clark met with Vice Admiral Marc Mitscher in San Diego and suggested using Marine F4Us aboard CVs until the Navy could fill the gap. Mitscher, recently relieved as the fast carrier commander, took the idea to Washington. Before the end of November a high-level conference in San Francisco resulted in approval from Admiral Ernest J. King, Chief of Naval Operations. Ten F4U squadrons were authorized for immediate carrier qualifications and deployment to the Fast Carrier Force.

As if to hasten the move, unsolicited comment came from ComAirPac. In an early December message to King, Vice Admiral George D. Murray characterized the fleet defense problem as "critical." Marine fighter squadrons were specifically requested, and they couldn't arrive soon enough.

Leading VMF-124 from the *Essex*, Lieutenant Colonel William A. Millington became the first carrier-based Marine pilot to shoot down an enemy plane. Millington describes the action to Rear Admiral Frederick Sherman after a strike against Formosa on 3 January 1945. (U.S. Navy)

Thus, in an atmosphere of frantic haste were Corsairs sent to carrier duty. Five *Essex*-class ships were each to receive two eighteen-plane F4U-1D squadrons over the next three months. At the time of the decision, these units were either in Hawaii or on the West Coast. All were still in various stages of training.

The first two squadrons were old Solomons outfits—at least in number if not in fact. These were VMF-124 and 213, led respectively by Lieutenant Colonel William A. Millington and Major David E. Marshall. Millington, being senior, would be in overall command of both units, which actually functioned as one aboard ship. As skipper of 124 for a year and a half, Millington was a popular leader and a respected aviator.

Both squadrons had been ferried to Hawaii in September, where further carrier qualification was conducted. This involved considerable field carrier landing practice at MCAS Ewa, and actual landings aboard the light carrier *Bataan*. By the time the Marines joined the Fleet, they had made about a dozen deck landings each, including a few aboard the *Saratoga* off the West Coast. There was simply no time to gain additional experience. And experience was something Millington's pilots needed.

118

The average age of his fliers was 22 to 23. One-Twenty-Four had only four combat veterans beside the CO; VMF-213 had only three, including the Hellhawks' top ace, Captain Gus Thomas.

Additionally, the Marines had to take their own intelligence and maintenance personnel with them. The latter were particularly important, since the F4U was largely unknown to carrier air service detachments. When Bill Millington finally took his troops aboard the *Essex* at Ulithi on 28 December, they numbered 178 in all: 54 pilots for 36 F4U-1Ds, 120 enlisted men, and 4 nonaviator officers.

Despite the haste and uncertainty, the Marines settled in immediately. Recalled Millington, "We were made to feel much at home aboard the *Essex*, from the admiral on down—Rear Admiral Frederick Sherman, commander of Task Group 38.3. Our officers and enlisted got along fine with our Navy shipmates, and VMF-124 and 213 became an integral part of Air Group Four." To the handful of South Pacific veterans, "there was nothing like being out of the mud, bugs, pests, and filth that we had in the Solomons. Carrier duty provided good food, clean bedding, showers, and all the conveniences."[8]

There was precious little time to enjoy the accommodations. On 30 December Task Force 38 sortied from Ulithi, bound for the Ryukyus and Pescadores. Recognizing the Marines' inexperience at carrier operations, the *Essex* landing signal officer, Lieutenant "Billy" Sunday, offered to help smooth out some of the rough spots in the Corsair pilots' technique. During practice the first day out, Lieutenant Thomas Campion apparently stalled at low level and crashed in flames off the starboard bow. The next day brought the loss of two more F4Us and one pilot, all within fifteen minutes.

Shortly past dawn on 3 January 1945 the *Essex* launched her Corsairs in earnest for the first time. Millington's job was to escort TBMs of Torpedo Squadron Four in an attack on Kagi Airfield, Formosa. The weather was a foreboding indication of things to come: a low, dark, gray overcast.

The *Essex* strike overflew most of the island and turned to approach from the west. As the Avengers nosed down into their attack the Marines stayed with them, pressing through the flak to suppress AA fire. TBM bombs erupted across runways, hangars, and parking areas. Dark blue Corsairs sped back and forth, shooting up gun pits and buildings. Then the *Essex* planes withdrew for rendezvous over the western mountains.

The filthy weather kept most Japanese aircraft grounded, and fewer than 30 were shot down by the carrier pilots. But Millington personally opened the Marines' account when he spotted two Nick twin-engine fighters near the rendezvous. Almost by reflex he turned his Corsair towards the hostiles and pulled deflection on the nearest. He fired a long burst which connected. The .50-caliber bullets struck sparks as they impacted

119

the Nick, and Millington knew he was scoring good hits. The Kawasaki lurched, dropped into a spin, and disappeared towards the cloud-wrapped mountains. Its companion immediately made for the cover of nearby cumulus.

But back aboard the *Essex* one Marine was missing. Later the pilots learned what had happened. Lieutenant Robert W. Mullins was last heard over the radio heading out to sea. A Navy pilot returning from a fighter sweep over Okinawa had attempted to steer Mullins to the task force, but evidently the lost Marine never heard the transmission. Another F4U disappeared the following day, trying to climb through a 5,000-foot overcast for a navigational fix from a radar picket destroyer.

From this initial combat exposure, the *Essex* Marines realized that the Japanese were so far the least of their worries. It was woefully apparent that they had nowhere near enough training in navigation, instrument flying, or carrier operations. But the press of events had been such— and would continue—that the young Corsair pilots literally received on-the-job training. During strikes against the northern Philippines on 6 and 7 January, the wretched weather continued to take a toll. Three pilots, all twenty-two-year-old lieutenants, disappeared into the murk over Luzon and were never seen again. During the same period four Corsairs were lost in landing accidents or ditchings, but providentially the pilots survived.

During their first nine days at sea, VMF-124 and 213 had lost seven pilots and thirteen Corsairs—none attributable to enemy action. Five had disappeared over open water under IFR conditions. But with losses and hard-won experience came knowledge and skill. The Leathernecks recognized that their car-quals in Hawaii were conducted under vastly different conditions from those encountered operationally. Flying in clear skies with reduced fuel and no ordnance was poor preparation for operating a fully loaded Corsair in zero-zero weather.

Yet there was some room for optimism. Lieutenant Sunday continued to exercize the Marines when weather and flight schedules permitted, and Millington attributed his squadrons' later performance in large part to the LSO's tutelage. As for the F4U itself, Millington believes it had the confidence of his pilots: "Certainly we felt the Corsair was superior in performance to the F6F, and it really was a good carrier plane in all respects. I personally thought the Corsair was *one fine aircraft*, and I'm sure most of our pilots felt the same. Our operational losses were largely due to insufficient instrument flying experience and navigational experience under fleet conditions. Also, losses on carrier takeoffs and landings can only be charged to lack of sufficient experience under actual fleet conditions. At least three such losses were simply due to stalling out after launch or during landing approach."[9]

By mid month the Marines seemed to have things sorted out. With better weather in the South China Sea, the F4U pilots were able to concentrate on destroying the enemy rather than merely surviving their environment. The first big opportunity came on 12 January during Admiral Halsey's ambitious antishipping strike against French Indochina. It was the first time in four years that Allied warships had ventured so close to the Asian mainland.

Task Force 38 made one of the biggest hauls of the war during its day-long strikes up and down the Vietnamese coast: 47 ships for some 150,000 tons. With almost no air opposition, the carrier planes sank entire convoys unhindered by anything but flak. The Corsairs flew fifty-seven sorties—nearly three missions per remaining F4U. Thirty-eight of these were ForceCap, but two sweep-strikes were made.

By now, with a depleted inventory, the Marines were flying mixed division formations. Millington led an eleven-plane airfield strike which included six of his own VMF-124 pilots and four of VMF-213. Each was armed with a 500-pound bomb. They hit runways and buildings at places with strange-sounding names which would become familiar to a later generation: Bien Hoa, Long Bin, Trang Bang. One portion of the strike hunted enemy shipping in the Saigon River and harbor. The best bombing was done by Major Fay Domke of 213 who put his 500-pounder on a medium cargo ship which was finished off by Navy planes.

Later that day Captain Gus Thomas hit Tan Son Nhut airfield with two divisions. Seven of the eight pilots were from 213. They spotted 25 to 30 planes on the field, and Thomas led his Corsairs down to strafe. In six passes the Kansas ace burned three stubby Tojos and a twin-engine transport, damaging several more. The other pilots destroyed five additional aircraft.

But it wasn't one-sided. The number four man in Thomas's division took several hits in his engine and splashed into a wheels-up landing in a rice paddy three miles west of the field. Lieutenant Joseph "Irish" Lynch was last seen standing by his Corsair as the other pilots turned towards the coast. Interned by the Vichy French, Lynch turned up safe in Kunming, China, two and a half months later.

Back aboard the *Essex*, the F4U pilots chattered among themselves, relating bits and pieces of what they'd seen and done during the day. This was definitely more like it—tolerable weather (the sun had even come out a few times), plenty of good targets, and no serious losses.

There was one sobering incident. Late that afternoon three Corsairs on CAP spotted a four-engine aircraft above the overcast near the coast. The flight leader was Captain Edmond Hartsock, one of the old-timers of 124. He had been involved in that long-ago dogfight near the Russells when Major Bill Gise, the squadron's first skipper, was killed.

At first Hartsock thought the multiengine plane was an Emily flying boat. Only 15 Japanese aircraft were shot down during the day, but it seemed possible this was a snooper reporting on the task force. As the three F4Us approached for a closer look, the stranger opened fire. Hartsock positioned his flight out of range to evaluate the situation. It was strange, but the bomber looked like a PB4Y Liberator.

The pilots had been briefed to beware of enemy-flown American aircraft. This one had no markings at all, which further reinforced the suspicion. Hartsock waggled his wings and tried to establish radio contact with the bomber. To no avail. The only response was more gunfire directed at the Corsairs. That did it. Hartsock and his wingman rolled in from starboard, and both made overhead gunnery passes which left the bomber trailing a thin smoke ribbon. The third man, Lieutenant Herbert L. Libby, turned in above and behind the target from port. He fired into the number two engine, which gushed flame. The bomber exploded. Its remains fell through the overcast near Phan Rang.

Hartsock's report stirred instant fear among air staff officers who knew that China-based B-24s of the Fourteenth Air Force had been in the vicinity. Proof was shortly forthcoming when Hartsock's gun camera film was developed. Though the Marines had naturally identified the Liberator as a PB4Y, it was in fact a B-24. Equally clear was the fact that it carried no national insignia. It was evidently painted olive drab, which the pilots reported as reddish-brown.

Much later, it became known that the B-24 had radioed its base that it was under attack by U.S. Navy aircraft. Why the Liberator should have opened fire on planes it recognized as friendly remains a mystery. And while the tragedy caused considerable grief, there were no recriminations. Correspondent Robert Sherrod, aboard the *Essex* at the time, overheard one major say, "I'd have done the same thing. If anybody shoots at me, I'm going to shoot back. I expect the other fellow to know his recognition as well as I do. There are ten lives in a B-24, but it can cause a thousand deaths aboard ship if there are Japs in it."[10]

Soupy weather returned, but by now the F4U pilots could handle it. On 15 January they flew in under a low ceiling against Takao on Formosa's southwest coast. Clouds of multicolored flak bursts wafted past the Corsairs as they dropped out of leaden gray skies to get at targets in the harbor area. Several Marines returned with holes in their planes, but all got back. In exchange for this damage, they dropped bombs on a factory and worked over two ships. One was identified as a destroyer —probably the 1,300-ton *Hatakaze*—which exploded when Lieutenant Charles Chop dropped his bombs. Chop didn't know if he or some SB2Cs had been responsible, and he probably didn't much care. It's an unsettling experience to have a ship blow up in your face.

Commander Otto Klinsmann, the thirty-four-year-old skipper of Air Group Four, was lost during the day. His plane was badly damaged by flak and he ditched near a destroyer but went down with his aircraft. Bill Millington, being the senior squadron commander aboard the *Essex*, was immediately promoted to CAG. He was certainly the first and probably the last Marine to command a Navy air group.

On the 16th Admiral McCain's carriers doubled back to the west. He launched a series of strikes against Hong Kong, Swatow, and Canton, while sending TG-38.3 squadrons against Hainan. It was over 250 miles to their targets at Yulingan Bay and Saifa Point, but the F4Us did well. Bomb-toting Corsairs sank one ship and left two burning as they withdrew, though not without difficulty. In a scuffle with Zekes, Lieutenant William E. Reynolds bagged one but Lieutenant George Strimbeck's plane was hit by another. When his belly tank exploded, Strimbeck bailed out and was seen parachuting safely. However, nothing more was ever heard of him.

Damage inflicted during these two days was disappointing. Only eight ships and fewer than 50 Japanese planes were destroyed, while the carriers lost 61 aircraft, fully half to operational causes. It was time to leave the South China Sea.

After waiting three days for the wretched monsoon weather to abate, Task Force 38 refueled and exited through Balintang Channel between Luzon and Formosa. This put the fleet within range of land-based bombers, and the CAP shot down 15 throughout the day. The *Essex* Corsairs were heavily engaged for two hours as seven pilots of 213 and five of 124 sighted ten Helens. The 12 F4Us flew as a unit, and shared the shooting more or less equally. Lieutenant William McGill, formerly a Nevada cowboy, rode herd on three Helens and splashed them all in three minutes. His partners accounted for five more confirmed and one probable, leaving only one to tell the tale. Admiral McCain was impressed. He signalled, "Three cheers for the Leathernecks!"[11]

There was less to cheer about on the 21st. Strikes were flown against Formosa and adjacent islands, drawing the wrath of the kamikazes. Suiciders crashed into two ships, including the *Ticonderoga* in the *Essex* task group. The light carrier *Langley* was hit by a bomb. The two carriers and a destroyer survived, but clearly the suicide threat was not diminished, as the Marines learned first-hand.

Gus Thomas took six Corsairs to beat up Kagi airfield and returned to the task force at 1115. The F4Us had been airborne a long time and were dangerously low on fuel, so Thomas allowed four other pilots to land ahead of him. He was still in the pattern with his wingman, Lieutenant F. J. Goetz, when bandits appeared. One bomber dived on the *Essex*, and though his fuel gauge registered a mere twenty gallons, Thomas unhesitatingly went to full power. He closed range and got in one burst when some F6Fs took over and made the kill. Thomas and Goetz landed aboard the *Enterprise* completely out of fuel and with no LSO on duty. They had been airborne six and a half hours. When they returned to the *Essex* that afternoon, nobody could doubt that by now the Marines were truly qualified carrier pilots.

Following a brief fling against Okinawa on the 22nd, the task force set course to the southeast for Ulithi. The three days en route gave the Marines time to evaluate their first month in combat. In 658 sorties, including 33 non-combat flights, they had logged nearly 2,000 hours, shot down 10 Japanese aircraft, and destroyed 16 on the ground. Eleven enemy ships had been damaged by F4U bombs.

Against this record were balanced the loss of eight pilots and 17 Corsairs. The aircraft losses amounted to half the original complement brought aboard at the end of December. And since there were no F4Us in the carrier resupply system, any replacements had to be obtained ashore. This would remain a problem for some time. Hellcats, being a mainstay of the carrier force, were usually available from CVEs at sea. The Marines were not so fortunate. As Millington said, "We did not receive replacement pilots or aircraft while at sea—only on return to Ulithi prior to our next sortie."[12]

Yet there was proof that the Corsairs could operate effectively despite the initial disadvantages. Once the pilots got the hang of instrument flying, overwater navigation and carrier landings, they improved quickly. Only two planes and one pilot had been lost to enemy action. Most important of all, the Marines were doing what was asked of them. They were meant to help stop the kamikazes, and they did. Their performance north of Luzon on 20 January was ample testimony.

And Millington's squadrons were no longer the only Marines in the task force. In preparation for the next sortie—now as Task Force 58 under Admiral Spruance—six more VMF units were on hand, and Navy Corsairs were also available. These new squadrons benefitted from 124 and 213's early grief by getting extensive navigation and instrument training while at Ulithi.

With 144 Corsairs embarked—mostly -1Ds—the eight Marine squadrons accounted for one-sixth of the total Task Force 58 fighter strength. They were going to need all the strength they possessed, for the next target was Japan itself.

chapter 7

Corsairs against Japan

So ends the bloody business.

Homer, *Odyssey*

Looking down from his F4U-1D, Major Herman Hansen, Jr., was fascinated. And he was a young man not easily impressed by sights or events. Not yet twenty-five, he had been CO of VMF-112 since mid-1943. Yet his combat experience predated even the Wolfpack's arrival in the Solomons. As one of two F4F-7 pilots on Guadalcanal in the fall of 1942, Hansen had flown unarmed reconnaissance missions for General Roy Geiger. In those days, there had been little percentage in flying without your guns.

The scene which captured Hansen's attention was Task Force 58. Upon Admiral Raymond Spruance's resumption of command, the fleet number had changed, and so did the carrier force when Vice Admiral Mitscher returned to relieve McCain. The *Bennington* was the new home of VMF-112, in company with Major Everett Alward's 123, but she was only a small part of the picture. "There had never before been such a collection of combat ships and there never will be again," Hansen said. "The fleet spanned the ocean from horizon to horizon. It was quite a sight."[1]

Indeed it was. There had been larger assemblies of ships, but they included transports and landing craft. For pure striking power, Task Force 58 was unexcelled. It included fifteen fast carriers—ten CVs and five CVLs—with eight battleships, seventeen cruisers, and destroyers too numerous to count. All deployed in five task groups. All headed for Japan.

The main objective was Iwo Jima, the sulphurous island in the Bonins which the Third, Fourth, and Fifth Marine Divisions would assault on 19 February. The carrier-borne Marine Corsairs were assigned tactical air support for the first time in the Iwo operation. Bill Millington had helped work out a massive strafing plan for D-Day, and the F4U squadrons had practiced with the assault troops in the short time available. But first, Tokyo.

Actually, the weather was the first consideration. In a word, it was terrible. But few of the task force sailors or aviators complained during the approach. Low ceilings, rain showers, and heavy seas kept the run-in a secret as the carriers neared their launch point in the small hours of 16 February.

Considering the weather and the target, it was a rough way to break into combat. Over half of the carrier pilots were embarked upon their first missions, as the flattops plowed through the swells, heading northwest. But the Marine squadrons were less experienced than the Navy. Though the fliers were well trained, it's a long way from training to combat. The *Bennington* and *Wasp* Corsair units were all of similar composition to the two *Essex* squadrons: a handful of veterans scattered among the youngsters. Hap Hansen had only three other pilots with combat experience in VMF-112.

Cloudy skies and choppy seas cut short a follow-up strike at Tokyo on 25 February 1945. These F4U-1Ds belong to VF-84 aboard the *Bunker Hill,* the first Navy squadron to operate in strength from a carrier. (R.M. Hill)

The noteworthy carrier, insofar as F4Us were concerned, was the *Bunker Hill.* She was proof of the faith the Navy now placed in the Corsair. For Air Group 84, under Commander G. M. Ottinger, boasted three F4U squadrons with a total of 71 Corsairs. There were also six F6F-5P photo planes. The skipper of VF-84 was Lieutenant Commander Roger Hedrick, erstwhile exec of VF-17. Hedrick had four other Skull and Crossbones alumni with him, and there was poetic justice in their assignment to the *Bunker Hill.* When Tommy Blackburn's squadron was bounced off the ship two years earlier, it seemed as if they would never complete their original mission.

The two Marine squadrons also included some familiar names from the Solomons. Among the pilots in Major Edwin S. Roberts's VMF-221 was Captain Jim Swett, the young Medal of Honor winner with fifteen kills in Wildcats and Corsairs. And in VMF-451 Major Henry Ellis could count on Major Archie Donahue, the veteran ace of VMF-112. At the end of January the three *Bunker Hill* fighter squadrons had 63 F4U-1Ds and 8 FG-1Ds. All sported the vertical white arrow on their tails and were flown interchangeably to simplify the maintenance program.

The more recent additions to the task force were undeniably better equipped to operate from carriers than the *Essex* Corsairs had been. Generally the car-quals had gone well. Hansen's Wolfpack had two fatalities during training, but neither was related to carrier flying. And though one F4U was lost from the *Bennington* after departure from Ulithi, the pilot was saved. Morale was good; even excellent. Certainly anticipation was mixed with some degree of apprehension, but after all, the target was Tokyo.

Launch commenced 60 miles off the Honshu coast on 16 February, 125 miles from Tokyo. At 0635 a division of VMF-112 was sent into the gray, drizzly sky from the *Bennington*'s windswept deck. The flight leader, Major David Andre, got in the Marines' first shooting of the day when vectored onto a Betty some 30 miles offshore. All four F4Us attacked and hit the bomber, but Andre and his wingman were credited with the kill.

Other *Bennington* Corsairs flew fighter sweeps and strike support. The weather prevented some formations from reaching their assigned objectives, but alternate targets were not difficult to find. Konoike and Hokoda airfields were strafed and rocketed by free-hunting Wolfpack pilots, and one Tojo was shot down. Meanwhile, Hap Hansen got through to his assigned targets with the *Bennington*'s first strike. He led an aerial stampede over O Shima, Mobara, and Katori airdromes, leaving an estimated 20 planes trampled behind it. A lone Nick was downed, but there was one loss. Lieutenant James Hamilton's plane took an AA hit in the belly. Hamilton got out beyond the coast where he ditched and was picked up by a U.S. destroyer.

One-Twelve's teammate, VMF-123, participated in a Task Group 58.1 sweep southwest of Tokyo. Major Everett Alward's "Eight-Balls" helped the *Hornet* and *Wasp* F6Fs in low-level attacks against parked planes and moored ships. They had hardly begun when somebody called out five bandits overhead. The Corsairs climbed to challenge the intruders, which proved to be Zekes. A short combat resulted in Alward dropping a Zero. But the Japanese flak was bad, and 123 lost three planes and a pilot.

The *Essex* Marines flew their first strike behind Bill Millington, who went for Vayzu airfield near Tokyo. Two-Thirteen was led by its skipper, Major Dave Marshall, who took the first F4Us over the Imperial City while escorting TBMs. But the combined elements of surprise, weather, and U.S. air superiority deprived the Hellhawks of aerial combat. Not till an afternoon sweep by 11 *Essex* Corsairs did 124 and 213 find airborne hostiles near Tokyo. Gus Thomas bagged a pair of Zekes, running his string to eighteen and a half, while a Val and another Zeke were also shot down. Seventeen Japanese planes were destroyed or damaged at Tenryu.

The *Bunker Hill* Leathernecks went after coastal shipping, with limited success. They hit a five-ship convoy, claiming damage to three cargo vessels. One plane of VMF-451 took an AA hit from a destroyer escort and made a water landing. The pilot got out alright, and rescue operations were put in motion, but the Marine was never found. During the day Air Group 84 claimed eight shootdowns; five by VF-84, two by VMF-221, and a lone Jake by 451.

Air Group 81 Corsairs aboard the *Wasp* had a rugged combat initiation. Major Jack Amende's VMF-217 division accompanied Navy planes to Hamamatsu airfield where some 60 enemy aircraft were observed. The "Bulldogs" burned a half-dozen. Then at the rendezvous point, Amende's Corsair was shot up by a Zeke. As the CO's plane turned away trailing smoke, Lieutenant Vernon Salisbury destroyed the bandit, but it was too late to save Amende. Nor was that all. Two other divisions made a sweep of Yokosuka and Tateyama airfields. One plane and pilot were lost on launch and two more F4Us failed to return, their pilots MIA.

So ended the 16th. The nine Corsair squadrons lost ten aircraft and eight pilots. Seventeen Japanese planes were shot down by F4Us on sweeps and CAPs, in addition to aircraft destroyed on the ground and several ships damaged.

On the 17th the weather worsened, and air strikes were canceled before the full schedule was completed. Pilots flew in long underwear, cursed the elements, and damned the rainwater which froze in gun breeches at

Major Herman Hansen, CO of VMF-112, spins a condensation trail from his propeller on takeoff from the USS *Bennington* on February 10, 1945. (R.M. Hill)

high altitude. The outside air temperature at 25,000 feet was 55 degrees below zero. But the local Tokyo weather was tolerable, and several formations broke through. The *Bennington* put the first Corsairs over the enemy coast as Hansen and Alward swept airfields around Tokyo Bay. Two divisions of VMF-112 bombed runways and Hap Hansen shot down an Oscar which attempted to intervene. The 123 CO equalled Hansen's feat, as Major Alward tangled with a Tojo and dropped it into Tokyo Bay. He then amused himself with a low-level rocket attack on a locomotive, with spectacular results. He recovered aboard the *Bennington* with mud caked on his windscreen. But one pilot never returned.

Fighting 84 equalled its first day's bag of five kills while *Essex* and *Wasp* pilots also scored. In all, another fourteen victories were recorded by Corsairs on the 17th, for a two-day total of thirty-one. But when the task force pulled away to the southeast, the pilots were vaguely dissatisfied. Their claims amounted to some 340 aerial victories and nearly 200 more Japanese planes were thought wrecked on the ground. Sixty American aircraft were lost to enemy action and almost half as many to noncombat causes. Considering the wretched weather and sea state, the operational losses could have been worse. Full-scale Japanese opposition had failed to develop, undoubtedly due to the weather. But everyone knew there would be another day.

Marine Corps history was made in the early morning of 19 February when Bill Millington led 48 fighter-bombers over Iwo Jima. The fast carriers had launched 24 Corsairs and 24 Hellcats from west of the island to provide the first Marine carrier air support for an amphibious landing. They operated on an artfully timed schedule which left little room for error.

The Fourth and Fifth Divisions churned towards Iwo's southeast beaches in their amtracs even as Millington's strike went to work. And there was work aplenty. The photo interpreters had identified 642 Japanese strongpoints and gun positions. The air support commander had told the fighter-bombers to go in and scrape their bellies on the beach, and that is pretty much what they did.

Iwo's terrain dominated the seven landing beaches on both flanks. Volcanic Mount Suribachi overlooked Green Beach at the southwest while a rock quarry 4,000 yards northeast controlled Blue Two. In between were the two Red and Yellow beaches, and Blue One. Millington deployed his formations in two parallel columns as he swung around to the south and approached the island on a northerly heading. Beginning at H-Hour minus 45 minutes, the F4Us and F6Fs executed continuous low-level attacks against the flanks of the landing area. On the first run they dropped napalm, then pulled out over the northern shore and turned port or starboard by divisions, orbiting back for another pass. For ten minutes the two opposite-circle patterns continued, rocketing and strafing. Naval gunfire then took over for thirty minutes.

Millington regrouped his formations and made south-to-north strafing runs all along the landing beaches. In line astern the Hellcats and Corsairs fired in steep dives, recovering with a right-hand turn to rejoin the circle. The pilots pulled out of their dives at 600 feet, as the bombardment from offshore was still in progress. When the amtracs hit the beaches, the fighters remained overhead, hosing down the area only 200 yards ahead of the assault troops. Once the Marines were ashore, the impact area was moved 500 yards inland. Amid the noise, smoke, and confusion it was difficult to tell just how much the Japanese return fire was diluted. But the combined effect of 278 .50 calibers, not to mention scores of rockets and napalm bombs, had to be considerable. Enemy resistance did not commence in full fury until after the first Marines were ashore.

That afternoon it was Air Group 84's turn as the *Bunker Hill* Corsairs strafed and napalmed troublesome strongpoints inland from the beaches. Millington's *Essex* squadrons remained as ForceCap during the remainder of the operation while the other air groups alternated on close support. *Bennington, Bunker Hill,* and *Wasp* squadrons were available for strikes against Iwo until early afternoon of the 22nd, when deteriorating weather forced an end to air operations. Next day the task force launched strikes against nearby Chichi Jima, where one Marine F4U fell to AA fire. The pilot parachuted and was last seen swimming ashore. Two weeks later the Japanese beheaded him with several other downed fliers. After the war, when atrocities including cannibalism were revealed, five senior Japanese officers from the Bonins were executed.

From Iwo the fast carriers returned to Empire waters for a second strike at Tokyo. Launch commenced at 0800 on the 25th, 190 miles southeast of the capital. Again opposition was spotty and weather miserable. In fact, it was so bad that further operations were canceled at midday. But during the morning several Corsair squadrons found combat.

Among the first were four *Essex* squadrons led by CAG-4, Bill Millington. Nine pilots of VMF-124 and seven of VMF-213 swept airfields north of Tokyo and met a mixed batch of 14 enemy fighters. In a series of brief combats the Marines claimed five kills and six damaged. They commented on the atrocious enemy gunnery which only damaged two Corsairs. Millington got one of two Tonys destroyed while two Zekes and an Oscar also went down. The *Essex* Corsairs concluded their mission by burning planes at Kamagaya and Matsuyama airfields, and strafing cargo ships off Cape Inubo. One F4U force-landed when it ran out of fuel from a gas leak and the pilot was taken prisoner. He survived the war.

133

Bennington F4Us also shot up shipping, concentrating on an 8,000-ton freighter in Tokyo Bay. Everett Alward, skipper of VMF-123, was on his fourth pass when his formation was jumped by an estimated 15 bandits. Eight days previously Alward had shot a Tojo into Tokyo Bay, but this time he was caught at a serious altitude disadvantage. The Eight-Balls' CO was killed when a Zeke knocked his Corsair into the water. Another pilot went down before the Marines could shoot their way out of trouble. Alward was the second carrier-based Marine squadron commander lost over Japan, and was succeeded by Major Thomas E. Mobley, Jr.

Roger Hedrick led 16 VF-84 Corsairs on a sweep to Katori airfield, armed with HVARs and external fuel. They took eight Franks by surprise and the tall, thin CO disposed of two in consecutive passes. The second exploded directly ahead of Hedrick's F4U and he flew through the fireball. Several Zekes which appeared were thwarted in an attack when Lieutenant Willis Laney turned his division into the threat. In a few minutes he claimed two destroyed and a probable. Hedrick ended the combat—his only one since the Solomons eleven months before—by sending a lone Zeke burning into the beach from low level. It was his twelfth victory. Fighting 84 had destroyed at least nine bandits, then expended its rockets on targets of opportunity. One yellow-nosed Corsair ditched 50 miles offshore with flak damage but the pilot was never found.

Most pilots returned to their ships reporting the same thing: few targets, freezing guns and gun cameras, lousy weather. Others complained that all they had to show for three hours over Tokyo was a case of frostbite. Of nearly 160 Japanese planes thought destroyed, only 37 were taken on the wing. Nine carrier planes were lost, including four F4Us.

Task Force 58 hit Okinawa on 1 March, encountering minimal opposition, and dropped anchor in Ulithi Lagoon three days later. During the stay at Ulithi, four Marine squadrons were detached with their air groups. Bill Millington's VMF-124 and 213 had shown much improvement during their two months with Air Group 4. Between them, they gunned down 23 airborne Japanese and wrecked 64 on the ground, losing nine pilots and 24 Corsairs. In five weeks aboard the *Wasp*, VMF-216 and 217 had destroyed 19 planes—including four airborne—and six small ships. They had lost nine F4Us and five pilots.

Many Marine maintenance personnel stayed behind to lend a hand: forty-six men aboard the *Essex* and twenty-eight aboard the *Wasp*, each group overseen by one officer. Colonel Millington, en route to duty in Hawaii with MAG-44, had high praise for these men. "I thought maintenance aboard the *Essex* was great," he said. "We had a number of highly experienced Marine non-coms in 124 who had service in the Solomons. They worked well with the Navy air group people, as well as with the ship's personnel. Our line chief, ordnance chief, and electronics chief were particularly top notch."[2]

Upon the Marines' departure, the *Essex* and *Wasp* each received a new fighter-bomber squadron. These were VBF-83 and VBF-86, arriving with their respective air groups. Both units flew F4U-1Ds, including some of the same aircraft left behind by the Leathernecks. Skipper of VBF-83 was Lieutenant Commander Fred A. Patriarca, a Rhode Islander out of the Annapolis class of '37 who had flown SBDs for two years in Scouting Six. Many of his pilots were also former dive bombers. When Fighting 83 was divided in early January to form the fighter-bomber outfit, thirty-two of Patriarca's fifty-four pilots came from VB-83. They converted from SB2Cs to Corsairs in time to qualify as F4U pilots aboard the *Essex*.

Two new air groups arriving in March were even more committed to the Corsair. These were Air Group 5 aboard the *Franklin* and Air Group 10 aboard the veteran *Intrepid*. Like the *Bunker Hill*, the *Franklin* flew three F4U squadrons: VF-5, VMF-214, and VMF-452. Two-Fourteen, the Black Sheep, was led by Greg Boyington's former exec, Major Stanley

Deck hands push a VBF-6 F4U-1D off the deck-edge elevator of the USS *Hancock* in March 1945. (R.M. Hill)

135

Bailey. But as correspondent Robert Sherrod noted, 214 "was full of new sheep, barely sooty."[3] No other Solomons pilots remained.

Air Group 10 was unique in the U.S. Navy. It was the only air group to fly three full tours aboard carriers. Fighting 10, originally Jimmy Flatley's "Grim Reapers," had flown F4Fs in 1942 and F6Fs in 1943–44, both times from the *Enterprise*. No other squadron would fly Wildcats, Hellcats, and Corsairs in combat. The Reapers were now led by Lieutenant Commander W. E. Clarke, who had a sprinkling of VF-10 veterans among his youngsters. The VBF-10 skipper was Lieutenant Commander W. E. Rawie, like Fred Patriarca a veteran combat pilot. Commander Air Group 10 was John J. Hyland, also F4U-mounted. His squadrons were fitted with antiblackout G-suits and the new 11.75-inch Tiny Tim air-to-ground rockets.

The other new Corsair outfit was Lieutenant Commander Robert W. Schumann's VBF-6 aboard the *Hancock*. Bob Schumann was yet another VF-10 product, having been exec and then CO of the Reapers during 1944. In all, there were now thirteen Corsair squadrons in the task force —seven Navy and six Marine. It would remain the zenith of fast carrier F4U strength during the remainder of hostilities.

Task Force 58 returned to Japan on 18 March. Forty-five Kyushu airfields were attacked, stirring up heavy local resistance at some points. By far the heaviest aerial combat among F4U squadrons was found by VBF-83. In fighter sweeps over southern Kyushu that day, Fred Patriarca's pilots bagged 17 Zekes and a Judy, plus 9 probables and 2 damaged. Three *Essex* Corsairs were lost over Tomikaka airfield.

The other Navy F4U squadrons fared poorly. *Intrepid's* VF-10 splashed a Judy during the afternoon CAP, but three planes and two pilots were lost on Sweep 1A. Japanese patrol planes had spotted the task force during its approach and the enemy was prepared. Some airfields were devoid of planes, anticipating the American strike, and the enemy had enough information to jam some radio frequencies. *Intrepid* pilots reported "many Jap voices" on 4475 kilocycles.[4]

Of 102 claimed shoot-downs, the Marine squadrons were credited with 14. *Franklin* Leathernecks splashed four against a loss of three Corsairs and two pilots. The *Bunker Hill* Marines dropped a pair of bandits during the day, losing a plane and pilot. But Hap Hansen's four divisions of VMF-112 had things entirely their own way. Approaching Kanoya East at 19,000 feet, the Wolfpack was met by some 20 Zekes. Five went down in the first pass, and in another several seconds four more were destroyed. Back aboard the *Bennington* Hansen's pilots found that their F4Us had suffered no damage. Later in the day, however, one failed to return.

Bombers and kamikazes went after the carriers, steaming 100 miles off-shore. There was no serious damage, but the suiciders were back the next day. With a vengeance.

Vice Admiral Mitscher raised his sights on the 19th, seeking enemy shipping around Honshu and Shikoku. Major Tom Mobley led 15 VMF-123 Corsairs on a dawn fighter sweep to Hiroshima and Kure, clearing the air for strikes against Japanese fleet units in the Inland Sea. Hearing another formation under attack, Mobley led his squadron over to lend a hand. Then the roof fell in.

An estimated 30 hostiles struck the Corsairs from six o'clock high. Two F4Us were shot out of formation, never to be seen again. Though a mixed bag of Army and Navy fighters—Zekes, Jacks, Georges, and Tojos—this bunch was vastly different from the sorry lot the *Bennington* Corsairs had clobbered the day before. The Japanese flew two- and four-plane sections, shooting accurately, employing coordinated tactics. In short, they were professionals. Outnumbered two to one, the Marines fought for their lives.

Mobley shot down one plane, then took 20-mm hits in his cockpit. He turned the lead over to Captain William A. Cantrel, a soft-spoken Oregonian who'd been with 123 on Guadalcanal. In his Solomons tour Bill Cantrel had fired at one Zeke and missed. In two minutes over the Inland Sea he shot down two big, rugged Georges. Then, with a painfully wounded foot and a damaged aircraft, Cantrel organized a withdrawal towards the coast. Eight Corsairs were badly shot up, and the aggressive Japanese pressed their attacks on stragglers. During this thirty-minute running combat, Cantrel protected the cripples, hitting two more bandits and driving them off. One F4U gave out near the radar picket destroyers and the pilot parachuted into the ocean. Of the returning Corsairs, three were beyond repair and pushed overboard. Nine Japanese planes were thought destroyed, but 123 lost six Corsairs and two pilots. Bill Cantrel received a Navy Cross.

Corsairs accompanied other planes on strikes against airfields and men-of-war for the rest of the day. *Bunker Hill* Marines and *Intrepid's* squadrons were among the F4Us which went after targets near Kure. At 0730 Commander John Hyland led ten of his fighter-bombers against Kure Air Depot with 500-pound bombs and HVARs. When intercepted near the target, Hyland splashed a Rex float fighter. Lieutenant (jg) R. H. Hill found one gun inoperative, his oxygen system out, and his belly tank wouldn't release. Nevertheless, he teamed with Ensign R. D. Erickson to destroy a Tojo and two Zekes. Hyland's formation then swept over three airfields, leaving ten single-engine planes destroyed and four damaged. Ninety minutes later another 14 *Intrepid* Corsairs under Lieutenant Commander Clarke found an escort carrier at Inno Shima, 40 miles east

Air Group 10 aboard the USS *Intrepid* achieved spectacular success against the kamikazes, with both the fighter and fighter-bomber squadrons equipped with F4U-1Ds. This VF-10 Corsair was photographed over Okinawa on 10 March 1945. (R.M. Hill)

of Kure. Eight fighters attacked, scoring four rocket hits and one bomb strike. The carrier was burning as the F4Us pulled out.

But the greater damage was inflicted upon American flattops. Task Group 58.2 was set upon by conventional bombers which, it was thought, got through because most F6Fs and F4Us were on sweeps or strikes. The *Wasp* took a bomb hit which ignited aviation gasoline, wrecked her hangar deck, and killed or injured some 370 men. She was saved from further destruction by efficient fire-fighting, and was able to recover her airborne planes.

At almost the same moment another Japanese plane dived out of the low clouds and put two 250-kilogram bombs through the *Franklin*'s flight deck. It couldn't have happened at a worse time. "Big Ben" had 31 planes spotted, ready to launch, including a dozen Corsairs. Bombs, rockets, and gasoline were all set off. Hard, jarring explosions tossed some aircraft over the side. A huge, boiling mass of smoke and flame enveloped un-lucky CV-13. Explosions wracked the 27,000-ton hull for five hours. Dead in the water 55 miles offshore, smoking like a volcano, the *Franklin* at-tracted more unwelcome attention but escaped further damage.

Most of the crew abandoned ship or were taken off by other vessels, leaving 700 men aboard as Captain Leslie Gehres fought to save the ship. One man who remained aboard was Don Russell, a Vought field service representative. His organizational efforts in leading fire-fighting teams earned him a rare Silver Star as a civilian.

Somehow, the *Franklin* survived. Her drastic starboard list was corrected, the major fires were extinguished, and after being towed out of range she proceeded to Ulithi under her own power. Over 1,100 men were injured, dead, or missing, including 65 Marine personnel killed. Some VF-5, VMF-214, and 452 pilots landed aboard other carriers to continue flying for a few more days, but the *Franklin* and her Corsairs were effectively out of the war.

Nor was that all. The *Enterprise* suffered considerable damage on the 20th, and all three stricken flattops withdrew to Ulithi. The Big E would return to combat before long, but the *Wasp* and Air Group 86 missed all but the last five weeks of the war. Corsair strength was now reduced to nine squadrons aboard six carriers.

Pre-invasion strikes against Okinawa were flown on 23 March, and for a week afterward as the fast carriers alternated between the Ryukyus and Japan. The first combat use of Tiny Tim rockets came on the 24th when Air Group 10 hit suspicious caves on Okinawa. After the *Franklin*'s early departure, the *Intrepid* was the only carrier with the big rockets. Twelve VBF-10 Corsairs flew the special sweep and eight had the special ordnance. One struck the propeller of a launching F4U, forcing an emergency landing aboard the *Yorktown*. John Hyland's Corsairs fired more Tiny Tims in succeeding days, with inconclusive results. The rockets were subsequently withdrawn as inaccurate and unreliable.

The invasion of Okinawa began on 1 April. Air Group 84 beat up the landing beaches with napalm and .50 calibers, as did the *Bennington* Marines. But two VMF-451 pilots were lost during the dawn launch from the *Bunker Hill*. Air action remained relatively calm until the 3rd, when three divisions of 451 accompanied 16 Hellcats in a strike at Amami O Shima, halfway between Okinawa and Kyushu. A wild gaggle of Zekes attacked, apparently intending to ram the Americans. The Marines splashed 11, of which Lieutenant William Peek got 3, and the F6Fs disposed of the others.

The first major kamikaze offensive of the long Okinawa campaign began on 6 April. Some 350 suiciders went after Allied shipping, and 288 were shot out of the sky by fast carrier and CVE fighters. Shipboard gunners accounted for 39 more, but 22 broke through the defenses and every one hit a ship. Three were sunk. Carrier-based Marines bagged 17 planes;

a dozen by the two *Bunker Hill* squadrons. Fighting 84 also got in some shooting. But the next day saw the biggest kamikaze of them all.

The 64,000-ton battleship *Yamato* departed the Inland Sea on the 6th with a light cruiser and eight destroyers. She was the largest warship in the world, mounting the world's biggest guns. The *Yamato* and her consorts had enough fuel for a one-way trip to Okinawa, hoping to destroy enough shipping to disrupt the invasion. It went without saying that none of these vessels were expected to return. Sighted by American submarines, the doomsday armada was vigorously sought by carrier aircraft.

Most of the Marine F4Us were involved in search and CAP. Major Edwin Roberts led VMF-221 on a sweep of Kagoshima Bay, hoping to find the dreadnought. She was by then far at sea, but the Fighting Falcons did find some items of interest. Six Rex floatplanes were bounced by Roberts and two wingmen, who downed five among them.

One Marine did get in a lick at the *Yamato*. Lieutenant Ken Huntington's was the only *Bennington* Corsair on deck when the strike was hastily launched. The 29 planes were the first to attack, arriving during the noon hour. They dived through spectacular flak in hues of red, blue, white, and yellow in addition to the more common black. The *Yamato* looked huge, as well she was, with her 863-foot length and 127-foot beam. Huntington pushed his dive as close as he dared, and was rewarded with a direct bomb hit on the A turret.

But other Corsairs were also involved. Air Group 10 departed *Intrepid* 280 miles south of the *Yamato* force: 16 Corsairs, 14 Helldivers, and a dozen Avengers. It was a five-hour round trip including time over target, in which the four VF-10 pilots each expended a 1,000-pounder on a destroyer. They scored one near-miss. The fighter-bombers went after the *Yamato* herself and the light cruiser *Yahagi*. Of fifteen bomb hits claimed by Air Group 10, six were credited to the Corsairs, including five by VBF-10. When it was all over, the *Yamato*, *Yahagi*, and four destroyers had succumbed to the massed air strikes. Ten U.S. carrier planes were lost.

Not all the TF-58 casualties were caused by enemy action. Four Marine pilots were assigned to VBF-83, operating as a division. They got lost over the sea and ran out of fuel. All survived the water landings, but only the flight leader and two wingmen were rescued. They were returned to the States without revisiting their short-term squadron mates aboard the *Essex*.

Elsewhere that day, more Marine Corsairs entered the picture. The Tactical Air Force on Okinawa arrived primarily by escort carrier, as MAG-31 put four squadrons ashore at Yontan airfield. Two CVEs—the *Sitkoh Bay* and *Breton*—launched the Corsairs and Hellcat night fighters in the midst of a kamikaze attack. A twin-engine Lilly bomber came in

140

low and straight for the carriers, hotly pursued by the CAP. But five F4U-1Cs of Major Perry Shuman's VMF-311 were not to be denied. They caught up and laced 20-mm shells through the big-bellied Kawasaki, setting it afire. Still flying, the Japanese pilot maintained his course towards the *Sitkoh Bay*, closing to 200 yards, then 100 yards. He couldn't miss.

Then the starboard wing folded up and the Lilly splashed in flames and spray only fifty yards from the little flattop. It was an exciting if heart-pounding introduction to Okinawa for the MAG-31 pilots. The pilots and support crews of VMF-311, 224, and 441 were accustomed to the Marshalls milkruns. Their first day in this new league demonstrated that the stakes were much higher.

Two days later the second wave of TAF fighters arrived. This was MAG-33, which included VMF-312, 322, and 323. A mixed batch of Vought and Goodyear Corsairs landed at Kadena airfield and quickly settled into the frantic lifestyle. With over 100 Corsairs now ashore, CAPs over the island and invasion fleet were flown regularly. Nor were the kamikazes and trigger-happy AA gunners the only concern. On 11 April an F4U ran through a soft spot on the Kadena runway and lurched out of control into another airplane. Three men were killed, two aircraft destroyed, and three damaged.

That same day the kamikazes returned in force. Such was Japanese confidence that a suicide pilot who was plucked out of the sea boasted that the attacks of the 11th would wipe out the whole fleet. They didn't succeed, but it was not from lack of trying. The *Enterprise,* recently back with the task force, was damaged slightly and two other ships were hit. Two task groups were kept on the line at any one time, with the other two refueling to the east. A 24-plane CAP was maintained throughout the daylight hours over each task group, with 12 fighters over each "Tomcat" radar picket destroyer. The increased flight schedule would be maintained almost indefinitely. Pilot fatigue became a major factor.

Yet there was no choice. Okinawa was within easy reach of Amami O Shima, and was little more than 350 miles from southern Kyushu. The fleet was committed to remain in a relatively small steaming area in order to support the troops on Okinawa. Consequently, the kamikazes had little difficulty finding their prime targets, the fast carriers.

There was a ghastly fascination about kamikazes, a compelling mixture of mystery and evil. Watching a lone suicider plunge through a storm of tracers and flak, some men were detached enough to wonder what the doomed Japanese pilot felt at that moment. For whether the kamikaze succeeded or failed, he still died.

Others shared the deadly fascination but were less inclined to philosophize about the enemy's emotions. Fighter pilots and shipboard gunners fought in a cold fury to stop the kamikaze short of his target. There was

141

only one way to do it: blow him out of the sky, shoot him into the water. It was twentieth century warfare, fought with fighter planes, radar, and proximity fuzes. But the objective was as old as war itself: kill him before he killed you. There was no other option. Neither surrender nor retreat existed in the kamikaze vocabulary.

To the airborne pilots and the relatively few sailors above decks, there was some small compensation in seeing and knowing what was happening. Black flak bursts against billowy white clouds, hails of red tracers criss-crossing the sky, crazily spinning smoke trails of destroyed suiciders, fountains and foam on the water. And all too frequently, smoking, burning ships.

For sailors below decks, for pilots in their ready rooms, an air attack could be even more distressing. Deprived of visual information, these men relied primarily upon their sense of hearing to know what drama was unfolding topside. When a CV's five-inch battery opened up, it was certain that enemy aircraft were approaching. But the kamikaze's target might be another ship; there was no way to tell. When the quad-mount 40-millimeters commenced fire, everyone knew the hostile was closer. The rhythmic rapid fire indicated that the suicider was within 4,000 yards. Perhaps twenty seconds later the 20 millimeters added their chatter to the din. At this point there was no longer much doubt as to the kamikaze's intended victim. If he survived to get that close, it was nearly certain he was bearing down on that particular carrier. Then there was nothing to do but wait. And waiting has always been one of the hardest parts of war.

No one could hope to relate the kamikaze campaign in detail—over 2,300 Imperial Navy planes alone were expended—nor is it necessary to do so. The battle peaked during April and May, and what follows is an attempt to hit the high spots of the Corsair's important role in that violent, eerie conflict, both ashore and afloat.

On 12 April most of the carriers had been at sea for sixty days. But the seagoing F4Us turned in one of their best performances against the kamikazes, despite increasing mental strain and physical fatigue of pilots, mechanics, and sailors. The four carrier-based Marine squadrons accounted for 51 hostiles in one of the largest suicide attacks of the war. The *Bennington* Leathernecks scored twenty-six victories during the day. Over Amami O Shima with three divisions of VMF-112 at 9,000 feet, Hap Hansen sighted some 30 suiciders approaching overhead. Climbing at full power, the Corsairs hit the Jack and Tony fighters escorting Kate torpedo planes. Hansen took his division into the fighters and treated himself to a twenty-fifth birthday present any fighter pilot might envy. His three quick kills made him an ace. The formations were broken up and a ratrace worked down to sea level. When it was all over, 20 Japanese planes had gone down without a loss to the Marines. And apparently none of the survivors molested any Allied ships.

The *Bunker Hill*'s Marines did very nearly as well, with twenty-five kills. At nearby Izena Shima, Major Archie Donahue of 451 had the best day of his career. His flight tangled with Vals and Zekes, and in the hassle he expertly gunned down four. Then he got a frantic call from one of his pilots, chasing another bandit. The Marine reported his guns jammed and screamed for Donahue to come down and finish the job. Donahue did, raising his wartime total to fourteen kills. Back aboard the *Bunker Hill*, the chagrined wingman admitted that he'd been so excited that he forgot to arm his guns.

So it went through the day as fighters stayed airborne to the endurance of their fuel and ammunition. The Navy squadrons made their presence felt, too. Fighting 84 claimed eight confirmed, and VBF-83 splashed seven, all bombers. The *Intrepid* Corsairs bagged 26 in three combats, losing three planes but no pilots. Of this total, twenty kills and two losses came on TargetCAP over Okinawa in mid-afternoon.

Fighting 10 put up 12 Corsairs whose pilots sighted 66 enemy aircraft and engaged 27. In a prolonged hassle all twelve *Intrepid* pilots scored kills. Two F4Us were lost, including one in a collision with a Wildcat, but the pilots survived. Nine victories were credited to four Marines. They had served with VMF-216 and 217 aboard the *Wasp* and were assigned to a pilot pool aboard a CVE. There they heard a rumor that the *Intrepid* needed replacements for its VMF squadrons. The "Evil I" had no Marine units embarked, but it didn't matter. When the Marines reported aboard—a total of eight in two groups—they were put to work. In all, thirteen flying Leathernecks served in Navy carrier squadrons, but the *Intrepid*'s were by far the most successful.

The Okinawa-based Marines had their first major combat on the 12th. Sixteen Japanese planes fell to MAG-31 Corsairs, including eight by Major Richard Day's VMF-312. But there were still problems to be worked out at Kadena and Yontan. Mud was a hazard in takeoff and landing, and the Army Corps of Engineers was slow in getting more fighter strips completed. Some Navy men claimed this showed the superiority of the Sea Bees, but the larger problem was administrative. The Army engineers were under orders to work on bomber fields first. Admiral Spruance, with a sense of priorities, went ashore and quickly set things straight.

On 16 April VF-10 fought one of the classic battles in Corsair history. Three divisions were launched for CAP over northern Okinawa at 0645, each with a different orbit point. Marine Lieutenant G. A. Krum, who had splashed two Zekes during the frantic dogfight on the 12th, kept his division as top cover. The skipper, Lieutenant Commander W. E. Clarke, circled one of the sixteen radar picket stations which surrounded Okinawa. After thirty minutes on station the division was vectored to the northwest, climbing hard. The Corsairs were attacked by Zekes and Tonys but negated the bandits' altitude advantage. They bagged five Zekes and two Tonys, including four kills by Lieutenant (jg) C. D. Farmer.

En route to the rendezvous three pilots heard a destroyer calling for help. Racing to the scene, Clarke found other VF-10 aircraft with F6Fs, FMs, and Marine F4Us. The *Intrepid* Corsairs sailed into a low, milling bunch of Vals and obsolete Nate fighters, burning one Val and probably another. Then Clarke and his wingman dived on a low-flying Betty pursued by some Hellcats. They hit it solidly, saw it splash into a controlled landing, and noted three Japanese climb out. Since the enemy airmen were within paddling distance of shore, the CO's division strafed them in the water and headed home with nine kamikazes destroyed without damage.

Ensign Alfred Lerch of VF-10, who accounted for seven of the twenty kamikazes shot down by his squadron in one mission near Okinawa on 16 April 1945. Note the debris caught in the oil cooler. (U.S. Navy)

Lieutenant (jg) Phil Kirkwood's division hit the aerial jackpot. Vectored towards two groups of suiciders, Kirkwood split the division. He stayed below the clouds with Ensign Horace W. Heath while Ensigns Norwald Quiel and Alfred Lerch went on top. Lerch called out Vals at 7,000 feet, which was above the Corsairs, but in the short combat three Vals and a Nate went down.

Kirkwood and Quiel were returning to their patrol station when they overheard the same radar picket's distress call. But they were closer and got there first, which was none too soon. The destroyer had already taken one hit, 20 more kamikazes were approaching from the north, and no other friendly planes had arrived. The two *Intrepid* pilots—and surely they were intrepid—immediately attacked. For the next hour, as the action report noted, "it was just a question of trying to get to the Japs before they attacked the DD in groups."[5]

Phil Kirkwood was already a veteran of one tour with VF-10. He'd scored four kills in F6Fs from the *Enterprise* in 1944 and had added two more from the *Intrepid*, cashing in on the offer of a businessman in his hometown for $100 per enemy plane. Defending the radar pickets during this single four-hour mission, Kirkwood strained the New Jersey gentleman's patriotic generosity to the limit. He added another $600 to his bank balance with four Nates and two Vals. Norwald Quiel had no such financial reward for his quartet of Nates.

Meanwhile, Heath and Lerch had returned to the orbit point when they saw some 30 Nates. They broke up the formation and chased the little fixed-gear fighters down to the water. The Japanese milled around in obvious confusion, allowing the two F4Us to pick off five. Heath and Lerch then chased three more across the northern tip of Okinawa, where one got away but the other two met incendiary ends.

In this aerial massacre Alfred Lerch shot down seven planes—six Nates and a Val. It was a feat of arms equalled by only four other Americans. Horace Heath confirmed two Nates and a Val. Therefore, Kirkwood's division destroyed 20 kamikazes. The combined toll of both divisions was 29 confirmed, plus probables. Seldom has 17,000 rounds of .50 caliber been more efficiently expended. The only damage was caused by debris striking two F4Us.

Later that day Air Group 10 Corsairs splashed 13 more hostiles, losing a plane and pilot over Kyushu. But jubilation over this lopsided victory was exceedingly short-lived. At 1330 the *Intrepid* launched a dozen F4Us on CAP when five kamikazes dived. Four were shot down by the ship's gunners. The fifth went into the flight deck aft. Twenty fighters were destroyed, ten men killed, and nearly 100 injured. The *Intrepid* burned for an hour, but the hole in her deck was covered with steel plate and her airborne "chicks" came to roost. The air group remained aboard all

A Marine pilot brought this shot-up Corsair back to the USS *Bennington* for a crash landing in April 1945. (R.M. Hill)

the way to Alameda dockyard, but by the time the *Intrepid* returned to WestPac the war was over. In thirty-four days, VF-10 had shot down 85 aircraft (including 8 by Hellcat night fighters), nearly matching the six-month record of the previous tour. Seven pilots and 14 Corsairs were lost to enemy action. The fighter-bombers added another dozen victories, plus two by the CAG, Commander John Hyland.

Land-based Marines also had plenty of action on the 16th. Corsairs of VMF-311, 312, 323, and 441 all fought off kamikazes and conventional bombers over the radar pickets. Among them, these squadrons splashed 36 planes, including 17 by Major Bob White's Yontan-based 441. Responding to cries for help from the destroyer *Laffey*, three divisions took on 25 Bettys, Vals, and Zekes. The beleaguered picket ship had been hit or nicked by five suiciders, but White's 12 fighters broke up the attack. Not before Corsairs of 311 arrived, however, and chopped off the tail of a 441 plane in the scramble for leftovers. Two F4Us and a pilot were lost. Lieutenant William Eldridge took out four kamikazes while Lieutenant Selva McGinty got a triple. So did Captain Floyd Kirkpatrick, a flint-eyed Oregonian flying a Corsair named "Palpitatin' Pauli."

Despite the success in the air, things were still not quite settled on the ground. Kadena and Yontan were under sporadic artillery fire, and facilities were far from permanent. One establishment which opened its doors early, however, was the dining hall of VMF-323 at Kadena: "Mayer's Mess, where the aces meet to eat." It was no idle boast. The Death Rattlers proved that conclusively on 22 April.

That evening elements of three land-based Corsair squadrons were sent westward to the radar picket line. Some 80 suiciders were threatening the destroyers, and in a swirling half-hour rat race over 50 were shot down by F6Fs and F4Us.

First on the scene were two divisions of 323, led by the CO and the exec: twenty-four-year-old Majors George Axtell, Jr., and Jefferson D. Dorroh. One pilot aborted en route with engine trouble. The other seven found 39 Vals flying at 500 feet towards two destroyers about 40 miles north of Aguni Shima. It was a turkey shoot. Three pilots who had never before seen a Japanese airplane emerged as aces. Axtell chased down five Vals and splashed them all in fifteen minutes, damaging three more. Lieutenant Jerry O'Keefe, a curly-haired, twenty-one-year-old Mississippian, easily dropped four and set afire a fifth. It turned back towards him, attempting to ram. O'Keefe squeezed hard on his trigger. Collision seemed certain. Then at fifty feet the Aichi fell off on one wing and crashed into the water.

Top gun was big, enthusiastic Jeff Dorroh. He had entered flight training in July 1941. Since then he had logged nearly 1,700 hours, and had been with 323 since the fall of 1943. He flew thirty-three missions at Okinawa, and in this respect he was not much different from thousands of other aviators during the war. But his ninth mission was the exception.

"I could see it was going to be a long day," he said, "so I switched off two of my guns."[6] He moved in behind one Val which pulled such a sharp turn that the exec had to drop wheels and flaps to stay with it. Using only four .50 calibers, he hit the bomber's cockpit from astern and watched it fall into the South China Sea.

That was the only no-deflection shot Dorroh got. In the next twenty minutes he made wide-angle gunnery passes on six more Vals, hitting each in succession. Two which went down burning were not seen to crash so Dorroh only claimed them as probables. Then he formed up with Lieutenant C. S. Allen of Axtell's division and spotted a lone Aichi scooting for safety. Dorroh told Allen to take it, but Allen was out of ammunition so Dorroh flamed it with another wide-angle shot. It was his sixth definite kill of the engagement.

The seven Death Rattlers returned to Kadena near dark with a bag of twenty-four and three-quarters kills. No other Corsair squadron came so close to matching VF-10's sensational record of six days before. Mess officer Sol Mayer was moved to scrounge a dinner of steak and eggs for the three instant aces. The F4Us of VMF-224 and 441 had accounted for another eight shootdowns.

On 28 April the emphasis shifted back to sea. *Bunker Hill* Corsairs were heavily engaged during the day, as VMF-221 batted down 14 hostiles. Lieutenant Jack McManus dropped behind his division when vectored to investigate a high-altitude bogey. As the other Fighting Falcons went to work on Zekes and Tonys, McManus wondered if his supercharger would stay in high blower. He soon had other concerns as the combat worked down to his level.

McManus joined Lieutenant Dean Caswell, fighting against heavy odds. Bright, garish splotches of fire lent an eerie effect to the hazy sky as Zekes and Tonys fell to the outnumbered Marines. Recalled Caswell, "All their losses had been huge, terrifying flamers, those colossal gouts of fire that so often ended the lives of Japanese pilots. . . . It probably tipped the balance in our favor that they did not get us and yet the two Corsairs, full of fight, kept coming at them and scoring flamers."[7] McManus had splashed four and Caswell killed three, matching his feat over Kyushu ten days earlier.

Fighting 84 intercepted 28 suiciders near Kikai Shima during the afternoon. The 16 Corsairs jettisoned their 500-pound bombs and climbed to engage at 10,000 feet. Lieutenant John M. Smith, a VF-17 veteran, bagged three Nates while his squadron mates took out 15 more bandits.

But there was more for the Corsair squadrons than aerial combat. Close support of U.S. infantry was a frequent mission, and the Marines performed it well. There were, however, inevitable errors. On 30 April three F4Us, evidently misreading grid coordinates, strafed behind the American lines on Okinawa. Seven men were killed and eighteen wounded. Other incidents were reported from time to time, but this one was the worst.

For a period of nearly four weeks, from mid-April to mid-May, no fast carriers were struck by kamikazes. Task groups were rotated to Ulithi or the Philippines for brief rest and replenishment. But the Okinawa Corsairs dealt with the threat every day. And some of them found novel means of doing so. On 10 May a division of VMF-312 on early CAP over Ie Shima saw the contrails of a Nick recon plane at 25,000 feet. As the Corsairs climbed, so did the Nick. Two F4Us had topped out by 36,000 feet but Captain Kenneth Reusser and Lieutenant Robert Klingman persisted. They fired most of their ammo to lighten their planes and closed on the twin-engine Kawasaki at 38,000 feet. Reusser expended the last of his .50 caliber load, damaging the Nick's port engine. The rear gunner returned fire.

Klingman got within fifty feet and pressed the trigger. Nothing happened. His guns were frozen. In the rarified atmosphere Klingman carefully continued his approach, being careful not to stall out. His propeller

The distinctive checkerboard design on nose and rudder marked the F4U-1Ds of VMF-312 on Okinawa. (R.M. Hill)

chewed up the Nick's rudder and rear cockpit. Positioning himself again, the aggressive Marine sawed off the remnants of the rudder. By now he doubted he could get back to Okinawa, 150 miles astern. But he made a third buzz-saw attack, and this one did the trick. With its right stabilizer gone, the Nick spun down to 15,000 feet where it shed its wings.

Out of fuel, Klingman nevertheless managed a dead-stick landing. The tips of his prop blades were missing and the airframe was punctured and dented from debris and bullet holes. But he'd knocked down his opponent, and in the fighter pilot trade, that's the main idea.

Next day the carriers' lucky streak ran out. On CAP over Kikai, eight VF-84 pilots jumped about 30 kamikazes from a 3,000-foot altitude advantage. In two passes the Corsairs splashed 11. Lieutenant John M. Smith was again top man with two Nates and a Zeke, running his wartime total to ten. The Navy pilots returned to the flagship as the *Bunker Hill* was recovering some of her Marine fighters. Minutes later a Zeke crashed near the aft elevator and seconds after that, a Judy splintered the deck at the base of the island. Gasoline-fed fires blazed on the flight and hangar decks as aircraft were incinerated. It took four hours to control the conflagration, and Vice Admiral Mitscher shifted his flag to the *Enterprise*.

The *Bunker Hill* remained mobile, but she was out of the war. Most of her planes were destroyed, their engines and propellers the only recognizable items in the smoking rubble. Far worse were the personnel casualties: nearly 400 dead or missing and some 260 injured. Major Archie Donahue had landed with his VMF-451 division at the same time as the eight VF-84 Corsairs. The Marines were bone weary from the unrelenting

149

flight schedule, and Donahue had told his pilots to forget the debriefing and get some rest. The order saved their lives. Most of the VF-84 pilots in their ready room were asphyxiated by smoke and fumes. Roger Hedrick's squadron lost nineteen officers and three ratings. Of the twenty-nine Marine fatalities, one was a pilot. The others were maintenance personnel on the hangar deck.

Fifteen pilots of VMF-221 and 451 were still in the air during the attack. They splashed four suiciders, including a Jill by Captain Jim Swett—his sixteenth and last victory. The surviving F4Us were recovered aboard the *Enterprise*, which was herself kamikazed three days later. She went home after a long, long war.

In just under three months the *Bunker Hill* Corsairs had accounted for 176 airborne hostiles. Ninety-two were credited to VF-84 and 84 to the two Marine squadrons, which lost thirteen pilots during the deployment. Four of the Marine fliers were victims of operational accidents. With the *Bunker Hill*'s departure, only the *Essex*, *Bennington*, and the newly arrived *Shangri-La* with Air Group 85 retained F4Us in the task force.

On 21 May the Tactical Air Force received further reinforcement. The initial batch of MAG-22 landed at Ie Shima, and by month's end VMF-

Corsairs of VF-5 aboard the USS *Yorktown* on 9 May 1945, still flying after Air Group 5 was knocked out of the war when the USS *Franklin* was bombed on 19 March. (R.M. Hill)

113, 314, and 422 were based there. Major Elkin Drew now led 422, the outfit which lost six pilots and twenty-two aircraft during an over-water flight in the Gilberts a year and a half before. Drew's squadron made the flight to Ie Shima in good shape, but VMF-314 lost three F4Us in heavy weather during the leg from Iwo Jima on the 24th.

Next day, 25 May, the TAF fighters made their biggest killing—seventy-five victories, of which the Marines claimed thirty-nine. But the 165 kamikazes which swept down on the transports and picket destroyers came too thick and fast. Two ships were sunk, nine damaged. Still, had it not been for the F4Us and Army P-47s, the carnage would have been much worse.

The suicide pilots helped defeat themselves in some cases, as when a division of VMF-312 intercepted 20 hostiles at 0730. The Japanese were so inexperienced that they allowed Major Richard Day's pilots to knock down 12 without loss or damage. An hour later, more of "Day's Knights" waded into a larger formation and picked off 16 for the loss of one F4U. Ten kills were credited to only two pilots, as Captain Herbert J. Valentine and Lieutenant William Farrell dumped three and one-half Vals, three and one-half Zekes (plus two probables) and three Tojos. Valentine's five and one-half in this combat made him the ninth and last Corsair "ace in a day." Corsairs of VMF-322, 323, and the newly arrived 422 also got in on the fat pickings.

Despite the happy hunting ground aspect of the Okinawa campaign, the squadrons lived a far from merry existence. Rain, mud, nightly bombing, and even suicide crash-landings by enemy commando aircraft were all features of life in the Ryukyus. But there were occasional happenings which served to perk up morale. When MAG-14 began arriving on 8 June from the Philippines, it brought a new-model Corsair to Kadena. This was the F4U-4, received by MAG-14 the previous month, distinctive with its four-blade prop and "chin" scoop for the larger carburetor on the 2,300-hp Twin Wasp engine. With an astonishing 450 mph speed and four 20-mm cannon in the -4B model, it was just the thing to bolster the anti-kamikaze defense.

That same day the last of the Marine fast carrier squadrons revisited the Japanese home islands. Major Hap Hansen led VMF-112 and 123 on a last look at Kanoya while Navy squadrons bombed the complex of airfields on southern Kyushu. Hansen considered Kagoshima Bay the best-defended area he'd seen in three years of war. "It was a jumping-off spot for kamikazes to Okinawa," he said. "How I hated that place!"[8]

When the *Bennington* turned out of formation that afternoon and headed for Leyte Gulf, the Marine fast carrier mission was accomplished. In nearly four months of constant combat, the Wolfpack and Eight Balls had flown over 2,500 sorties and destroyed 231 Japanese aircraft—82 on the wing. Over 4,000 rockets, 100 tons of bombs, and nearly a million rounds of .50-caliber ammo had been expended. Their losses were equally noteworthy. The two squadrons counted eighteen pilots killed or missing; a third of the original complement. Of 48 F4U losses, 31 were attributable to enemy action.

In all, the ten VMF squadrons had been credited with 201 Japanese planes in air combat while flying from the fast carriers. Over 80 Corsairs and forty-six pilots were lost to all causes. They had been put aboard fleet carriers as an expedient. Their main mission was to help stop the kamikazes. Reflecting upon that chilling menace, Hansen said, "Early in 1945 we had heard of such stuff but I don't believe any of us really believed it. We learned! We started out with ten *Essex*-class carriers when we headed for Tokyo. Four months later every one except the *Bennington* that started out with us had been hit by a kamikaze."[9]

The land-based Corsairs now devoted more of their time to tactical ground support of the Army and Marine troops. Bombs, rockets, and napalm were liberally distributed over Okinawa, particularly in the hilly cave-riddled areas where the Japanese were well entrenched. On 14 June a massive strike of 64 F4Us burned out a suspected enemy troop concentration along a ridge-dominated ravine. Throughout the campaign, Corsairs spread 152,000 gallons of "hell jelly" across the island. It would be impossible to calculate the number of American lives saved by ground support sorties of the Second Marine Air Wing on Okinawa.

On 21 June Okinawa was declared secure. But the air defense mission remained till the end of the month. On the 22nd Captain Ken Walsh of VMF-222 pushed his F4U-4 to overtake a suicide Zeke. Like 20 Japanese planes before it, this one also fell to the Solomons ace. It was Walsh's last victory. In fact, it was about the last of MAG-14 as well. The group's three fighter squadrons recorded only nine claims during their brief service at Okinawa. The kamikaze threat was not ended, but it was clearly mastered.

The Tactical Air Force recorded 637 shoot-downs during the campaign, of which the dozen F4U squadrons contributed 436. The clear leader in the competitive scoring race was VMF-323, George Axtell's "deadly passel of kids."[10] They were all of that. Though the squadron had over half its pilots transferred early in the year, they still made an outstanding team with replacement personnel. Their 124½ victories were followed by VMF-311 with 71, VMF-312 with 59½, and 224 with 55. No other Marine squadron topped 50 kills.

For most of June the only fast carrier Corsair squadrons were VBF-83 aboard the *Essex* and the two Air Group 85 outfits on the *Shangri-La*. But four other F4U squadrons went to sea aboard escort carriers about

Four Marine squadrons flew F4U-1Ds and FG-1Ds from escort carriers in 1945. This VMF-351 aircraft nearly lost a wingtip upon recovery aboard the USS *Cape Gloucester*. (R.M. Hill)

this same time. They were the product of Colonel Al Cooley's Marine carrier program back on the West Coast. First was Marine Carrier Air Group 1 (MCVG-1), led by veteran Lieutenant Colonel John Dobbin aboard the *Block Island* (CVE-106). The fighter squadron was VMF-511, which operated eight F4U-1Ds with a similar number of Hellcats. The unit got its combat baptism on 10 May off Okinawa.

Close behind was MCVG-2 under Lieutenant Colonel W. R. Campbell aboard the *Gilbert Islands* (CVE-107). The Corsairs of VMF-512 first struck the Sakishima Gunto on 21 May and were similarly engaged till the end of the month, when the action moved south. Both jeep carriers were teamed in Task Group 32.1.3 from the first of June, when they supported Allied landings at Balikpapan.

Yet another Solomons veteran led MCVG-4. This was Lieutenant Colonel Don Yost, aboard the *Cape Gloucester* (CVE-109). His F4U contingent was VMF-351, which also cut its teeth on the Okinawa bone during early July. Operating with a Navy task group, the *Cape Gloucester* struck the China Coast during August, and stirred up more activity than the other Marine carriers. Three Japanese planes were shot down, including two by Yost himself. They were his seventh and eighth victims since Guadalcanal.

Arriving in WestPac out of sequence was the *Vella Gulf*'s (CVE-111) MCVG-3. Lieutenant Colonel Royce Coln's air group, including VMF-

513, made two strikes in the Marianas during late July and proceeded to Okinawa. Administratively, the four Marine CVEs were Carrier Division 27, but they never operated as a unit. There would have been four more had the invasion of Japan been necessary, but thankfully their services were not required.

So the majority of F4U operations in the last two months of the war were from the fast carriers. Two long-displaced fighter-bomber squadrons returned to work in June and July. The *Hancock*'s VBF-6 participated in a practice strike against Wake Island en route to the task force on 20 June. So did the *Wasp*'s VBF-86 four weeks later.

There was new blood as well. The *Bennington* now flew the reorganized Air Group 1, with two F4U squadrons. Air Group 88 went aboard the *Yorktown* at the end of June, with 37 F4U-1Ds in the fighter-bomber contingent. And the last Corsair squadron to arrive on the firing line was VBF-94, flying F4U-4s from the *Lexington*.

By now the U-Bird was firmly established and fully appreciated aboard carriers. Operational experience had shown that in a given deck space more F4Us could be parked (wings folded) than F6Fs. It was hard work for the plane handlers, interlocking wing stubs and stabilizers, but it was true. And the F4U-1D, not to mention the -4, was proving superior to the Hellcat in most tactical considerations—especially speed and offensive payload.

Recognizing this, some air admirals pushed for more and more Corsairs. Admiral Halsey, ComThird Fleet, called for 80 percent fighters aboard CVs. Vice Admiral Mitscher wanted only F4U-4s aboard his CVLs, owing to their greater speed and climb over the F6F-5, until the outstanding new F8F Bearcat arrived. Had the war continued, the F8F would have become the fleet's only pure fighter, with Corsairs taking over much of the strike duty. Hellcats would have been phased out completely over several months.

But it was not to be. Corsairs never did fly combat from CVL decks during World War II, and the F6F remained the dominant shipboard fighter until V-J Day.

During July and August the carrier planes roamed over most of Japan, largely in control of enemy airspace. Strikes against remaining Imperial Navy warships figured prominently, especially in the July raids against Kure. The main opposition was flak—heavy, multihued, spectacular—but Navy Corsairs pressed through to deliver their share of the bombs and rockets. The log of VBF-83 is typical of squadron entries during this period. Attacks on the Tokyo area on 30 July. Weather-aborted strikes on 2 and 8 August. Northern Honshu targets on the 9th and 10th. Back to Tokyo three days later. There were three losses during these two weeks: two operational, one probably to AA. One pilot was rescued. In six months aboard the *Essex*, VBF-83 received 129 Corsairs, three-quarters of which were destroyed, jettisoned, or transferred out with heavy damage.

Japanese aircraft were being destroyed on their airdromes in scores and hundreds, but few threatened the fleet. Most of those which fell to patrolling F6Fs and F4Us were snoopers or high-altitude recon planes. Several combats were fought above 30,000 feet.

On 15 August two strikes were sent against Tokyo again. Heading inbound, the new CO of VBF-83, Lieutenant Commander T. H. Reidy, bagged a long, lean Myrt recon plane. He may have been the last Corsair pilot to shoot down an airplane in the Second World War. As the first strike group reached the coast, both waves were recalled. The Japanese had capitulated.

On V-J Day, 2 September, there were nine F4U squadrons with the task force, embarked in seven CVs. Other ships were en route to WestPac when hostilities had ended. They included the *Intrepid*, returning to the war with John Hyland's Air Group 10; the *Boxer* with Air Group 93 flying F4U-4 fighter-bombers, as was the *Antietam* with Air Group 89. Southerners insisted upon calling her "*Sharpsburg*," after the Confederacy's name for that Civil War battle. But for the moment—and only for a moment, for such is human nature—thoughts of battles past and present were set aside.

During the Second World War the F4U underwent a dramatic evolution. The progression was almost poetic: from promise to disappointment

Two F4U-4s of VF-6 off the USS *Hancock* in August 1945, the last month of hostilities. (R.M. Hill)

to triumph. As a pure fighter the Corsair hung up one of the best records of all time. In thirty months of combat with the U.S. Navy and Marines it was credited with 2,140 Japanese planes destroyed in aerial combat. The known loss of 189 Corsairs to enemy aircraft translated into a kill-loss ratio of 11.3 to 1. Total Corsair losses in American service amounted to 1,624, of which 922 were operational casualties on both combat and training flights. In other words, 56 percent of U-Bird losses were not related to enemy action. Until finally modified, the Corsair was its own worst enemy.

Slightly over 64,000 combat sorties were flown by the Vought, Goodyear, and Brewster fighters. Of these, about two-thirds were logged in the Solomons. For this reason, the Corsair will always be associated with the Marine squadrons of the South Pacific. But as fine a job as the F4U did from Guadalcanal to Bougainville and beyond, it should be remembered that the Corsair was designed, built, and finally operated as a carrier aircraft. Despite delays which amounted to years, the Corsair did ultimately fulfill its intended role. As a fighter-bomber it had no superior, ashore or afloat.

These seven pilots of VMF-323 shot down 25 Val dive bombers near Okinawa on 22 April 1945. Rear: Major G.C. Axtell, Jr., the CO (5 Vals); Major J.D. Dorroh (6); Lieutenant J.J. O'Keefe (5); Lieutenant W.L. Hood (3½); Front: Lieutenant C.S. Allen (1); Lieutenant N.T. Therlault (2¼); Lieutenant E.L. Abner (2). (J.D. Dorroh)

Credit for the bent-wing bird's eventual vindication belongs to many men. Unfortunately, most of them remain anonymous: pilots and mechanics at the squadron and air group level who tasted the F4U's potential and proved its worth; Vought personnel who worked long and hard with their customers. For reasons which may never be completely understood, it took too long to bring this wonderful flying machine to its full capability. That is an undeniable fact of the F4U's career. But it is equally certain that those who believed in Rex Biesel's design refused to be satisfied until its promise was realized. And that is what made the Corsair what it was: a world-beater.

chapter 8

Korea

For those that fly might fight again.

Samuel Butler, 1678

By V-J Day, Corsair production had been drastically cut back. The last FG-1Ds were accepted in September 1945, whereas the final F4U-1Ds had been delivered in February. Thus, at war's end, Vought's efforts were almost wholly devoted to the F4U-4, having produced over 1,900 before Japan's surrender.

Goodyear had won a contract for 2,500 FG-4s, and had actually completed 12, ready for production flight test. But the contract was canceled and since the Navy didn't need the aircraft, they were scrapped. However, the Vought remained in limited production until the summer of 1947, when 2,356 F4U-4s had been delivered.

The follow-on Corsair was the -5. It first flew in April 1946 as a modified -4, and a layman could not easily tell it from the previous model. But the differences were important. The F4U-5 had Pratt and Whitney's R-2800-32W engine, the Twin Wasp series E, with "chin" inlets on the cowl for the twin auxiliary blowers. The forward fuselage was wider than on the -4 to accommodate this arrangement. Also, the engine was mounted at over two degrees downthrust to improve longitudinal stability, which improved forward vision.

For the first time in the Corsair line, the outer wing panels were metalized instead of being fabric covered. This resulted in a significant reduction in aerodynamic drag, and was partially responsible for the F4U-5's maximum speed of over 460 mph. Pilots appreciated the choice of manual or automatic operation of cowl flaps, supercharger, and other equipment. And spring tabs on elevators and rudder could reduce control input by as much as 40 percent. Furthermore, electrically heated guns and pitot tubes enabled the -5 to operate around 45,000 feet. A winterized model, the -5NL, featured deicer boots and improved cockpit heater. Some -5s were even fitted with cigarette lighters, colloquially called "spot heaters" to avoid drawing attention to the nonstandard equipment.

Despite this high-altitude capability, in actual use the F4U-5 would not require such an option. Its combat would be nearly all low-level, where the tremendous payload was eminently useful. When necessary, over 5,000 pounds of ordnance could be carried on the twin underwing pylons and the centerline rack. And there were times when it was necessary. The North Koreans invaded South Korea in June of 1950.

The only American fast carrier in WestPac at the instigation of hostilities was the *Valley Forge* (CV-45). One of the postwar *Essex* class, she embarked Air Group 5 with two Corsair squadrons, VF-53 and 54. The "Happy Valley" operated with the HMS *Triumph*, the beginning of what would thereafter be known as Task Force 77. Despite a considerable diversity of ship and aircraft performance—F9F Panther jets and Fairey Fireflies, for instance—the Anglo-Americans planned a strike against the

North Korean capital of Pyongyang. This important target was then beyond the range of available tactical aircraft.

At dawn on 3 July the two carriers were only 75 miles off the west coast of Korea, in the Yellow Sea. At 0600 the *Valley Forge* commenced launch: 16 rocket-armed Corsairs, 12 bomb-toting AD Skyraiders, and finally 8 Panthers. The faster Grummans arrived first, taking the Communists by surprise. They bagged two airborne Yakelov fighters, then shot up Pyongyang airfield. When the F4Us and VA-55 ADs arrived, they did a thorough wrecking job. Runways were holed, all three hangars destroyed, and the fuel depot set ablaze. No Allied planes were lost. Thus began three years of carrier operations against the Asian enemy. TF-77 exploited the carrier's traditional advantages of mobility and territorial independence, striking all around the Korean peninsula the rest of the month.

Not only the fast carriers were involved. On 3 August the escort carrier *Sicily* (CVE-118) arrived in Tsushima Strait with VMF-214 embarked. The Black Sheep's F4U-4Bs hit Chinju near the south coast with rockets and incendiary bombs, for the North Korean advance had been swift. On the 6th they were joined by the *Badoeng Strait* (CVE-116) flying VMF-323, also equipped with -4Bs.

But the enemy advance was too massive to halt with the limited forces on hand. Thirty days after the war began, the United Nations command had lost virtually all its in-country airfields—either overrun or rendered untenable. Air support had to come from the carriers or from Southern Japan. By September the Allied troops were cornered in the small Pusan pocket. In order to retrieve the situation, General Douglas MacArthur accomplished a tricky amphibious landing at Inchon on the west coast, which threatened to catch the Red army in a large pincers.

Before the landing, however, a minor confrontation occurred in the Yellow Sea. At 1330 on 4 September, TF-77 was 100 miles from the Chinese mainland and little more from Russia's naval-air complex at Port Arthur, on the tip of the Liaotung Peninsula. Thus, the task force was easily within fifteen minutes of Communist airfields, as the jet flies. Shipboard radar detected a bogey at 60 miles range, approaching from Manchuria. A few minutes tracking showed the unidentified aircraft making 200 mph at about 12,000 feet. Evidently it had taken off from Port Arthur. A VF-53 division on CAP was vectored towards the bogey to intercept and report.

Radar now showed the blip to diverge. There were two aircraft. One turned north while the other proceeded towards the task force. Only 30 miles out the four Corsairs eyeballed the bogey. It was definitely hostile—a twin-engine aircraft sporting the red star of the Soviet air force.

The Russian, realizing he'd been spotted, made a run for it. He nosed down, added power, and headed east toward North Korea. The division leader, Lieutenant (jg) Richard E. Downs, followed. As the F4Us over-hauled the hostile, it opened fire. Downs informed the *Valley Forge* and was told he could shoot back. Downs made a firing pass and missed the target, but his wingman didn't. The four 20-millimeters set the plane afire, and it spun into the Yellow Sea. Shortly a U.S. destroyer pulled up to the burning wreckage and retrieved the body of a Russian airman. No other bogies approached the task force.

Supporting the Inchon operation on 15 September were the *Valley Forge* and *Philippine Sea* (CV-47), by now veterans of Korea, and the newly arrived *Boxer* (CV-21.) All embarked two to four Corsair squad-rons. The *Boxer*, with a scratch-built air group, numbered 64 F4U-4Bs. Detachments of F4U-5Ns from Composite Squadron Three were also available. They included some old hands at the night-fighter business. The CO was Commander Richard E. Harmer—"Chick" Harmer of the *Enterprise*'s F4U-2s. In the *Valley Forge* was Lieutenant Commander William E. Henry, who had been the Navy's top night-fighter ace in F6F-5Ns during 1944–45. Nocturnal strike and heckler missions were part of VC-3's duties, but there were specialized daytime jobs, such as skipping bombs into enemy-occupied caves.

Joining the invasion fleet were the escort carriers *Sicily* and *Badoeng Strait* with their Marine squadrons. Like Lieutenant Colonel Bill Mil-lington's *Essex* Corsairs at Iwo Jima five and a half years before, the flying Leathernecks provided close-in support for the assault troops. They hit the beaches with bombs and rockets, then strafed the area with "20 mike-mike" immediately before the landing craft beached.

Caught at a strategic disadvantage, in three weeks the Reds were pushed back to the 38th Parallel. For naval air, things moved even quicker. Kimpo Airfield, between Inchon and Seoul, was taken on the second day of the landing and made available to tactical aircraft on D-Plus-Three. A Marine night-fighter squadron, VMF(N)-513, flew up from Itazuke Air Base, Japan. Its main equipment was F7F-3N Tigercats, but F4U-5Ns were also available. The skipper was another old-timer, Major Hunter Reinburg, formerly of VMF-121 and 122.

Reinburg's squadron was attached to MAG-12, then under Colonel Richard C. Mangrum. The group commander was impressed with 513's work. Destroying enemy transport was a major chore, made no easier when the truck convoys moved at night and doused their lights whenever aircraft were heard. Therefore, the nocturnal prowlers carried parachute flares to keep their targets lit up for brief periods. Dick Mangrum ex-plains the procedure:

"Spotting a truck convoy from a distance, we would start dropping flares to keep it illuminated while an attack section went to work. We got the Navy to provide patrol aircraft to provide the flares and they did a great job—we couldn't carry enough flares of our own to provide continuous illumination.

"Attacking ground targets under the dim, eerie light of flares over rugged terrain was just about the hairiest way to earn a living there ever was. Pilots were on instruments immediately on pull-up to climb for another run, and only the most competent were effective. Burning and exploding trucks were the only reward, but we had good reason to conclude that these operations contributed to disruption of enemy supply traffic, and were worth the effort."[1]

From 1951 to 1953 the squadron was credited with eleven night-fighter victories, including two by Corsairs. But the far larger effort was devoted to intruder and strike missions.

In October came the first indication of Red Chinese participation. By the end of that month there was no doubt. The ChiComs were heavily committed, pouring men and supplies across many of the seventeen structures spanning the Yalu River which separates North Korea from Manchuria. At this point, unrestricted air strikes would certainly have impeded the enemy advance by taking out the vital spans. They would not have stopped the Chinese, but the immediate result could only have been beneficial. Air Force B-29s had been targeted against the Sinuiju bridges but were unable to destroy them from high altitude. So TF-77 was called in to do the job—by halfway measures. Absurd political restrictions en-

The USS *Leyte* (CV-32) launches F4U-4s against targets in Korea on 10 October 1950. (U.S. Navy)

abled the carrier pilots only to hit the southern portion of the bridges. China was already in the war; "violation" of her airspace to do the job properly would hardly have complicated the diplomatic situation.

The Sinuiju strikes of early November achieved some success. The "bridge busters" worked in teams of eight ADs, each with a ton of bombs backed up by two to four divisions of F4Us as flak suppression. Enemy AA batteries were well deployed around the approaches, making each attack a risky venture. As many as 16 F9Fs orbited high overhead on MiG CAP. Sinuiju's highway bridge was knocked down by the TF-77 fliers, operating over 200 miles inland, but the railway spans stayed up. Throughout the rest of the month the Yalu bridges were attacked along the southern bank, allowing AA from the opposite shore to fire unhindered. Even worse, Communist personnel and supply concentrations on the north bank enjoyed total immunity. The Navy and Marine squadrons' task was akin to trying to stop a milk delivery. They had to break each milk bottle as it arrived instead of killing the cow.

The Chinese continued spilling men and materiel into North Korea, partially with the aid of pontoon bridges. When the weather turned cold enough, the river froze and the Reds went across on the ice. Embittered aviators pondered how soon they would be allowed to bomb the southern portion of the ice pack. Then, with their supply buildup accomplished, the Chinese launched a massive assault on 26 November: a quarter-million men. They more than compensated for the depleted North Korean army, which had almost ceased to exist.

Outnumbered about two to one, the UN troops were forced to give ground. Many units were isolated and enveloped by the onrushing Chinese. Tactical air power was limited at the time, owing to the temporary absence of several carriers. The *Valley Forge* had departed for a long-delayed overhaul, and the CVEs were engaged in ferrying replacement aircraft. But the CVs *Leyte* and *Philippine Sea* were reinforced in mid-December by the light carrier *Bataan* (CVL-29) while the hard-working *Sicily* and *Badoeng Strait* returned. The Black Sheep, who had been flying ground-support missions from Yonpo, flew out to the *Sicily* off Hungnam on 7 December without interrupting their operations schedule. On the 17th VMF-212 was aboard the *Bataan* covering the Hungnam evacuation. It had taken over five years for the air admirals to finally get Corsairs aboard a CVL.

All along the line of enemy advance, fighter-bombers delivered their ordnance at point-blank range. The Marines' patented close-support techniques were never closer. GIs still remark on the pinpoint accuracy of the bent-wing planes which bombed, strafed, and rocketed within fifty yards of the American lines. The wretched 100-degree heat of the summer had given way to the wicked freeze of winter, hitting as low as 25

164

degrees below zero. In such conditions, napalm could safely be used close to friendly troops. In some instances, Navy and Marine planes fired so close to American lines that expended .50-caliber and 20-mm cases were scattered among the infantrymen.

The pace of operations was unrelenting. The *Leyte*, for instance, was engaged almost continuously in strikes and support missions from 19 November to 12 December. In this twenty-four-day period, 16 were devoted to air ops—the others to refueling and resupply. The majority of sorties were flown against the hard-pressed Chosin Reservoir. Three fast-carrier planes were lost during this period—all from the *Leyte*'s Air Group 3.

The first was a Skyraider, damaged by ground fire and force-landed. The pilot was scooped up by the enemy. Both Corsair losses occurred on 4 December, in perhaps the most poignant episode of the war.

Ensign Jesse L. Brown, the Navy's first black aviator, crash-landed northwest of the reservoir, five miles behind the Chinese lines. His VF-32 squadron mates circling above could see that he was caught in the wreck, which began to burn. An incredibly courageous Massachusetts pilot, Lieutenant (jg) Thomas J. Hudner, Jr., decided to land and try to pull Brown to safety. There was no question of a safe landing in the rugged terrain. Hudner bellied in, scrambled from his Corsair, and ran over to Brown's F4U. There he found Brown's leg pinned by the buckled fuselage. Ignoring the sub-zero temperature and nearby enemy troops, Hudner scooped up enough snow to temporarily protect Brown from the flames.

Hudner then tried to pull his friend from the plane, but it was useless. He dashed back to his own F4U, radioed an urgent request for a helicopter with an axe and fire extinguisher, and returned to Brown. A Marine chopper arrived shortly, and with the helo pilot Hudner renewed his efforts to save his squadron mate. But even these supreme efforts were unavailing, as Brown had died. The Navy said that Tom Hudner's "exceptionally valiant action and selfless devotion to a shipmate sustain and enhance the highest traditions of the United States naval service."[2] The only conceivable award was the Congressional, which Hudner received in April 1951. He was the fourth and last Corsair pilot so decorated, and surely few men have ever been as deserving.

By February 1951 the Communist forces were withdrawn to defensive positions above the 38th Parallel. The see-saw war up and down the peninsula was now over, and the battle lines stabilized about where the prewar border had been. The truce talks began in July and would drag on for twenty-four months.

Corsairs with other Navy and U.S. Air Force planes, plus British Commonwealth squadrons, had played a substantial role in retrieving the desperate situation during the first year. True, enemy troops and supplies

President Harry S Truman presents the Medal of Honor to Lieutenant (jg) Thomas J. Hudner, the fourth Corsair pilot to receive the decoration and the only carrier pilot so honored during the Korean war. (U.S. Navy)

had still gotten through, but nobody on the ground wanted to know what would have happened without tactical air. And F4Us had proven the most useful aircraft to date. In the first ten months of hostilities the Voughts flew 82 percent of all Navy and Marine close-support sorties. They possessed two advantages over the jets: longer loiter time, especially at low level, and greater payload. The Douglas Skyraider enjoyed similar or even greater capability, but was far outnumbered by the F4U.

Among the Navy Corsair squadrons active during this time was VF-113 with Air Group 11. The CO, Commander John O'Neill, wrote his mother in Dallas, saying "Would you please get the Chance Vought test pilot on the phone and tell him I said my plane has had three tails, sixty-six patches, and two engines in it, but I'll get it back to the Vought plant if I have to swim and tow it."[3]

Like many of the pilots, some of the Corsairs were involved in their second war. Among the F4U-4s aboard the *Essex* and *Bon Homme Rich-*

ard were some with logbooks which showed missions over Okinawa and Japan. A -4 of VMF-212 which flew 107 missions in 1945 added another 150 in Korea. And by this time the U-Bird was becoming a multigenerational aircraft. A Marine lieutenant was overheard in the officer's club of a Korean airfield: "The Corsair was good enough for my old man, so it's good enough for me."[4]

So the Navy and Marines settled down to two years of dreary, dangerous, dirty work. Proportionately, their job was three times as important to the overall American air effort as in World War II. As one Com-TaskForce-77 admiral said, it was "a day-to-day routine where stamina replaces glamor and persistence is pitted against oriental perseverance."[5]

The last F4U-5, a night fighter, was delivered in October 1951, but a special Corsair was not far behind. Originally the -6, it was redesignated the AU-1. Strictly a ground attack aircraft (A for attack), it incorporated the lessons of Korean combat. Some 110 were delivered from February to October of 1952. They had the -83W engine with only the crankcase blower as a two-speed, single-stage supercharger. High-altitude performance was unnecessary. Twenty-five sheets of armor plate were installed, affording increased protection from ground fire. As a further precaution, the oil coolers which normally faced forward in the wing air inlets—causing the F4U's characteristic whistle—were placed in the wingroots facing inboard. Armament consisted of four M-3 20-mm cannon, plus ten five-inch rockets or six to ten bombs under the wings, and a centerline rack. Nearly all AU-1s went to the Marines.

There was plenty of work for the "Able Uncles." With more or less static positions, the Reds were able to beef up their AA defenses. These were usually small to medium caliber, largely fired under optical control, and were both fixed and mobile. But they could throw up torrents of fire, and what the Chinese lacked in accuracy was often compensated for by volume. Deeper in enemy territory, particularly around bridges and permanent facilities, heavy weapons were encountered, occasionally radar-directed. Veteran pilots may have groused about the tropical climate in the Solomons and Central Pacific, but Korea five to eight years later was no better. The flak was often as bad or worse, and biting cold, repetitious missions, and a drab, dreary landscape made the "police action" a frustrating undertaking. Nor was the situation much improved by some ordnance. Perhaps the majority of bombs used by the Navy and Marines were left over from World War II stocks. Some squadrons reported as high as 30 percent duds among 500-pounders.

But infrequently there were events which broke the routine. The light carrier *Bataan* operated the checkerboard-nosed F4U-4s of VMF-312. The first CO, Major D. P. Frame, was killed in action on 4 April 1951 and was succeeded by Major Frank H. Presley, who was wounded by small-caliber

AA on the 20th. Next day the squadron flew forty-two sorties for over 123 hours, including nine armed recon sorties. Captain Phil DeLong, the eleven-plane ace of VMF-212 in the Pacific, led his division near Chinnampo, on the Yellow Sea southwest of Pyongyang.

The flight split by sections, and at about 0645 First Lieutenant Godbey in the second section reported engine trouble. He bailed out over land, and DeLong contacted the *Bataan*'s CAP to relay the call for a helicopter. Two other recon F4Us diverted to cap Godbey until the chopper arrived.

DeLong and his wingman, First Lieutenant H. Daigh, proceeded north to drop their ordnance. Then Daigh noticed four aircraft closing on DeLong from astern. Almost simultaneously, DeLong called that his plane had been hit, and he split-essed to evade. While DeLong pulled up into the fight, Daigh jumped the first hostile and shot it down. He recognized it as a Yakelov fighter, probably a Yak-9.

In the short combat, DeLong expertly dispatched two more Yaks. Daigh hit the fourth one, but it was last seen heading into the glare of the sun, trailing smoke. It was claimed a probable, and while a downed enemy pilot was reported 20 miles north of the combat position several days later, confirmation was not forthcoming. Caught at a disadvantage, the Marines' training and experience in a superior aircraft had totally reversed the situation.

Lieutenant Godbey was retrieved by South Korean troops and returned to the *Bataan* by helicopter. During three days in late April, VMF-312 flew 128 sorties of all descriptions: strike, recon, CAP, close air support,

Six years and one war later, the F4U-4s of VMF-312 still sport their checkerboard insignia. The bleak surroundings of Kimpo Airfield are obvious. (U.S. Marine Corps)

The constant chore of arming Corsairs for repeated strike sorties is demonstrated, as bombs and rockets are loaded on F4U-4s. (U.S. Marine Corps)

rescap. Only three resulted in aborts—barely 2 percent. The F4U had become one of the most maintainable aircraft in the inventory.

By June 1952 MAG-12 was operating from K-6, the airfield at Pyongtaek on Korea's west coast. The group commander was now Colonel Robert E. Galer, a veteran fighter pilot who had won the Medal of Honor as CO of VMF-224 on Guadalcanal ten years earlier. The group numbered about 100 aircraft; F4Us and ADs.

Galer's deputy was Lieutenant Colonel George C. Axtell, the "Big Ax" of Deathrattler fame from Okinawa. Normally Galer and Axtell flew ADs, but a special strike was assigned that month which required all available Skyraiders. So the CO and exec each took a Corsair.

The target was a North Korean Army headquarters about 125 miles north of K-6. An ambitious plan called for simultaneous low-level and dive-bombing attacks. Surprise was achieved, and just as the strafers pulled off the target, Galer and Axtell led the dive bombers down. The compound was well smothered with bombs and rockets, but one AA gun must have been overlooked.

"He hit me as I made a treetop run up the valley, knocking out the engine," Galer recalled. The group commander was able to pull up over the ridge before he abandoned the crippled Corsair. But he had trouble getting out, and hit the tail when he jumped. The sharp blow broke three ribs and dislocated one shoulder. Galer hit the ground next to his crashed F4U, "and played hide and seek for the next four or five hours."[6]

Axtell took charge and organized a CAP, directing the Corsairs and Skyraiders in strafing runs to keep Communist troops from locating Galer. But at length the fighter-bombers ran low on fuel and returned to base. However, Galer was not abandoned. He remembered, "All afternoon, everyone who was heading south, including Air Force and I believe some South Africans, swung by to expend any available ammunition."[7]

Meanwhile, the injured Marine had found temporary safety in a cave. A Navy helicopter crew operating off an LST in Wonsan Harbor volunteered to attempt a rescue, and entered the area at dusk. Four Corsairs from Axtell's old unit, VMF-323, provided ResCap and led the chopper in.

Galer coached the helicopter to his cave by emergency radio. "They lowered a sling. I got into it, and away we went down the valley with everyone shooting," he said.[8] The Death Rattlers strafed visible gun positions during the daring escape, allowing the helo to clear the first two ridges. Further along, however, it took some small caliber hits and the pilot began to autorotate in an emergency landing. Providentially, the engine picked up and the Navy pilot, Lieutenant McEachren, climbed to safety above a fog bank.

A PBY out of Japan met the whirlybird well after dark and guided it back to Wonsan. Said Galer, "From my very biased point of view, I thought everyone who participated—the Marines, Navy, and Air Force —did a hell of a job."[9]

In the fall of 1952 a new menace threatened carrier-based fighter-bombers. MiG-15 jets made some of their deepest penetrations yet into Korean airspace. Royal Navy pilots off the HMS *Ocean* fought back-to-back combats with the enemy jets on 9 and 10 August. The Hawker Sea Furies claimed one kill, a probable, and three damaged in exchange for one loss and one damaged. The Russian jets were not employed effectively, but the implication was clear: MiGs could bounce the Corsairs at any time.

MAG-12, now under George Axtell, laid plans. Tactics for fighting the faster, better-climbing MiGs were formulated and pilots briefed accordingly. It appeared their new tactics would be put to the test on 7 September during a recon north of Taedong Estuary. "Postcard," the advanced radar station on Cho-do Island, informed a flight of F4Us that hostiles were high overhead. Subsequent reports indicated the enemy jets splitting to either side, obviously intending to bracket the Corsairs. The Marines initiated a defensive weave at 2,500 feet, waiting for the Reds to pounce. But nothing happened. Apparently the MiGs preferred less wary opponents.

Two days later the Marines made contact. Two flights of VMA-312 (redesignated from VMF) off the *Sicily* had expended their ordnance on Communist shipping near Chinnampo, southwest of Pyongyang. Thus, the Corsairs were in their best maneuvering configuration when four MiGs appeared from the northwest, over the Yellow Sea.

The MiGs attacked by sections. As the first two began a run, two Corsairs turned into them, forcing a nose-to-nose confrontation. Rather than trade gunfire, the jets climbed upsun. The Marines dived for the deck and headed west, keeping a close watch on their assailants. The MiGs separated, going for both flanks as they had on the 7th. But by the time the F4Us were over Cho-do they had descended through 1,000 feet and the jets turned north.

Next day, 10 September, VMA-312 again tangled with MiGs near Chinnampo. And this time the Communists were more aggressive. Captain Jesse G. Folmar and First Lieutenant Willie L. Daniels launched at 1610 on a two-plane strike against some 300 North Korean troops reported on the south shore of the Taedong River. A TarCap flight was also dispatched, with all Corsairs guarding the same radio frequency in case of trouble.

Coasting in at 10,000 feet, Folmar test-fired his four 20-millimeters and Daniels his six .50 calibers. They located the target area and broke away to explore the estuary before attacking. Three miles east of U.S.-occupied Sock-to Island, Folmar began a turn in his weave. Then he saw two MiG-15s in loose echelon, heading for the Corsairs. In the next few seconds several things happened. Folmar called, "Tally ho, bandits!"[10] He went to combat power, jettisoned his ordnance and belly tank, and hollered over the guard channel that he was engaged. At the same time he turned towards the threat, telling Daniels to stay close.

Four hundred yards to port, Daniels shot a look over his right shoulder. A MiG was diving in astern of Folmar. Daniels broke into it and traded gunfire in a brief head-on pass. The MiG turned left and disengaged, allowing Daniels to reverse his turn and complete the weave off Folmar's starboard beam. Daniels glanced at his airspeed indicator and saw he had only 140 knots on the dial.

While Daniels swapped gunfire with his MiG, Folmar saw two more. They closed rapidly from eight o'clock, and Folmar desperately turned left, trying to bring his guns to bear before the bandits opened fire. But the deflection angle was too great, the closing speed too fast. Tracers passed ahead of the -4B; the Reds had over-deflected.

Apparently one MiG passed between Folmar and Daniels. Folmar rolled into a right-hand bank and found the jet in a climbing left turn. The MiG was temporarily vulnerable. "I pulled up, got him in my gunsight, gave him about twenty mils lead, and held a five-second burst," Folmar reported. "I could tell I had him boresighted by the blinking flashes along the left side of the fuselage."[11]

The MiG emitted a gray stream of smoke which turned black in seconds. As it pitched down slightly and decelerated, the pilot ejected in a tumbling ball of smoke. When the parachute opened, Folmar and Daniels passed close enough to see the MiG driver's G-suit was afire. The flaming jet went vertically into the water from 7,000 feet.

As the two Corsairs resumed their weave, four more MiGs approached in loose column. Three or four remained overhead, making ineffective high side passes, but others pressed the attack. A MiG came down on Folmar from six o'clock high. "There's one on your tail," screamed Daniels,[12] who weaved towards the jet and fired a quick burst. The bandit passed ahead of the F4Us, out of range.

The odds were now seven against two. Folmar decided that was all the advantage he wanted to concede, and called, "Break hard left, down." The two Marines dived for the water at about 35 degrees, Daniels weaving to the right, when another MiG attacked. "There's another one on your tail," Daniels told his leader, but Folmar already knew.[13]

The 33-year-old captain had just begun accelerating in his dive when he saw tracers passing to his left. He felt a severe explosion in the port wing, which shuddered violently. The wing had taken 37-mm hits which gutted it to the inboard gun, knocking off the aileron and four feet of the tip. Folmar had trouble holding the Corsair level; it wanted to roll to port. Yet another MiG began a pass, but Daniels turned towards it and the jet shied away.

Folmar had applied full right stick but the F4U was becoming uncontrollable. He knew he'd never land it in this condition. He transmitted the distress signal, gave his position, and prepared to jump. Between 2,500 and 3,000 feet he rolled out the right side of the cockpit, fell clear, and pulled his ripcord. "I heard an earsplitting cracking sound and I saw another MiG fly by me at very close range, his guns blazing at the tight-spinning Corsair," Folmar recalled.[14] American antiaircraft guns on nearby Sock-to Island opened fire and the seven MiGs withdrew to the northeast. Folmar dropped into the water only a quarter-mile offshore.

Daniels circled, noting a landing craft and amphibian speeding towards his leader, and headed for the ship. En route, Daniels called the

MiG killer. Captain Jesse Folmar of VMF-312 shot down a MiG-15 jet fighter over the west coast of Korea on 10 September 1952. Folmar's Corsair was badly damaged in the combat, and he bailed out but was rescued and returned to duty. (U.S. Marine Corps)

rescue plane and learned Folmar was aboard, in good shape except for an injured arm. The combat had lasted less than eight minutes, and Folmar was rescued in a similar time.

After losing one of their valuable jets to Corsairs, the Communists were not so aggressive for the next few weeks. "Bandit tracks" were seen high over Pyongyang, but not until 29 September did they become belligerent again. A 312 division was heading west out of Chinnampo when four MiGs surprised the Corsairs by attacking out of the sun. They were spotted just as they opened fire, and the Marines broke hard right to evade the attack. Before the Reds completed their pass, the F4Us dived behind the cover of a mountain range. They waited until the jets withdrew to the north. After that, MiG attacks became increasingly rare.

Jesse Folmar and Willie Daniels's one-sided combat demonstrated the elements of success in fighting jets. A sharp lookout, teamwork, flying skill, and radio discipline defeated the tremendous advantage held by

An F4U-5N of Composite Squadron Three aboard the USS *Princeton*, probably in 1953. (U.S. Navy)

the MiGs. Folmar's victim was the last enemy jet to fall to a piston-engined aircraft during the war.

There were, however, a few more air combats. In June 1953 the U.S. Fifth Air Force requested a detachment of Corsair night fighters "on loan" to combat the Communist nocturnal hecklers. These were obsolescent prop planes which harried UN troops, flying low, dropping occasional bombs, and depriving many personnel of sleep. They were much too agile for night interception by jets such as the Marine F3D or Air Force F-94.

Two pilots of VC-3 from the *Princeton*'s Air Group 15 flew to Kimpo on 25 June for briefing and orientation. The F4U-5Ns would be working with Air Force controllers, and it was necessary to establish operating procedures. The Corsairs were then deployed to K-6 at Pyongtaek, south of Seoul. Their patrol area was established along the UN side of the front lines.

The detachment leader was a blonde Louisiana pilot, Lieutenant Guy P. Bordelon, who made the only contacts. In three missions over a three-week period, from 29 June to 16 July, he claimed and was credited with five victories. The record is somewhat unclear. They have variously been reported as four Yak-18s and a Yak-11, or two Yak-18s and three Lagg-9s or -11s. Bordelon and his partner, Lieutenant (jg) Ralph Hopson, returned to the *Princeton* and left their planes at K-6. Bordelon's Corsair, named "Annie-Mo" for his wife, was written off by an Air Force pilot shortly thereafter. Impressed with the Navy's success, the Air Force gave some thought to adopting the F4U as a night intruder since it had no single-engine prop-driven night fighters of its own. By then, however, it didn't really matter. The uneasy armistice went into effect on 27 July.

In all, Navy and Marine Corps Corsairs were credited with ten aerial victories in Korea. Another veteran F4U pilot, Major John Bolt of Boyington's old flock, matched his South Pacific total in Korea with six MiG-15s while flying F-86s as an exchange pilot with the 51st Fighter Wing.

At least seven Marine and twenty-eight Navy squadrons flew Corsairs in Korea, but by the end of 1953 only three Marine and seven Navy units retained them. From then on, the U-Bird was steadily replaced. A year after the Korean unpleasantries, only VC-3 and VC-4 still had F4Us, and the latter was the final employer of the old warhorse, in December 1955.

Corsairs were active in the Navy and Marine air reserve program after Korea, but the last of these were stricken from the rolls in mid-1957. Excluding service in reserve squadrons, the F4U's operational life had lasted over thirteen years. At the time, it was a record for longevity in naval aviation matched only by the Martin PBM flying boat.

It was truly the end of an era.

chapter 9

Other wars

It is a homicidal civilization.

Hilaire Belloc

The Corsair's third war began shortly after the first and outlasted the second. And like both previous conflicts, it involved an oriental enemy.

In July 1952 the F4U-7 made its first flight. Like the late-model -4, it had the R-2800-43W engine, but the airframe was nearly identical to the AU-1. In many ways the -7 was the most specialized Corsair of all, for it was built specifically for a foreign customer with a specific job in mind. The customer was the French Navy. The job was Indochina.

France had been fighting insurgents and Communist rebels in its Asian protectorate since 1946. Among the aircraft employed in this prolonged struggle were British Seafires and a variety of American aircraft. The Aeronautique Navale, using three former U.S. Navy carriers to begin with, flew SBDs, F6Fs, and SB2Cs. Likewise, the French Air Force had about 100 F8F Bearcats. Except for the Bearcats, most of these planes were second-line equipment—high-time castoffs. The Aero-Navale wanted something newer.

French naval aviators transitioned to F4U-7s at NAS Oceana, Virginia, in October 1952. Three months later the last of nearly 100 new Corsairs had been delivered. The French were absolutely delighted with their new Voughts.

One of the early squadron commanders, now Rear Admiral Pierre Menettrier, explains some of the reasons. "[The F4U-7] was the first brand-new, straight-out-of-the-factory aircraft to be delivered to the French Navy since 1945, as opposed to the Seafire Mark III straight from the junkyard on the basis of one for flight, two for spares. The veteran F6F-5s had logged 2,000 hours at delivery. Second, the F4U-7 came in with a complete and well-computed set of spares, tools, and special support equipment providing for four squadrons, two naval air stations, and two carriers. Thirdly, the prestige and terrific good looks of the long-nosed, gull-winged Corsair had a tremendous appeal to the young pilots flying Hellcats for the preceding years. And last but not least, the speed, cockpit sophistication, new technology, and considerable increase in military capabilities were all reasons for enthusiastic welcome."[1]

In comparing the Corsair to the Seafire and Hellcat, the French saw advantages for each. The F6F was considered easier to land aboard ship, and the Seafires were "pure jewels" in the air. However, the British fighter's landing characteristics were notorious. Menettrier recalled, "The Seafire IIIs or XVs which were in use in the French Navy had catapult hooks and tail hook, but the landing gear struts seemed unchanged from the land version. This gave them a superb capability to play pogo-stick in the first contact with the flight deck, to bounce gracefully direct into the barrier, if not over it."[2]

Therefore, the F4U's speed, payload, and advanced technology (such as power-folding wings) made it readily welcomed into the French Navy.

These Flotille 14F AU-1s are loaded with 500-pound bombs and napalm for strike sorties against Communist forces in Indochina. (Icare)

And little time was wasted putting the new fighter-bombers to use. One squadron, 14 Flotille, was stationed at Karouba, Tunisia, in the spring of 1954. On short notice it was moved, minus aircraft, to Tourane, Indochina—later famous and notorious as Da Nang. No French carriers were available, as two were already in Southeast Asian waters and the third was in overhaul. The squadron personnel were flown by U.S. Air Force transports while the light carrier *Saipan* (CVL-48) delivered 25 AU-1s. These aircraft were from Marine Air Group 12 in Japan, and were flown into Tourane by Marine pilots on 26 April. A week later 14F was operational at the French Air Force field of Bach Mai, near Hanoi.

Initial missions were flown in support of the besieged French paratroopers at Dien Bien Phu. The mountainous outpost had been occupied since late November, but the Viet Minh had isolated the garrison, requiring constant reinforcement and supply by air. The ridges overlooking Dien Bien Phu were loaded with artillery and AA guns. The Corsairs arrived too late to help very much, as the garrison surrendered on 7 May. It was a major military coup for the Communists, but it was not militarily decisive. Like the Tet offensive against the Americans fourteen years later—which was actually a military defeat for the enemy—Dien Bien Phu was important for its political consequences. Less than three months later the armistice was signed, partitioning the nation into northern and southern camps.

In about eleven weeks of operations, 14F had flown 1,422 sorties, dropped 1,567 tons of bombs, and expended 850 rockets and 130,000 rounds of 20-millimeter. Of the twenty-five AU-1s and twenty-five pilots, six aircraft and two aviators were lost. Following the cease-fire on 21 July

179

Safety first. An Aeronavale Corsair starts up while a crewman stands by with a fire extinguisher. (Icare)

1954, the Corsairs were returned to the U.S. Navy in the Philippines. The F4U-7s left behind in Tunisia were ferried to 14F by the light carrier *Bois de Belleau,* but the entire squadron was back in Tunisia twelve months later.

Three other Corsair squadrons were engaged in North African operations, opposing Algerian guerrillas. It was only the second time in its thirteen-year combat career that the F4U had been used against non-Asians. Squadrons 12F, 15F, and 17F flew from Oran, Telergma, Bizerte, and off the British-built *Arromanches* during 1955–56, with some loss. Several of the AU-1s that had been returned to the U.S. Navy were overhauled and sold to the French during the Algerian fighting.

Nor was Algeria the last combat use of French Corsairs. In October 1956 the smouldering Egyptian-Israeli dispute over border lands reached the flash point. Israel initiated a preemptive invasion of the Sinai Peninsula to forestall an Egyptian thrust. Britain and France called upon both nations to cease fire, allowing continued international access to the strategic Suez Canal. Since the Israelis had already captured considerable territory, they agreed. The Egyptians, under President Nasser, refused. The fighting continued.

Britain and France, with their own national interests in keeping the Suez open, embarked on a joint military venture against Egypt. This involved land-based air power from Cyprus and Malta, plus three Royal Navy carriers and two French CVLs: the *Arromanches* and *LaFayette* (nee USS *Langley*). Between them, the French ships embarked a total of 36 F4U-7s of 14F and 15F.

Operation Musketeer, as the Anglo-French project was called, remains a unique incident in military history. It was the only time British and French carriers worked together and was not without its peculiar aspects. For instance, the French knew that Israel would launch an attack into Egypt, but the British did not. And as if to demonstrate that European politicians can be as obtuse as any other, the British government restricted its aviators to 250-pound bombs, in hopes of "not overly antagonizing" the Egyptians.[3] Whether one is killed by a half-ton bomb or one weighing a quarter as much seems irrelevant, to say the least. Yet few nations seems to lack diplomats and bureaucrats gifted with such insight.

At any rate, carrier air operations began on 1 November. Though the Egyptians possessed MiG-15s and Il-28 jets, equal or superior to the Allied forces, none were used effectively. Most were destroyed or disabled on the ground by noon of the second day. Even antiaircraft fire was sporadic and ineffective. Allied air supremacy was never in doubt. The Corsairs, sporting black and yellow recognition stripes, ranged back and forth along the coast, seeking targets of opportunity. There were slim pickings, but the F4Us did sink a torpedo boat.

No French aircraft were lost during the first two days, and British carrier squadrons had light casualties. The pilot of a flak-damaged Sea Hawk crashed on landing, and another jet was damaged. The entire operation ended on the 7th when the British and French heeded a United Nations cease-fire demand. They had put paratroopers and amphibious troops ashore, but their late arrival and a lack of willingness to exploit the situation impaired Musketeer's usefulness. With more decisive political leadership, the British might have used their long-time influence in Egypt to guarantee international access to one of the world's most important waterways.

Not all the Corsairs survived the Suez operation. One was wrecked in an operational accident, and the commanding officer of 14F was killed by AA fire over Cairo. But considering that the carrier pilots flew as many as four sorties daily, the loss rate was exceptionally low.

The Suez incident was the Corsair's last major combat operation. A full 25 percent of the carrier strike aircraft had been F4U-7s. The U-Birds remained in French service for another eight years, providing an excellent means of transition to more modern aircraft. The -7 and AU-1, with their high-speed performance and modern equipment, helped simplify the

Yellow and black striped F4U-7s of Flotille 15F during the Anglo-French Suez crisis of 1956. (Icare)

French Navy's step into the jet age. Even then, the Aero-Navale looked to Dallas, opting for the F-8E Crusader. A satisfied customer usually returns to do business again.

With French retirement of the Corsair, Latin America became the last stronghold of the long-lived Vought. The Argentine Navy flew F4U-5s for a while, but the theater for the final performance was north of the equator.

One of the quirks of the Corsair's career is that of the six nations that flew the type in combat during four wars and several "incidents," two of those air forces used Corsairs against each other. But it is only slightly less peculiar than the war in which they were engaged.

The U.S. military assistance program of the 1950s and 1960s covered most Central American countries. But not all these Latin neighbors were on friendly terms. In one incident, two banana republics staged cross-border raids one night, robbing each others' supply depots. Next morning the respective American military attachés were on the phone, pondering how to remedy the statistical impossibility of mismatched supply lists.

Finally, in a moment of inspired paper-shuffling, they decided to exchange inventory sheets, and the records tallied once more.

Vought and Goodyear-built Corsairs went to Honduras and El Salvador during this period. In the former case, 18 F4Us were supplied from 1956 to 1961. The largest batch was ten F4U-5s ferried 2,500 miles from Litchfield Park, Arizona, to Tegucigalpa, Honduras, during 1956. Four -4s were delivered both in 1960 and 1961. About the same time, El Salvador received some FG-1s.

Thus did the "Tipo Corsario" arrive in Central America.

Unfortunately, Honduras and El Salvador did not enjoy amicable relations. A series of political and cultural differences culminated in the "Soccer War" of 1969. Newspaper accounts of the cause and execution of this conflict were generally as inaccurate as they were simplified. Though it may have made good reading, the confrontation did not result solely from a flare-up of Latin tempers during a soccer match. Nor did the aerial phase of the war involve any Republic P-47s. It involved North American P-51s on a small scale limited to the Salvadorian side. Nearly all the air combat—what little there was—pitted Corsair against Corsair.

On 11 July 1969 the Honduras Air Force was informed of possible impending hostilities. Therefore, early on the 12th, four F4U-4s were detached to San Pedro Sula on the north coast while eight F4U-5s and one -4 were kept at Tegucigalpa. No combat occurred during the next two days.

The Argentine Navy flew F4U-5s from the *Independencia* (formerly HMS *Warrior*) from 1958 to 1965. (U.S. Navy)

About 1700 on the 14th, the Tegucigalpa pilots were ordered to return home long enough to pack such clothes and supplies as they might need for the duration. They were all home packing their bags—except for the lone T-28 duty pilot—when bombs began falling on the capital's airport. An El Salvador C-47 transport with a rectangular hole cut in the fuselage floor was found to be the "bomber." The Honduran pilots rushed to the base and several took off about 1815, looking for the now-departed intruder. But this was the first time they had flown Corsairs at night, and with no cockpit lights installed there was little they could do. Not surprisingly, no further enemy aircraft were seen, and the F4Us returned to base, guided by searchlights from the field.

Ground support and strike sorties were flown during the next four days. Early on the 15th, eight Tegucigalpa Corsairs were away flying their scheduled missions when two El Salvador Mustangs and an FG-1 attacked the airport, dropping 100-pound bombs. The only ready defense was Lieutenant Roberto Mendoza, aloft in a T-28A on warning duty. Lieutenant Colonel Jose Serra took off in the remaining F4U-5 but could do no good because of inoperable guns. Mendoza managed one diving pass at the hostile Corsair, hitting it with his .30-caliber guns. The FG-1 made off at high speed, streaming visible smoke, but escaped.

Meanwhile, the four north coast F4U-4s had taken off about 0445 to strike the coffee port of Acajutla. Employing bombs and rockets, they burned an oil refinery but missed an electric plant. One plane, flown by Captain Walter Lopez, took a hit and headed west to land in Guatemala, where he and the aircraft remained until the cease-fire. But the Guatemalans repaired the Corsair and returned it to Honduras after the shooting stopped. The grateful Hondurans awarded Navy wings to the Guatemalan P-51 pilot who delivered the F4U!

Though the arena of conflict was a small one—only 450 statute miles at its widest point—aerial confrontations were few. One C-47 was the only El Sal aircraft seen in the northern zone. Lieutenant Marco Tulio Rivera shot it up in his Corsair, but did no serious damage. On another occasion, however, two San Pedro Sula F4U-4s destroyed nearly forty buses delivering Salvadorian troops to the front.

Early on the 17th, Captain Fernando Soto took off from Tegucigalpa with two other F4U-5s flown by Captains Edgardo Acosta and Francisco Zepeda. "Sotillo" Soto was one of the more experienced Honduras fighter pilots, with 400 hours in Corsairs since 1960. He led his wingman down on ground targets near the border for a strafing attack, but Zepeda's guns jammed. Soto ordered Zepeda to pull up and wait for rendezvous.

Then, recalled Soto, "All of a sudden Zepeda called us to say he has two P-51s on his back."[4] Soto and Acosta abandoned their strafing and raced to Zepeda's assistance.

"Number 609," the F4U-5 flown by Captain Soto of the Honduras Air Force in the 1969 war with El Salvador. (Bassett)

"I got there pretty quick," Soto said. When in range he fired and the El Sal Mustangs broke, one right and one left. Soto was confident the Corsair could defeat the P-51 below 10,000 feet, and pursued the engagement. He followed the Mustang to starboard and turned inside, "real, real easy."[5] On the inside of the 51's turn, Soto fired three bursts from his four 20-millimeters and knocked off the left wing. The Mustang crashed on the Honduras side of the border before the pilot could bail out. When Soto looked around for the other P-51, it was gone.

Soto's fourth mission of the day, late in the afternoon, was to San Miguel in El Salvador. He and Acosta were flying alone when they saw two Corsairs approaching from the north. Figuring they were FG-1s, the Hondurans jettisoned their bombs and climbed rapidly. By the time they reached 13,000 feet they were directly above the two hostiles, which were flying steadily 2,000 feet below.

Still unseen, Soto and Acosta split-essed to attack, coming in behind and above. Soto hit the first FG-1, which caught fire, and the pilot bailed out. Soto's speed from the dive carried him beyond the second Salvadorian, but Soto was confident Acosta would take him out. Soto was quickly disillusioned when he looked back, for the enemy Corsair was in range and gunning. Radio problems had plagued the Hondurans, and Soto hadn't heard Acosta call out two more bandits which hadn't been seen.

Sotillo wracked his Corsair through tight turns, dives, and zoom-climbs in a downhill battle, trying to shake the blue-and-white cockaded Corsair

Captain Fernando Soto of Honduras with his F4U-5, showing two El Salvador Corsairs and a P-51 shot down in the "Soccer War." (Bassett)

behind him. Finally he rolled over to begin a split-ess but turned out to one side. The Salvadorian continued down to complete the maneuver, leaving Soto on top. He fired several bursts, then hit the port wing and shot off the aileron. As he closed the range, he fired again and the enemy fighter exploded. Soto was sure the FG-1 pilot had neglected to depressurize his fuel system.

As he turned back towards Acosta, Soto passed a parachute at 2,000 feet. It was the first FG pilot, headed towards a safe landing. The dogfight had lasted only long enough for the chute to descend about 9,000 feet, but to Soto "it was like a century."[6]

More ground support sorties were flown on the 18th but no more air combat developed. When hostilities ceased on 19 July, Fernando Soto had done all the shooting of consequence in either air force. Apparently neither side lost any planes to AA fire, and Soto's three kills on the 17th were the only ones recorded.

After 1969 the Honduras Corsairs were flown only thirty-five to forty hours annually. They were maintained in good condition but by 1978 only nine were left intact. And though Honduras has acquired jets, it will probably keep the F4Us until the newer equipment is fully assimilated. Meanwhile, the Corsairs remain a popular attraction for American military assistance pilots. Colonel James Bassett, who logged over 100 F-105 missions in Vietnam, considered his Honduras assignment the best of his career. "This is a fighter pilot's paradise," he wrote a friend in the States. "It's practically illegal not to do a loop to a landing."[7] At one time Bassett was the only jet-qualified pilot in the country, and was asked to demonstrate Honduras's silver and blue F-86. He willingly complied, but confessed that he had more fun flying the Corsairs.

Probably no other combat aircraft has ever remained in operational service as long as the Corsair. The Honduras F4Us were still active thirty-eight years after the prototype's first flight. The seven nations which flew the bent-wing birds in that period had employed them in virtually every mission, climate, and type of conflict possible for a fighter-bomber.

In 1979 Rear Admiral Menettrier, the French Naval Attaché to Washington, spoke for everyone who was ever privileged to strap into an F4U when he said, "I do not know of any former Corsair pilot who does not keep a tender and loving memory of this beautiful aircraft."[8]

Appendices

Appendix A. Surviving Corsairs

More Corsairs have survived than the combined number of F6Fs, FMs, SBDs, and SB2Cs. Only the TBF-TBM series outnumbers Vought and Goodyear Corsairs among remaining carrier aircraft of the World War II era. The 1974 edition of *Veteran and Vintage Aircraft*—the "what's where" of historic airplanes—lists 62 F4Us, FGs, F2Gs, and AUs. Such compilations can seldom be complete or totally accurate, but this volume is probably the best source of its kind.

An itemized listing would be difficult to compile, and space considerations are prohibitive. But some general observations are possible. In 1978, 15 Corsairs were licensed as airworthy in the United States including seven F4U-4s. To these should be added several others which are basically airworthy but not flown. The Marine Corps Museum at Quantico, Virginia, is under the capable direction of retired Colonel Tom D'Andrea.

An FG-1D arrives at Bridgeport, Connecticut, by way of a U.S. Army CH-54A Flying Crane. The Corsair, donated by the El Salvador Air Force in 1969, was restored as a permanent memorial at the airport to honor those who built the Corsair in nearby Stratford. (Sikorsky Aircraft)

Bob Guilford's Corsair, variously identified as an F4U-7 or an AU-1, known in racing circles as "Blue Max." Everett, Washington, 1972. (F.A. Johnsen)

The F4U-7 restored to French Navy markings and flown by Gary Harris. (F.A. Johnsen)

The museum's enlightened attitude is worth emulation. No aircraft is flown unless there are at least two of any one variant (i.e., two F4U-4s or two F4U-5s) which are airworthy.

In private hands, Corsairs are best known to the public from the recent television series *Black Sheep Squadron*. Allegedly based upon Greg Boyington's autobiography, the plots ranged from barely plausible to patently ridiculous. Former VMF-214 personnel publicly disclaimed the NBC production. But partially offsetting the gross inaccuracies and absence of research were as many as seven Corsairs: FG-1Ds with F4U-4s and a -7. The controversial series was canceled in its second season, but much of the aerial photography was excellent. Among aviation circles, there was never any doubt as to who (or what) were the genuine stars.

191

John Schafhausen and F4U-7 Corsair at Skagit Regional Airport (Bayview) Washington, May 14, 1977. (Frederick A. Johnsen)

The claim has been made that several F4U-7s remain in France, but apparently none do. The French naval attaché to Washington said in 1979, "Unfortunately, none of these old warriors which had flown over Korea, Indo-China, and Algeria in war missions was saved for museums. They were scrapped in Cuers, France, around 1964." Several -7s and one or two AU-1s are still flying in the United States, but only one Corsair remains in Europe. The Fleet Air Arm Museum at Yeovilton, Somerset, maintains a Corsair Mark IV (FG-1D). At least one FG-1D is flown by the Canadian Warplane Heritage.

Another FG-1D has been restored in recent years at the New Zealand Museum of Transportation and Technology in Auckland. It is the only remaining Corsair in the country, as another was exported to the United States in 1971, unfortunately to be modified as a racer. Not surprisingly, the Corsair has been widely employed in air racing. To purists and historians, the modifications required to make an aircraft competitive usually render it virtually useless from an historical viewpoint. Nevertheless, by far the greatest successes attained by racing Corsairs were in the postwar Thompson Trophy events, when highly modified F2Gs captured two championships.

No final plans had been made for the nine remaining Honduras F4U-4s and -5s by 1978. The -5 flown by Fernando Soto in the "soccer war" of 1969 will be retained as a museum aircraft or as a monument. Most likely the others will eventually be sold in a block or traded for an equal number of more useful aircraft. In any event, the Hondurans are aware of the value of their Corsairs, and no bargains are likely to be had.

The only other Corsair known outside the United States is an F4U-5 at Rio Parana Delta, Argentina.

Corsairs will continue to be flown for many years, almost exclusively by civilian owners. But the Navy and Marine Corps, along with such institutions as the National Air and Space Museum, can ensure that the bent-wing birds will always be with us.

192

Appendix B. Corsair variants

Interesting variations of the Corsair include this F4U-4XB having a wing-tip tank installation. (Ling-Temco-Vought)

Unusual, indeed, is this XF4U-4 with an Aero Products counter-rotating propeller installation for a propeller vibration survey. (Ling-Temco-Vought)

Likely origin of World War II squadron readyroom tales concerning the existence of a "straight-wing Corsair" was this Vought Sikorsky Model VS-326, an
XTBU modified to accommodate a pressure tank. It was also used as a test bed
for the 3,000-hp R-4360 Wasp Major engine which later powered the F2G. The
family resemblance to the F4U in the background is distinctly evident. (Ling-
Temco-Vought)

The Goodyear XF2G-1 was intended as a low-level interceptor but was canceled
with the end of the war. (U.S. Navy)

A two-seat F4U-1 which was built in 1946 by Vought in an effort to generate
more orders for the plane. The two-seater was designed to be a trainer.

Possibly unique among all WWII aircraft was Corsair 122 of Marine Squadron VMF-111, the only plane known to receive an official citation for its individual contribution. Number 122 logged over 400 flight hours in completing 100 missions in the Marshall Islands area. (Arthur Schoeni)

Damnant quod non intelligunt (They condemn what they do not understand.) (R.G. Smith)

Appendix C. Specifications

	F4U-1	F4U-4
Wing area	314 sq. ft.	314 sq. ft.
Wingspan	41 ft.	41 ft.
Span folded	17 ft.	17ft.
Length	33 ft. 4 in.	33 ft. 8 in.
Height	16 ft. 1 in.	14 ft. 9 in.
Empty weight	8,982 pounds	9,205 pounds
Gross weight	14,000 pounds	14,670 pounds
Engine	P-W R-2800-8	P-W R-2800-18W
Engine rating	2,000 h.p.	2,100 h.p.
Top speed	417 mph @ 19,900 ft. (360 kts.)	446 mph @ 26,200 ft. (385 kts.)
Cruise speed	182 mph (159 kts.)	215 mph (187 kts.)
Climb rate	2,890 ft. per min.	3,870 ft. per min.
Service ceiling	36,900 ft.	41,500 ft.
Range	1,015 statute miles	1,005 statute miles
Standard armament	Six .50-cal. machine guns	Six .50-cal. machine guns
Maximum ordnance		Eight 5-inch rockets under wings. Up to 4,000 pounds on centerline and pylon racks.

F4U-5N	AU-1
314 sq. ft.	314 sq. ft.
41 ft.	41 ft.
17 ft.	17 ft.
33 ft. 6 in.	34 ft. 1 in.
14 ft. 9 in.	14 ft. 10 in.
9,683 pounds	9,835 pounds
14,106 pounds	19,398 pounds
P-W R-2800-32W	P-W R-2800-83W
2,300 h.p.	2,300 h.p.
469 mph @ 26,800 ft. (408 kts.)	238 mph @ 9,500 ft. (207 kts.)
227 mph (197 kts.)	184 mph (160 kts.)
3,780 ft. per min.	920 ft. per min.
41,400 ft.	19,500 ft.
1,120 statute miles	484 statute miles
Four 20-mm cannon	Four 20-mm cannon
Ten 5-inch rockets under wings, and up to 5,000 pounds of ordnance on centerline and pylon racks.	Ten 5-inch rockets or up to 3,000 pounds under wings, plus centerline ordnance or fuel.

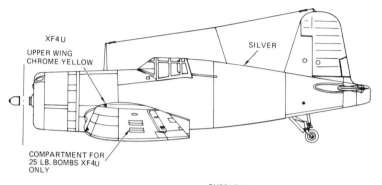

XF4U

UPPER WING
CHROME YELLOW

SILVER

COMPARTMENT FOR
25 LB. BOMBS XF4U
ONLY

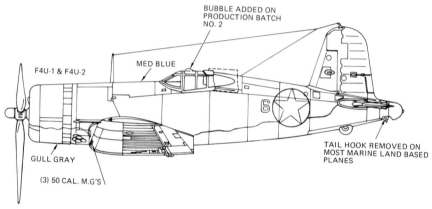

BUBBLE ADDED ON
PRODUCTION BATCH
NO. 2

F4U-1 & F4U-2

MED BLUE

GULL GRAY

(3) 50 CAL. M.G'S

TAIL HOOK REMOVED ON
MOST MARINE LAND BASED
PLANES

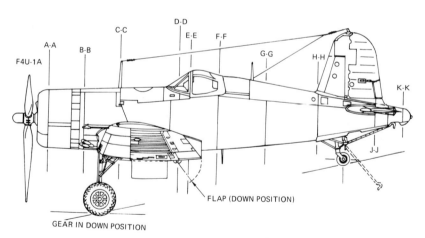

A-A

B-B

C-C

D-D

E-E

F-F

G-G

H-H

K-K

F4U-1A

J-J

FLAP (DOWN POSITION)

GEAR IN DOWN POSITION

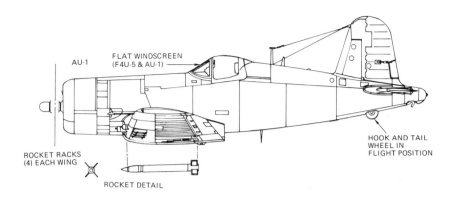

AU-1

FLAT WINDSCREEN
(F4U-5 & AU-1)

ROCKET RACKS
(4) EACH WING

ROCKET DETAIL

HOOK AND TAIL
WHEEL IN
FLIGHT POSITION

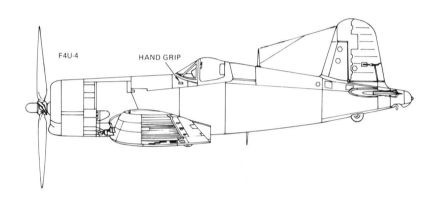

F4U-4

HAND GRIP

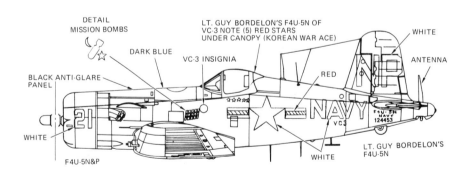

DETAIL
MISSION BOMBS

DARK BLUE

VC-3 INSIGNIA

LT. GUY BORDELON'S F4U-5N OF
VC-3 NOTE (5) RED STARS
UNDER CANOPY (KOREAN WAR ACE)

WHITE

ANTENNA

BLACK ANTI-GLARE
PANEL

RED

WHITE

F4U-5N&P

WHITE

NAVY

F4U 5N
NAVY
124453

LT. GUY BORDELON'S
F4U-5N

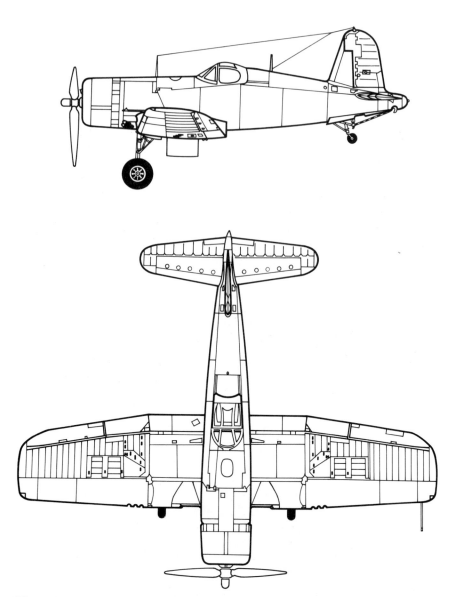

The "clipped wing" Corsair of the Royal Navy, modified so that it could be accommodated in the lower overhead of British carrier hangar decks.

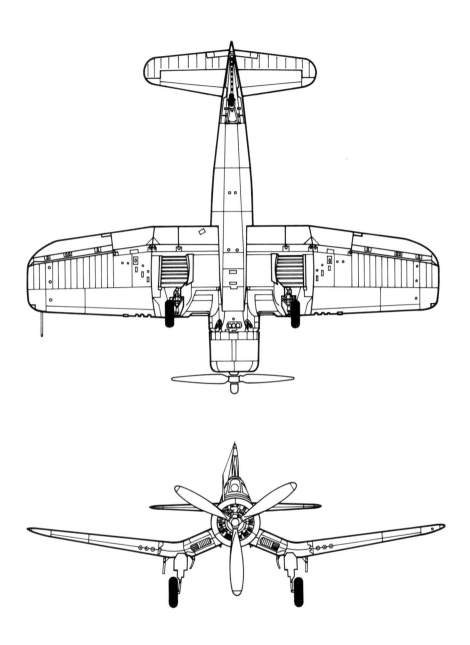

World War II Monthly acceptances of Corsairs

Note: Navy acceptances will approximate, but not duplicate, manufacturers' monthly aircraft production.

Month/year	Vought	Goodyear	Brewster	Totals
July 1942	2			2
August	9			9
September	13			13
October	31			31
November	55			55
December	68			68
	178			178
January 1943	39			39
February	75			75
March	77			77
April	113	2		115
May	132	7		139
June	156	16	2	174
July	171	22	3	196
August	176	30	0	206
September	186	77	8	271
October	195	63	27	285
November	230	78	28	336
December	235	82	68	385
	1785	377	136	2298
January 1944	224	150	61	435
February	225	147	78	450
March	256	222	100	578
April	230	220	119	569
May	254	220	122	596
June	169	160	102	431
July	300	170	17	487
August	220	168	0	388
September	210	180	0	390
October	217	182	0	399
November	197	145	0	342
December	163	144	0	307
	2665	2108	599	5372

World War II Monthly acceptances of Corsairs (Continued)

Month/year	Vought	Goodyear	Brewster	Totals
January 1945	118	103		221
February	152	178		330
March	268	262		530
April	279	205		484
May	302	195		497
June	300	179		479
July	303	180		483
August	210	151		361
(As of V-J Day)	(1932)	(1453)		(3385)
September	41	68		109
October	31	0		31
November	21	0		21
December	21	0		21
	2046	1521		3567

The Goodyear total does not include eight F2Gs delivered in 1945.

Appendix D. The top Corsair aces

Name and rank	Squadrons	Aerial victories	Comments
First Lieutenant Robert M. Hanson	VMF-214, 215	25	2 with 214. KIA February 1944
Major Gregory Boyington	VMF-214	22	POW January 1944
Captain Kenneth A. Walsh	VMF-124, 222	21	1 with 222
Captain Donald N. Aldrich	VMF-215	20	KIFA May 1947
Captain Wilbur J. Thomas	VMF-213	18.50	KIFA January 1947
Lieutenant Ira C. Kepford	VF-17	16	
Captain Harold L. Spears	VMF-215	15	KIFA December 1944
Captain Edward O. Shaw	VMF-213	14.50	KIFA July 1944
Captain Philip C. DeLong	VMF-212, 312	13.16	2 with 312 in Korea
Major Archie G. Donahue	VMF 112, 451	12	
Major James N. Cupp	VMF-213	12	
Lieutenant Commander Roger R. Hedrick	VF-17, VF-84	12	3 with VF-84
Captain Harold E. Segal	VMF-221, 211	12	2 with 211
Lieutenant Commander John T. Blackburn	VF-17	11	
Lieutenant Commander T. Hamil Reidy	VBF-83	10	
Lieutenant (jg) John M. Smith	VF-17, VF-84	10	7 with VF-84
Major Donald H. Stapp	VMF-222	10	

Only victories obtained while flying F4Us are included. Of the eleven Marine and five Navy pilots who scored ten or more victories in Corsairs, 81 percent of the kills were made in the Solomons.
KIA: Killed In Action
KIFA: Killed In Flying Accident
POW: Prisoner Of War

Notes

Chapter one

1. Vought *Profile*. 20 May 1976.
2. Correspondence with Boone T. Guyton. November 1978.
3. Correspondence with Kenneth A. Walsh. 4 November 1977.
4. Correspondence with Robert G. Dose. December 1978.
5. Interview with M. W. Davenport. 1 November 1978.
6. Wolfgang Langewiesche, "What It Takes to Fly an F4U," *Flying*, June 1977.
7. Guyton correspondence, November 1978.
8. Correspondence with William N. Leonard, 31 October 1978.
9. Correspondence with Bernard M. Strean, 10 June 1978.
10. Conversation with Rex T. Barber, 1977.
11. William Askins, "The Ultimate Fighter Pilot," *Air Progress*, September 1970.

Chapter two

1. James Michener, *Return to Paradise* (New York: Random House, 1951), p. 177.
2. VMF-124 action report, 14 February 1943.
3. Correspondence with Kenneth A. Walsh, 22 April 1978.
4. Walsh interview, March 1977.
5. Jiro Horikoshi, et al., *Zero* (New York: Ballantine, 1971), p. 161.
6. Walsh interview.
7. Walsh correspondence, 22 April 1978.
8. R. F. Toliver, *Fighter Aces* (New York: Macmillan, 1965), p. 213.

Chapter three

1. Gregory Boyington, *Baa Baa Black Sheep* (New York: Bantam, 1977), p. 120.
2. Ibid., p. 139.
3. Ibid., p. 154.
4. USMC news release, October 1943.
5. Robert Sherrod, *History of Marine Corps Aviation in WW II* (Washington: Combat Forces Press, 1952), p. 183.
6. Davenport interview, 1 November 1978.
7. "The F4U-2 in the Solomons," U.S. Navy study, 1943.
8. Sherrod, *History*, p. 195.
9. Interview with Marion E. Carl, 1 November 1978.
10. John DeChant, *Devilbirds* (New York: Harper and Brothers, 1947), p. 130.
11. Ibid., p. 131.
12. Carl interview.
13. VMF-215 action report. 14 January 1944.
14. Ibid.
15. Ibid.
16. Charles A. Lindbergh, *The Wartime Journals of Charles A. Lindbergh* (New York: Harcourt, Brace, Jovanovich, 1970), p. 818.
17. Ibid., p. 822.

18. Carl interview.
19. Lindbergh, *Wartime Journals*, p. 847.

Chapter four

1. Richard Abrams, "The Night Fighters, VMF(N)-532," *AAHS Journal*, Spring 1973.
2. DeChant, *Devilbirds*, p. 154.
3. Lindbergh, *Wartime Journals*, pp. 919–20.
4. Ibid., p. 922.
5. DeChant, *Devilbirds*, p. 151.
6. J. Hunter Reinburg, *Combat Aerial Escapades* (Reinburg, 1966), p. 134.

Chapter five

1. Owen Rutter, *The British Navy's Air Arm* (New York: Penguin, 1944), p. 30.
2. Vice Admiral Sir Philip Vian. Victoria Cross recommendation, 1945.
3. Leonard correspondence.
4. Carl interview.

Chapter six

1. Correspondence with Richard E. Harmer, 1977–78.
2. Ibid.
3. VF(N)-101 action report, 24 April 1944.
4. VF-10 action report, 19 June 1944.
5. VF(N)-101 action report, 28 June 1944.
6. Ibid.
7. Thomas H. Moorer, editorial, *Wings of Gold*, Fall 1978.
8. Correspondence with William A. Millington, 27 August 1978.
9. Ibid.
10. Sherrod, *History*, p. 340.
11. Ibid., p. 342.
12. Millington correspondence.

Chapter seven

1. Correspondence with Herman Hansen, Jr., 29 October 1978.
2. Ibid.
3. Sherrod, *History*, p. 359.
4. VF-10 action report, 18 March 1945.
5. VF-10 action report, 26 April 1945.
6. Interview with Jefferson D. Dorroh, October 1978.
7. Toliver, *Fighter Aces*, p. 210.
8. Hansen correspondence.
9. Ibid.
10. DeChant, *Devilbirds*, p. 227.

Chapter eight

1. Correspondence with Richard C. Mangrum, 9 January 1979.
2. Congressional Medal of Honor citation.
3. Ling-Temco-Vought, "Corsair Outline."
4. Ibid.

5. *U.S. Naval Aviation 1910–1970*, p. 179.
6. Correspondence with Robert E. Galer, 8 November 1978.
7. Ibid.
8. Ibid.
9. Ibid.
10. VMA-312 action report, 10 September 1952.
11. Ibid.
12. Ibid.
13. Ibid.
14. Ibid.

Chapter nine
1. Correspondence with Rear Admiral P. Menettrier, 9 January 1979.
2. Ibid.
3. Norman Polmar, *Aircraft Carriers* (Garden City: Doubleday), p. 577.
4. Recorded interview with Colonel Fernando Soto, 13 July 1977.
5. Ibid.
6. Ibid.
7. Correspondence with Colonel James Bassett, 1976.
8. Menettrier correspondence.

Sources

Official

The Corsair story is a long and varied one, requiring diverse sources of information. But as always, an excellent starting point is the Navy's Operational Archives in the Washington Navy Yard. Consultation of numerous Navy and Marine Corps squadron action reports provided much of the primary research material. Other valuable documents included *The F4U-2 in the Solomons*, a contemporary account of VF(N)-75's activities, plus an air intelligence summary titled *The Combat Tactics of Major Gregory Boyington*. Korean War action reports were also available from Dr. Dean C. Allard's archives branch, though not in the quantity of World War II.

Further assistance was provided by the Marine Corps historical branch, with special thanks to Colonel J. E. Greenwood. This office kindly provided a large selection of photos in addition to requested documentation.

An official chronology titled *U.S. Naval Aviation 1910–1970* was useful for the Korean War chapter. Also helpful were back issues of *Naval Aviation News*. The current staff, especially Captain Ted Wilbur and Commander Zip Rausa, deserve particular mention.

Among foreign users of the F4U, official assistance came from France and Honduras. Frigate Captain Michel C. Debray, the French Assistant Naval Attaché in Washington, kindly passed along a request for assistance. And the Fuerza Aero Honduras sent documents on early Corsair deliveries which were decipherable to anyone with passable high school Spanish. Mr. L. F. Murray of the Canadian War Museum rendered photographic assistance.

Unofficial

The line between official and unofficial sources is sometimes literally paper-thin. Whether documents originate from the Navy or elsewhere, in most cases during research for this volume they have all been in some sense "official." This is certainly true of Ling-Temco-Vought, which has been receptive to all requests. A lengthy if somewhat incomplete summary titled *Corsair Outline* was sent by Louise Gilbreath of LTV's public affairs office, as were a substantial number of photos. And Vought's "official unofficial historian," Art Schoeni, took an active interest from the beginning. The F4U-1D pilot's handbook was consulted in a few instances.

One other Vought publication deserves mention. Richard W. DeMott, alias Caleb Flerk, wrote a priceless piece of Corsair fantasy called *Some*

Trouble of a Serious Nature. It has gone through at least nineteen printings by LTV, and should be considered required reading for any U-Bird enthusiast.

Documentation on British and New Zealand Corsairs came from Chris Shores and E. C. Calcinai, respectively. Detailed information on aviation armament was obtained from two excellent sources: Mr. C. E. Harris of the National Rifle Association, and the legendary Elmer Keith of Salmon, Idaho.

Frank Olynyk in Chelmsford, Ohio, probably has the most thorough documentation on Marine Corps fighter claims, and he shared his information unstintingly. And as always, my friend Dick Hill of Milwaukee, Wisconsin, was on hand to help with photos and squadron histories. Bill Hess, secretary of the American Fighter Aces Association, also lent assistance.

Below is a list of those former Corsair pilots who provided first-hand knowledge. Foremost among these is Ken Walsh, whose interest and enthusiasm have been unmatched. In addition to writing the foreword and reading most of the manuscript for accuracy, he unhesitatingly provided new or additional material. In some cases he has been more of a co-author than contributor.

Two other Solomons veterans deserve recognition. Marion Carl and Butch Davenport, those stalwart elk hunters, took time out from stalking the Blue Mountains to discuss their experiences and impressions of the F4U. Next winter there will be one more hunter in camp at Table Springs, as the author has no intention of missing another season.

Finally, sincere thanks to my friend and flying buddy, Colonel Jim Bassett. His efforts on my behalf while serving as Air Force advisor to Honduras were exceptional. In addition to sending photos and status reports, he made an invaluable contribution by recording an interview with Colonel Fernando Soto, the top gun of the Honduras Air Force.

Colonel Robert M. Baker, USMC—VMF-121
Colonel James R. Bassett, USAF—USMAG, Honduras
Major Gen. Marion E. Carl, USMC—CO VMF-223
Commander M. W. Davenport, USN—VF-17
Major Jefferson D. Dorroh, USMC—XO VMF-323
Captain Robert G. Dose, USN—CO VF-12
Brigadier General Robert E. Galer, USMC—CO MAG-12, Korea
Mr. Boone T. Guyton—Chance Vought chief test pilot
Colonel Herman Hansen, Jr., USMC—CO VMF-112
Captain Richard E. Harmer, USN—CO VF(N)-101; CO VC-3, Korea
Lieutenant (jg) Robert M. Kraus, USN—VF-10

Rear Admiral William N. Leonard, USN—Task Force 38 operations officer

Lieutenant General Richard C. Mangrum, USMC—CO MAG-12, Korea

Rear Admiral Pierre Menettrier, French Navy—CO Flotille 14F

Brigadier General William A. Millington, USMC—CO VMF-124; Commander Air Group 4

Colonel Robert Bruce Porter, USMC—VMF-121

Colonel J. Hunter Reinburg, USMC—CO VMF-122; CO VMF(N)-513, Korea

Lieutenant Commander Edward O. Schiess, USN—VBF-83

Colonel Fernando Soto, HAF—Tegucigalpa

Lieutenant Colonel Kenneth A. Walsh, USMC—VMF-124, VMF-222

Bibliography

Books

Boyington, Gregory. *Baa Baa Black Sheep*. New York: Bantam Books, 1977.

Brown, David. *Carrier Operations in World War II. Volume 1: The Royal Navy*. Annapolis: Naval Institute Press, 1974.

DeChant, John A. *Devilbirds*. New York: Harper and Brothers, 1947.

Dial, Jay Frank. *The Vought F4U-1 Corsair*. Profile No. 147. *The Vought F4U-4 to F4U-7 Corsair*. Profile No. 150. Both Leatherhead, Surrey: Profile Publications, 1965.

Green, William. *Famous Fighters of the Second World War*. London: Macdonald, 1962.

Hill, Richard M. *Markings of the Aces, U.S. Navy*. Book 2. (Series 3, No. 7). Victoria, Australia: Kookaburra Publications, 1972.

Jackson, Robert. *Air War Over Korea*. New York: Scribners, 1973.

Lindbergh, Charles A. *The Wartime Journals of Charles A. Lindbergh*. New York: Harcourt, Brace, Jovanovich, 1970.

Morison, Samuel Eliot. *History of U.S. Naval Operations in World War Two. Volume VI: Breaking the Bismarcks Barrier*. Boston: Little, Brown and Company, 1969.

Okumiya, Masatake, et al. *Zero!* New York: Ballantine, 1971.

Polmar, Norman. *Aircraft Carriers*. Garden City: Doubleday, 1969.

Reinburg, J. Hunter. *Combat Aerial Escapades*. Reinburg, 1966.

Reynolds, Clark G. *The Fast Carriers*. New York: McGraw-Hill, 1968.

Rutter, Owen. *The British Navy's Air Arm*. New York: Penguin, 1944.

Sherrod, Robert. *History of Marine Corps Aviation in World War Two*. Washington, D.C.: Combat Forces Press, 1952.

Swanborough, Gordon and Bowers, Peter M. *U.S. Navy Aircraft since 1911*. Annapolis: Naval Institute Press, 1968.

Toliver, R. and Constable, T. *Fighter Aces*. New York: Macmillan, 1965.

U. S. Navy. *U.S. Naval Aviation 1910–1970*. Naval Air Systems Command, 1970.

Winton, John. *The Forgotten Fleet: The British Navy in the Pacific*. New York: Coward-McCann, 1969.

Articles

Abrams, Richard. "The Night Fighters, VMF(N)-532." *AAHS Journal*, Spring 1973.

Askins, William. "The Ultimate Fighter Pilot." *Air Progress*, September 1970.

Farmer, James H. "Art and the Airman." *AAHS Journal*, Fall 1973.

Guyton, Boone T. "Old Hog Nose." *Airpower*, September 1971.

Langewiesche, Wolfgang. "What It's Like to Strap On an F4U." *Flying*, June 1977.

Langstaff, Hap. "Sweathogs of the Solomons." *Airpower*, January 1978.

Moorer, Thomas. Editorial. *Wings of Gold*, Fall 1978.

Regan, John. "RNZAF Corsairs." *Wings* [New Zealand], September 1972.

Shores, C. F. and Brown, J. D. "Fleet Air Arm Fighter Operations in World War II." *Air Pictorial*, April 1971.

Walton, Frank E. " 'Baa Baa Black Sheep' Is Pulling the Wool over Our Eyes." *TV Guide*, 23 April 1977.

Index

Ellis, H. A., 32, 129
Elwood, Hugh, 67
Eniwetok Atoll, 76
Enterprise (CV-6), 13, 108–14, 124, 136, 139, 141, 150
Erickson, R. D., 137
Essex (CV-9), 50, 119–23, 134, 135, 150, 152, 166
Everton, Loren, 77, 79

Farmer, C. E., 144
Farrell, William, 151
Folmar, Jesse, 171–73
Fontana, Paul, 31
Ford, Ken, 36
Formidable (British CV), 96, 99, 101, 102
Formosa, 119–20, 122
Foss, Joseph J., 57
Frame, D. P., 167
Franklin (CV-13), 135, 136, 138, 139
Freeman, Calvin B., 82
Freeman, D. C., 52–53

Galer, Robert E., 169–70
Gambier Bay (CVE-73), 67
Gilbert Islands (CVE-107), 153
Gile, Clement D., 51
Gise, William E., 10–12, 29, 30, 33
Glory (British CVL), 105
Godbey, First Lieutenant, 168
Goetz, F. J., 123–24
Goodyear Aircraft, 7–8
Gordon, Alfred, 67
Gray, R. H. (RCN), 96, 101–2
Guadalcanal, 26, 33, 35, 104
Gutenkunst, D. H., 61
Guyton, Boone T., 4, 5, 8, 16, 23

Hacking, Albert, 37
Hamilton, James, 130
Hamilton, Weldon, 33–34
Hancock (CV-19), 154
Hansen, Herman, 128–30, 132, 136, 142, 151
Hansen, John, 75
Hanson, Norman (RN), 98
Hanson, Robert M., 49, 60–61, 62–63
Harmer, Richard E., 53, 108–14, 162
Hartsock, Edmond, 121, 122
Hatakaze (Japanese DD), 122
Hay, R. C. (RM), 98, 99
Heath, Horace, 145
Hedrick, Roger, 49, 51, 63, 129, 134, 150
Henry, William E., 162
Hill, R. H., 61, 137
Holden, Robert F., 110, 112, 113, 114

Hopson, Ralph, 175
Horikoshi, Jiro, 35
Hospers, Jack, 9, 11, 17
Hudner, Thomas J., 165
Humberd, William C., 90
Huntington, Kenneth, 141
Hyland, John J., 136, 137, 139, 146, 155

Illustrious (British CV), 96–100
Indefatigable (British CV), 98
Independence (CVL-22), 50
Indochina, 121–22, 178–79
Indomitable (British CV), 96–98
Intrepid (CV-11), 108, 110, 135, 137, 139, 145–46, 155
Iwamoto, Tetsuzo, 55
Iwo Jima, 128, 132–33

Jeans, Cloyd, 76
Jensen, Alvin, 41
Jerome, Clayton, 91
Johns, R. L., 54
Johnston, William, 40

Kaiyo (Japanese CVE), 101
Kalinin Bay (CVE-68), 74
Keller, Robert P., 67
Kepford, Ira C., 51–52, 61–62, 65–67
King, Ernest J., 117
Kirkpatrick, Floyd, 146
Kirkwood, Philip, 145
Klingman, Robert, 148–49
Klinsmann, Otto, 123
Krum, G. A., 143
Kullberg, Cecil L., 108, 110
Kwajalein Atoll, 76

LaFayette (French CVL), 181
Laffey (DD-724), 146
Laney, Willis, 134
Lang, Frank C., 78
Langewiesche, Wolfgang, 15
Langley (CVL-27), 123
Lausen, Christian, 75
Leeds, James, 36
Lehnert, Robert, 75
Leonard, William N., 17, 103
Lerch, Alfred, 145
Lexington (CV-16), 154
Leyte (CV-32), 165
Libby, Herbert L., 122
Lindbergh, Charles A., 68–70, 82–83
Logan, Samuel, 34
Lopez, Walter (HAF), 184
Lynch, Joseph O., 121
Lyon, Second Lieutenant, 30

McCain, John S., 123, 128
McClurg, Robert, 45
McEachren, Lieutenant, 170
McElhaney, Boyd, 69
McGill, William, 123
McGinty, Selva, 146
MacLaughlin, John S., 74–76
McManus, John, 148
Magda, John, 13
Mangrum, Richard C., 162–63
Marshall, David E., 118, 130
Mayer, Sol, 147
Mendoza, Roberto (HAF), 184
Menettrier, Pierre, 178, 187
Michener, James, 28–29
Millington, William A., 37, 39, 118–21,
    123, 124, 128, 130, 132–34
Mitscher, Marc A., 117, 128, 149, 154
Mobley, Thomas E., 134, 137
Moore, D. J., 56
Moorer, Thomas H., 116
Morrell, Rivers, 55
Mullins, R. W., 120
Munda, 27, 37, 38

Nashi (Japanese DD), 101
Naval Aircraft Factory, 21
Neefus, James, 38
New Georgia, 27, 36

Ocean (British CVL), 170
Oerth, Karl, 90
O'Hare, Edward H., 18, 19
O'Keefe, J. J., 147
Okinawa, 99–100, 134, 139, 140, 143
Olsen, Theodore, 90
O'Neill, H. D., 54
O'Neill, John, 166
Otis, James C., 84
Owens, Robert G., 60, 63

Pace, William, 45
Palau Islands, 85–87
Patriarca, F. A., 135, 136
Pearson, John, 17
Pearson, Lloyd B., 30
Peek, William, 139
Percy, Gilbert, 34–35
Peyton, Monford, 32
Philippine Islands, 87–91, 120
Philippine Sea (CV-47), 162, 164
Porter, Robert Bruce, 36
Porter, Sam, 9
Presley, Frank H., 167
Princeton (CV-37), 174
Pyongyang, Korea, 161, 173

Quiel, Norwald, 145

Rabaul, New Britain, 44, 50, 55, 56, 60,
    63, 66, 67, 69, 105
Railsback, Eldon, 90
Rawie, W. E., 136
Reid (DD-369), 89
Reidy, T. H., 155
Reinburg, Joseph H., 85–86, 162
Reusser, Kenneth, 148
Reynolds, William E., 123
Ridderhoff, Stanley, 11
Rivera, Marco Tulio (HAF), 184
Roberts, Edwin S., 140
Royal Navy
    1830 Squadron, 94, 96, 97, 99
    1833 Squadron, 94, 96, 97, 98
    1834 Squadron, 95, 97, 98, 99
    1836 Squadron, 95, 97, 98
    1837 Squadron, 97
    1841 Squadron, 96, 100, 101
    1842 Squadron, 96
Royal New Zealand Air Force
    14 Squadron, 103, 104, 105
    16 Squadron, 105
    20 Squadron, 103, 104
    26 Squadron, 103
Russell, Donald, 139
Russell Islands, 27, 31, 33

Saipan (CVL-48), 179
Salisbury, Vernon, 131
Sanderson, Lawson, 45
Sangamon (CVE-26), 9
Santee (CVE-29), 84
Saratoga (CV-3), 13, 96, 118
Schumann, R. W., 136
Serra, Jose (HAF), 184
Shangri-La (CV-38), 103, 150, 152
Sharpe, W. S., 91
Shaw, Edward O., 40
Sheppard, D. J. (RCN), 98, 99, 100
Sherrod, Robert, 122, 136
Shuman, Perry, 36, 141
Sicily (CVE-118), 162, 164, 171
Sinuiju, Korea, 163–64
Sitkoh Bay (CVE-86), 140–41
Smith, John L., 17
Smith, John M., 148, 149
Soto, Fernando (HAF), 184–86
Sovik, Edward A., 78–79
Spatz, Donald, 78
Spears, Harold, 62, 63
Stewart, Second Lieutenant, 30
Stout, Robert F., 85, 87
Strean, Bernard M., 17

VF-53, 160, 161
VF-54, 160
VF-84, 129, 131, 132, 134, 143, 148, 149–50
VF-113, 166
VF-301, 17
VF(N)-75, 22, 53–54, 108
VF(N)-101, 22, 53, 108–14

Valentine, Herbert J., 151
Valley Forge (CV-45), 160, 161, 162, 164
Vaughan, Everette H., 77
Vella Gulf (CVE-111), 153
Victorious (British CV), 95, 97, 98, 99, 100
Vroome, Raymond, 31

Walsh, Kenneth A., 12, 29–31, 33, 34, 38–40, 152

Warner, A. T., 61
Wasp (CV-18), 128, 131, 133, 134, 138, 139, 154
Weissenberger, Gregory, 31, 36
White, Robert, 146
Widhelm, W. J., 53–54, 108
Williamson, Herbert, 49
Wilson, Walter, 75
Witonski, Stanley, 88
Wright, T. K., 17

Yahagi (Japanese CL), 140
Yamato (Japanese BB), 140
Yorktown (CV-10), 139, 154
Yost, Donald K., 153

Zepeda, Francisco (HAF), 184